Reforming the Russian Industrial Workplace

Based on extensive original research, this book explores how far the Soviet pattern of industrial workplace organisation, characterised by a high level of management discretion, authoritarian control and the use of punitive methods on the shop-floor, has been replaced by internationally established practices, with a greater emphasis on a lean organisation and employee involvement in quality improvement. The book explores how the market reforms of the 1990s raised companies' attention to product quality but did not lead to a change in the management methods, which only began with the increased internationalisation of the Russian economy in the 2000s. The book includes a rich in-depth study of multinational and domestic companies, and argues that a move from the Soviet pattern of workplace organisation to new practices is only likely to occur in companies with strong ties to international partners, who provide support for, and audit the implementation and upholding of, international management standards. The research shows that local companies not exposed to such international collaboration continue with the old methods.

Elena Shulzhenko is a lecturer at the Department of Organization at Copenhagen Business School. She was formerly a researcher at the WZB Berlin Social Science Research Center.

Routledge Contemporary Russia and Eastern Europe Series

65 Democracy, Civil Culture and Small Business in Russia's Regions
Social Processes in Comparative Historical Perspective
Molly O'Neal

66 National Minorities in Putin's Russia
Federica Prina

67 The Social History of Post-Communist Russia
Edited by Piotr Dutkiewicz, Richard Sakwa and Vladimir Kulikov

68 The Return of the Cold War
Ukraine, the West and Russia
Edited by J.L. Black and Michael Johns

69 Corporate Strategy in Post-Communist Russia
Mikhail Glazunov

70 Russian Aviation, Space Flight and Visual Culture
Vlad Strukov and Helena Goscilo

71 EU–Russia Relations, 1999–2015
From Courtship to Confrontation
Anna-Sophie Maass

72 Migrant Workers in Russia
Global Challenges of the Shadow Economy in Societal Transformation
Edited by Anna-Liisa Heusala and Kaarina Aitamurto

73 Gender Inequality in the Eastern European Labour Market
Twenty-five Years of Transition since the Fall of Communism
Edited by Giovanni Razzu

74 Reforming the Russian Industrial Workplace
International Management Standards meet the Soviet Legacy
Elena Shulzhenko

Reforming the Russian Industrial Workplace

International Management Standards meet the Soviet Legacy

Elena Shulzhenko

LONDON AND NEW YORK

First published 2017
by Routledge
2 Park Square, Milton Park, Abingdon, Oxon OX14 4RN

and by Routledge
711 Third Avenue, New York, NY 10017

Routledge is an imprint of the Taylor & Francis Group, an informa business

© 2017 Elena Shulzhenko

The right of Elena Shulzhenko to be identified as author of this work has been asserted by her in accordance with sections 77 and 78 of the Copyright, Designs and Patents Act 1988.

All rights reserved. No part of this book may be reprinted or reproduced or utilised in any form or by any electronic, mechanical, or other means, now known or hereafter invented, including photocopying and recording, or in any information storage or retrieval system, without permission in writing from the publishers.

Trademark notice: Product or corporate names may be trademarks or registered trademarks, and are used only for identification and explanation without intent to infringe.

British Library Cataloguing in Publication Data
A catalogue record for this book is available from the British Library

Library of Congress Cataloging in Publication Data
Names: Shulzhenko, Elena, author.
Title: Reforming the Russian industrial workplace : international management standards meet the Soviet legacy / Elena Shulzhenko.
Description: 1 Edition. | New York : Routledge, 2017. | Series: Routledge contemporary Russia and Eastern Europe series ; 74 | Includes bibliographical references and index.
Identifiers: LCCN 2016045401| ISBN 9781138692022 (hardback) | ISBN 9781315533377 (ebook)
Subjects: LCSH: Industrial management–Russia (Federation)–History. | Total quality management–Standards–Russia (Federation) | Quality control–Standards–Russia (Federation)
Classification: LCC HD70.R9 S564 2017 | DDC 658.4/0130947–dc23
LC record available at https://lccn.loc.gov/2016045401

ISBN: 978-1-138-69202-2 (hbk)
ISBN: 978-1-315-53337-7 (ebk)

Typeset in Times New Roman
by Cenveo Publisher Services

 Printed in the United Kingdom
by Henry Ling Limited

To my grandfather, Alexander V. Shulzhenko,
who worked at Soviet industrial plants from the age of
16 up to 65

Contents

List of figures	x
List of tables	xi
Acknowledgements	xii
List of abbreviations	xiii

1 Introduction   1

    1.1 Continuity and change in the Russian industrial workplace 1

    *1.2 Internationalisation of the Russian automotive industry
and new quality management standards 6*

    *1.3 Theoretical perspective: change in the Russian industrial
workplace as breaking path dependence 10*

    1.4 Research questions 15

    1.5 Empirical data collection and analysis 17

    1.6 Overview of the chapters 21

**2 Evolving persistence: the socialist path of industrial work in
Russia (1920s–80s)**   23

    *2.1 The 'scientific organisation of labour' in the
early twentieth century 23*

    *2.2 Forced-pace industrialisation and worker
mobilisation campaigns 27*

    *2.3 The quality turn: Complex Systems of Management of Output
Quality in the 1970s and 1980s 30*

    *2.4 Self-financing brigades and workers' self-management under
Gorbachev 43*

    *2.5 Conclusion: the socialist path of industrial work by the start of the
transition to a market economy 44*

viii   *Contents*

3   Still there: the industrial workplace in Russia after the market reforms   48

   3.1 Compliance with rules and standards in production 49

   3.2 Quality management and lean production 51

   3.3 Group work and employee empowerment 54

   3.4 Worker qualification and development 56

   3.5 Remuneration systems 60

   3.6 Representation of employees' interests 65

   3.7 Conclusion: industrial work in Russia after the market reforms 67

4   The new times: international quality management standards in the Russian car industry   70

   4.1 The origins of international quality management standards: from Taylorism to total quality management 70

   4.2 Lean production and standardised production systems in the international automotive industry 77

   4.3 International quality management standards ISO 9000 and ISO/TS 16949 80

   4.4 Quality management in the Russian automobile industry during the first decade after the market reforms 84

   4.5 Dissemination of the 'local' and the international versions of ISO/TS 16949 in Russia 86

   4.6 Enforcing new quality management requirements through supply chains 91

   4.7 Conclusion: international quality management standards in the Russian automotive industry 101

5   What about the workers? Impact of international quality management standards on the Russian industrial workplace   104

   5.1 Production processes and workers in the plants under study 105

   5.2 Reforming quality assurance in production 112

   5.3 Work organisation and assignment of quality assurance tasks 138

   5.4 Employee development and quality assurance competencies 147

   5.5 Remuneration, bonuses and sanctions for performance quality on the shop-floor 156

   5.6 Conclusion: impact of international quality management standards on the path of industrial work in Russia 168

Contents ix

6 Conclusion   173

*6.1 Decomposing path dependence in the Russian
industrial workplace 173*
*6.2 Supporters and challengers of the international quality
management standards 174*
6.3 Change in the Russian industrial workplace 176
6.4 Prospects 178

Appendix   179
References   182
Index   194

List of figures

1.1	Production of foreign and Russian passenger car brands in Russia (in thousand units)	8
1.2	Sales of Russian and foreign brands of automobiles in Russia (share of total number of units sold)	9
3.1	Lean manufacturing tools applied at Russian enterprises	52
3.2	Dynamics of employment and real wages at medium and large enterprises in 1991–2006	61
5.1	The composition of personnel at Westauto	107
5.2	The share of different categories of employees at Rusauto and Rusmet	108
5.3	Average age of employees at Rusmet	109
5.4	Gender distribution in employment at the plants studied in Russia	111

List of tables

1.1	Research dimensions	5
1.2	Production and sales of automobiles in Russia (in thousand units)	7
1.3	Major industrial policies supporting the localisation of foreign car manufacturing in Russia	8
1.4	Motor vehicle production by Russian OEMs in 2006–9 (with production exceeding 10,000 units in at least one of the years)	10
1.5	Case studies conducted in Russia	18
1.6	Interviews statistics	19
1.7	Interviews conducted for the case studies of automotive plants in Russia	20
2.1	The range of variable incentives used in the Soviet automobile industry	41
3.1	Application of personnel appraisal systems at Russian firms	63
3.2	"On whom does the size of your wage depend mostly?"	64
4.1	Prominent personalities in the debate on quality management	74
4.2	Diffusion of the ISO/TS 16949 standard in Russia	88
5.1	Basic data about the enterprises studied in Russia	105
5.2	Organisational hierarchies in production at the studied plants in Russia	109
5.3	Average monthly wages at the plants studied in Russia (2007–8)	110
5.4	Importance of forms of control in QM systems at the studied plants (%)	119
5.5	Share of quality department employees in the total in employment at the studied firms	120
5.6	Causes of defects at the three plants, as estimated by the managers	129
A.1	Overview of the sources of data complementing the interviews	179
A.2	Supplementary expert interviews	180
A.3	Pilot interviews at metal industry and automotive plants	181
A.4	Pilot case studies of German-owned automotive plants	181

Acknowledgements

I am indebted to many people and institutions that supported this study. First and foremost I want to thank the Alexander von Humboldt Foundation and the WZB Berlin Social Science Center for financing my work on the project. In particular, I am indebted to Ulrich Jürgens, who headed the Research Group "Knowledge, Production Systems, and Work" at the WZB up to his retirement. His support went far beyond the formal obligations.

I also want to thank my 62 interview partners at industrial plants and other organisations in Russia, Germany and Poland, who remain anonymous as a condition of their involvement. The knowledge they shared allowed me to understand the complexity of manufacturing quality in the Russian industrial workplace and to put it into a comparative perspective.

A number of colleagues and friends discussed early ideas and drafts of this study and provided me with valuable critique and encouragement. My wholehearted gratitude goes to Simon Clarke, Professor Emeritus at Warwick University, Martin Krzywdzinski, Sebastian Botzem and Dieter Plehwe from the WZB, Christian Wittrock from Aarhus University and to my friends Julia Ulyannikova and Marina Nistotskaya. I am also indebted to John Jennings, who struggled to improve the English language in the first draft of this book.

The cover artwork is a fragment of a Soviet poster by Vasiliy V. Suryaninov, 'Everyone – to the collective, the collective – to everyone!', 1960. I would like to express my gratitude to Ruben V. Suryaninov, the artist's son, for his generous permission to use it in the book.

This book would not have reached its readers without a publisher. I am grateful to Peter Sowden and Lucy McClune from Routledge for their support and patience.

I thank my partner, David Dahl, for sharing the ups and downs of the project with me; my father – for teaching me audacity; and my mother – for always giving me a hand when I need it.

Elena Shulzhenko
Copenhagen

List of abbreviations

AFNOR	Association Française de Normalisation
AS	appraisal score (used for employees at Rusmet)
CEO	chief executive officer
CKD	completely knocked down
ETKS	*Soviet Wage Rate and Qualification Handbook for Workers* (*Edinyi tarifno-kvalifikatsionnyi spravochnik*)
FMEA	failure mode and effects analysis
FTT	first-time-through
GOST	Technical standards by the Russian Federal Agency for Technical Regulation and Metrology
GOST 51814.1	Russian version of ISO/TS 16949 standard
HR	human resources
IATF	International Automotive Task Force
ISO	International Organization for Standardization
ISO 9000	Family of Quality Management Standards by ISO
ISO/TS 16949	Particular Requirements for the Application of ISO 9000 Standards for Automotive Production and Relevant Service Part Organizations
JV	joint venture
KTU	Coefficient of Labour Participation (*Koeffitsient trudovogo uchastiya*)
NAMI	Research Institute for Automobiles and Automotive Engines (*Nauchno-issleedovatel'skiy Avtomobil'nyy i Avtomotornyy Institut*)
NAPAK	National Association of Automotive Component Manufacturers (*Natsional'naya Assotsiatsiya Proizvoditeley Avtomobil'nykh Komponentov*)
OAR	Association of Russian Automobile Manufacturers (*Ob"edinenie Avtoproizvoditeley Rossii*)
OEM	original equipment manufacturer
OICA	Organisation Internationale des Constructeurs d'Automobiles
PPAP	production part approval process
QA	quality assurance

xiv *List of abbreviations*

QM	quality management
RSS	managers, specialists and office employees (*rukovoditeli, spetsialisty, sluzhashchie*)
SPC	statistical process control
TQM	total quality management
VDA	Verband der deutschen Automobilindustrie
VDA-QMC	Verband der deutschen Automobilindustrie – Qualitätsmanagementcenter
VNIIS	All-Russian Research Institute of Certification (*Vserossiyskiy nauchno-issledovatelskiy Institut Sertifikatsii*)
WG	working group
WPS	Westauto Production System
WQOS	Westauto Quality Operation System
5M	Change programme including five components: method, machines, materials, man and *mir* (Russian for 'environment')
5S	Japanese workplace organisation method, which includes five terms: sorting, streamlining, systematic cleaning, standardising and sustaining

1 Introduction

1.1 Continuity and change in the Russian industrial workplace

The character of work on the shop-floor in Russian industry shows a remarkable continuity despite the radical institutional reforms in the national economy since the early 1990s. Russia's transition to a market economy and development of market competition urged enterprises to improve the quality of manufactured goods. The companies achieved that rather by intensifying work and disciplining workers on the shop-floor than by introducing new approaches to organisation of production, quality management (QM) and work. Most of the literature on production work in Russia agrees that the market reforms had a weak impact on companies' approaches to organisation of production and work in the 1990s and early 2000s. The post-socialist workplace remained dominated by the principles inherited from the planned economy. Provision of skills and competences was not modernised. The production machinery was largely obsolete. Remuneration systems were frequently changed but their arbitrary and punitive character continued to prevail. In the mid-2000s production work in Russian enterprises was still characterised by low formalisation of work processes, high discretion of line management, authoritarian control over workers and the use of punitive methods on the shop-floor.

Since the early 2000s, however, the popularity of the concepts of 'lean production' and 'total quality management' (TQM) has been growing in the Russian manufacturing sector. These management concepts became widespread in the capitalist economies at the end of the twentieth century. They integrated ideas about organisation of production and QM with the aim of increasing the involvement of production employees, foremen and workers in QM. The development of these concepts started in the USA and received a strong boost from Japan, where a complex approach to quality control evolved in the 1960s and 1970s (Cole 1979; Womack, Jones and Roos 1990). Japanese companies attempted to improve product quality by preventing defects with the help of workers instead of checking the quality of ready-made products. These principles evolved in a complex system of company-wide QM aiming at continuous improvement of product quality and production processes on the basis of all-employee participation in these activities. The diffusion of the new QM ideas in the West peaked in the

2 Introduction

1990s (cf. Cole 1999; Jürgens, Malsch and Dohse 1993); they became the basis for the international QM standards established around that time.

The aim to reduce control over employees' performance through quality inspectors and to involve workers in QM, which was fundamental to the international QM concepts diffused in Russia, contrasted with the reliance on punitive methods to discipline workers common in the Russian industry. This contradiction represents the starting point of the present study. The study is motivated by the question of whether the introduction of international QM standards has led to a weakening of the punitive character of production work in Russia. The study will analyse the determinants of the introduction of new QM standards and their impact on the character of production work in Russia. The dissemination of new QM standards is a significant trend influencing the entire Russian manufacturing sector. Given the magnitude of this area – over 10 million people are employed in this sector in Russia[1] – the problems discussed in this study are of great social importance in Russia today.

The research on Russian industrial enterprises points at quality control as an important field of tensions in industrial work in the post-socialist period. The study of QM allows analysis of how Western management concepts promising increased efficiency and product quality were confronted with the workplace realities of a post-socialist enterprise. In this enterprise production management had to ensure that production processes ran smoothly while machinery was old, the status of production in the organisation was low, the workforce was ageing and lacked new competencies and the companies' resources were directed towards marketing and sales departments. Line managers were under pressure to meet the output targets and ensure workers' compliance with process requirements, but lacked incentives for motivating workers. Tensions between the quality department and production workers persisted from the planned economy period, as workers' earnings still depended on the acceptance or rejection of the product by quality inspectors. Therefore, QM is a field where different actors' interests meet and collide and the study of it is suitable for gaining an insight into general mechanisms governing production work in Russia.

After the market reforms, enterprises have paid much greater attention to the quality of the product than before, but cases when domestic enterprises carried out systemic change in organisation of production and quality control are rather rare (Clarke 2007:209–210). Instead, the traditional Soviet system of quality control, in which punishment played a central part, has prevailed. This applies to both traditional privatised enterprises and new private companies. Schwartz and McCann have referred to this approach to manage quality as a 'punitive quality regime':

> SMEs also tend to enact strict and punitive quality regimes, with shop managers or directors immediately involved in fining the individuals or groups of workers.
>
> (Schwartz and McCann 2007:1543)

Introduction 3

Fining and sanctions can affect individual workers and whole groups, called 'brigades', on the shop-floor due to the popularity of collective piece-rate systems. While workers are considered 'responsible' for product quality and their earnings directly depend on it, this responsibility does not imply having control over production processes or their quality. Instead, it implies that workers are blamed when something goes wrong, although their actual authority and scope of action is rather restricted, their competencies and skills are not updated, supplied materials are often of a poor quality and production machinery is worn-out:

> The majority [of studied companies] rely on the skills and commitment of their inherited labour force to overcome the difficulties of achieving high quality standards with inferior materials and worn-out equipment and use punitive methods in an attempt to maintain quality standards and minimise losses.
>
> (Clarke 2007:210)

Quality control and the use of remuneration and sanctions in Russia has significantly shaped the work situation on the shop-floor and given it an arbitrary and dramatic character. Clarke has pointed out that the continuity in production work in Russia has been a result of several intertwined causes. Employees lacked competencies relating to new ways to work and assure quality; inferior materials and supply parts hindered reduction of quality checks by inspectors; and worn-out machinery led to frequent failures in production processes and required deviation from formal rules on the shop-floor in order to adjust to process disturbances.

The absence of systemic change found in the qualitative studies outlined above is confirmed by the survey by Kononova on modernisation of production systems in Russia, the most comprehensive survey on the topic to date (Kononova 2006). According to the survey, only 5 per cent of all enterprises surveyed aimed at improving the organisation of production processes systematically and consistently (ibid.:122). Yet, some change took place: 32 per cent of the enterprises in the sample introduced 'some elements' of production systems on the basis of lean manufacturing and 23 per cent of the enterprises improved their production systems on the basis of their own ideas (ibid.:124). TQM has been the most popular concept in modernisation of production at Russian enterprises. Burnyshev *et al.*, who have analysed modernisation of QM systems at Russian industrial enterprises, observe that some companies strove to certify their QM systems for compliance with international standards (Burnyshev, Vandyshev and Priamikova 2006). Most of the firms studied, however, still adhered to 'traditional' ways to control quality.

There is little research on Western manufacturing enterprises operating in Russia. The available evidence shows that Western companies differ from Russian-owned enterprises with regard to production systems and human resource (HR) practices (Björkman, Fey and Park 2007; Jürgens and Krzywdzinski 2016). Foreign-owned companies strive to transfer their production systems, based on lean principles, to their Russian locations (Jürgens and Krzywdzinski 2016). These

4　*Introduction*

companies also apply internationally established HR instruments, such as formalised recruitment and performance appraisal systems, across different locations (Björkman, Fey and Park 2007; Jürgens and Krzywdzinski 2016). Yet, there is evidence that the Russian employment system and traditional work culture still influence the workplace at a deeper level (Jürgens and Krzywdzinski 2016).

Little is known on how collaboration with Western partners in the introduction of international concepts of organisation of production and QM affects the workplace. The case study of a Russian plant that attempted to start supplying its products to Britain shows that partnership with the prospective British customer represented an important resource for the Russian enterprise (Dickenson and Blundell 2000). The Russian plant succeeded in introducing the Western approach to QM and in qualifying as a supplier to the British partner. The achieved change outcome, however, did not prove to be sustainable and exporting eventually failed. According to the authors, there were multiple differences between the Western and Russian approaches to organisation of production and QM, which included production equipment, the role of formal rules, the system of incentives and competencies available on the shop-floor. The major cause of the failure was, however, the Russian managers' inability to pass the new knowledge and new work attitudes down to the employees. Yet, Jürgens and Krzywdzinski came to different conclusions in their study of the Russian automotive giant GAZ (Jürgens and Krzywdzinski 2013, 2016). The authors state that GAZ's cooperation with international automotive companies Magna and Chrysler provided the motivation for modernisation of the company's production system (Jürgens and Krzywdzinski 2013:121). According to them, it succeeded in adopting the principles of lean production and significantly changing personnel management, although involvement of workers in problem-solving and improvement was very limited. These studies point to the importance of collaboration with Western companies for modernisation of production and QM in Russia and to difficulties of involving workers in QM in Russia.

The available studies show that although principles inherited from the socialist period dominated organisation of production, QM and work in the Russian industry, some modernisation efforts have taken place. The change in organisation of production and QM at industrial enterprises in Russia, however, has not been researched much. In particular, there is a lack of research looking specifically at how the introduction of new QM ideas affects production work. The present study will contribute to filling this research gap. It will analyse the complex causes underlying the continuity of the principles shaping production work in Russia using path dependence theory as a conceptual lens.

In the present study production work will be understood as activity aimed at manufacturing a material product in the context of an industrial enterprise. The analysis will concentrate on four dimensions of production work affected by the TQM movement in the West (see Table 1.1; cf. Chapter 4, Section 4.1–4.3).

Introduction 5

Table 1.1 Research dimensions

1. Organisation of quality assurance and workers' role in it
Organisation of quality assurance; workers' role in quality assurance; content
of work on the shop-floor and integration of quality-related tasks into the
responsibilities of direct workers.

2. Work organisation
Principles underlying group work; degree of integration of the quality assurance
tasks into the groups' responsibilities on the shop-floor.

3. Workers' competencies and personnel development systems
Qualification requirements for workers; organisation of employee training; quality-
related competencies on the shop-floor.

4. Systems of remuneration and sanctions applied to workers
Remuneration rules on the shop-floor; system of bonuses and sanctions applied in
production and their link to quality assurance.

Source: Data compiled by author

When speaking about QM and production organisation standards that were being
implemented at Russian enterprises, the study uses a rather broad definition of
'standards'. In accordance with Brunsson and Jacobsson, standards will be understood as a specific kind of voluntary rules:

> Standards are related to other ideas and rules, but they have characteristics requir-
> ing special attention. Standards possess some qualities that can affect the ease with
> which they travel between and within organizations and organizational fields: they
> consist of explicit statements and they are presented as being voluntary.
> (Brunsson and Jacobsson 2002a:9)

The term 'standards' may, in some places, be substituted by 'concepts' with the
same meaning implied to avoid repetitions.

Three terms are used throughout the study to signify enterprises' efforts aimed at
manufacturing high-quality output: 'quality control', 'quality assurance' and 'quality management'. 'Quality control' is used for quality-related standards and
processes under the planned economy in Russia and before the 'total quality revolution' in the West. 'Quality management' and 'quality assurance' refer to quality-
related rules and processes in contemporary enterprises. While QM signifies the
principles that apply to the whole organisation, 'quality assurance' refers to the
standards and processes that are in place in production.

The study will concentrate on one industry – the automobile industry. In the
2000s, the automotive industry in Russia underwent a rapid shift from being
protected from imported international brands to becoming an arena of competition
with and between major international automobile manufacturers that established
production in Russia. The international automakers' attempts to increase
localisation of production in Russia drove them to support the diffusion of international QM standards in the country. At the same time, the rising competition in
the internal market motivated local automakers to reconsider both their own
approaches to QM and those applied by their suppliers. Thus, the internationalisation

6 Introduction

represented an important shift that could potentially become a starting point for unlocking the persistent path of production work in this industry. The following section will provide a short overview of the internationalisation of the Russian automotive industry.

1.2 Internationalisation of the Russian automotive industry and new quality management standards

The year 2005 marked the end of the era of domestic brands in the Russian automotive market. Two important events took place this year: a new industrial policy fostering foreign direct investment (FDI) into the Russian automotive industry was adopted and local automakers lost over half of the market to foreign brands. The internationalisation of the Russian automotive industry led to a growing interest in international QM standards.

The market reforms carried out in Russia in the early 1990s did not challenge the domination of domestic car manufacturers in the local market. Domestic automakers remained protected from the international competition and continued to reign in the Russian market during the 1990s. However, the demand for cars grew and, by the late 1990s, production of automobiles by local manufacturers was not able to cover the demand of the local market, both in terms of volume and quality of cars. The presence of foreign brands in the Russian market grew rapidly after 2001, when import duties were decreased to 25 per cent of the cars' value under pressure from the World Trade Organization (Kozichev 2009). This led to import of over 400,000 cars into the country in 2001 compared to c. 100,000 cars a year earlier (see Table 1.2).

The same year, the share of foreign brands sold in Russia (both new and used) exceeded that of local brands (calculated in US dollars), according to the Ministry of Industry and Energy of the Russian Federation (Ministry of Industry and Energy of the Russian Federation 2004). Around this time, the assembly of the first foreign brands in Russia started, mostly as licensed assembly of completely knocked down kits (CKD). Despite these changes, the Russian OEMs were able to keep their production volumes relatively stable until 2004. This gave the Russian OEMs an illusion of stability, despite the fact that internationalisation of the automotive industry in Russia was gaining momentum.

The next phase of internationalisation of the Russian automotive market started in 2005, when the Russian Government began to support localisation of automobile assembly by foreign OEMs (see Table 1.3).

First, customs duties on car components imported by OEMs for 'industrial assembly' in Russia were reduced. To qualify for 'industrial assembly', OEMs had to carry out welding, painting and assembly operations locally, and to gradually increase the share of locally purchased parts. In 2006, the localisation of automotive suppliers was supported by reduction of the import duties on certain car components and materials used in car component production in Russia.

Table 1.2 Production and sales[1] of automobiles in Russia (in thousand units)

	1990	1991	1992	1993	1994	1995	1996	1997	1998	1999	2000	2001	2002	2003	2004	2005	2006	2007	2008	2009
Total production	1103	1030	963	956	798	835	868	985	839	954	969	1022	980	1010	1110	1068	1176	1293	1470	596
Total sales	n/a	n/a	n/a	n/a	n/a	1506	1282	1886	1328	1047	1087	1428	1500	1388	1484	1714	2022	2764	3274	1402

Sources:[2] Aleshin 2006; Verband der Automobilindustrie 2006; Bundesagentur für Außenwirtschaft 2008; Gesellschaft für Außenwirtschaft und Standortmarketing mbH 2010; Verband der Automobilindustrie 2010

Notes:
1. Sales include used imports
2. In case of differences in data in different sources, more recent sources were given priority

8 Introduction

Table 1.3 Major industrial policies supporting the localisation of foreign car manufacturing in Russia

Date	Introduced policies
March 2005	Reduction of customs duties on car components imported by OEMs for 'industrial assembly' in Russia (Russian Government Decree No. 166)
August 2006 and October 2006	Introduction of Special Economic Zones (FCS Orders No. 750 (9 August 2006) and 1072 (31 October 2006))
September 2006	Reduction of import duties on certain car components and materials used in car component production in Russia (Russian Government Decree No. 566)
December 2008	Increase of import duties for cars from 25% to 30% on the average to protect Russian-based manufacturers

Sources: Ernst & Young 2007; Kozichev 2009; *Automobilproduktion Newsletter für Osteuropa* 2005–8

The new industrial policy contributed to the localisation of assembly operations in Russia by international OEMs. Among others, the top-five leading OEMs according to OICA[2] – Toyota, GM, Volkswagen, Ford and Hyundai – had established production in Russia by 2007. In total, 16 international OEMs decided to establish production in Russia during the first two years after the introduction of the new policy (Ernst & Young 2007:21). The share of international OEMs in the Russian automotive market started to grow both in terms of production and sales volumes (see Figures 1.1 and 1.2).

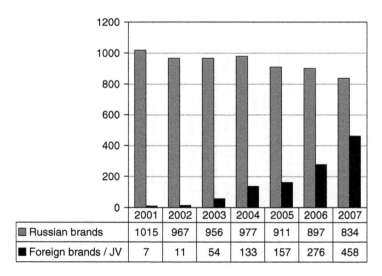

Figure 1.1 Production of foreign and Russian passenger car brands in Russia (in thousand units)
Sources:[1] Aleshin 2006; Ernst & Young 2008
Note: 1. In case of differences in data in different sources, more recent sources were given priority

Introduction 9

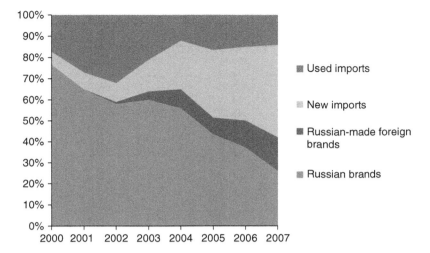

Figure 1.2 Sales of Russian and foreign brands of automobiles in Russia (share of total number of units sold)
Sources: Ernst & Young 2008; Institut kompleksnykh strategicheskikh issledovaniy 2005

The position of the domestic manufacturers rapidly deteriorated, starting from 2005 – when the Russian brands occupied 43.5 per cent of the market counted in number of units sold. The same year, the production volume of the Russian automobile manufacturers sank by over 60,000 units and kept falling further in the following years.

The present empirical study will concentrate on the period between 2005 and 2008. In 2008 the global financial crisis started to affect the Russian automotive industry and therefore changed the context for the enterprises. After 2005 the production volumes at domestic automobile manufacturers fell drastically; some plants were closed by 2009. In 2006, there were 11 Russian-owned OEMs with production exceeding 10,000 units annually (see Table 1.4).

AvtoVAZ (formerly VAZ) in Togliatti was by far leading in the Russian automotive industry in terms of number of passenger cars produced. The second largest Russian OEM was GAZ in Nizhny Novgorod; it manufactured over 200,000 vehicles in 2006, but its position significantly deteriorated during the subsequent years.

The decline of the Russian car manufacturers was, to a great extent, determined by the poor technical characteristics of their cars compared to the international brands. However, Russian brands were rejected by consumers even in the niche of simple but cheap cars. The low quality of these cars led to frequent breakdowns and need for repair. Low quality was characteristic for both Russian brands and locally supplied parts. Russian OEMs purchased 91 per cent of the suppliers' content locally in 2005 (Roland Berger Strategy Consultants 2005). According to a study by Ernst & Young, the Russian domestic industry average defect rate was over 1,000 parts per million (ppm), whereas the international

10   *Introduction*

Table 1.4 Motor vehicle production[1] by Russian OEMs in 2006–9 (with production exceeding 10,000 units in at least one of the years)

	OEM, location	2006	2007	2008	2009
1	AvtoVAZ, Togliatti (Lada)	765,627	735,897	801,563	294,737
2	GAZ, Nizhny Novgorod	237,445	237,221	178,321	53,401
3	Izh-Avto, Izhevsk	65,024	78,802	64,19	10,966
4	UAZ, Ulyanovsk	64,147	74,766	72,181	32,636
5	TagAZ, Rostov Region	48,397	72,3326	100,13	24,336
6	KAMAZ, Naberezhnye Chelny	42,851	52,847	51,006	23,062
7	Avtotor, Kaliningrad	39,853	106,368	108,458	60,338
8	PAZ, Pavlovo (belongs to GAZ Group)	14,215	15,031	13,912	7,259
9	SeAZ, Serpukhov	11,338	4,901	1,291	–
10	AZ Ural, Miass (belongs to GAZ Group)	9,952	15,754	15,158	6,829
11	Sollers, Naberezhnye Chelny	9,653	21,804	36,006	5,359

Source: Verband der Automobilindustrie 2010
Note: 1. Including all types of vehicles

industry standard was below 70 ppm (Ernst & Young 2007:21). Out of about 200 Russian component manufacturers, less than 5 per cent (under ten firms) supplied international OEMs in the West or their locations in Russia and only 1 per cent (two firms) had export activities in 2007 (ibid.). These crucial differences in product quality divided the industry into two segments in terms of supply chains – international and domestic.[3] Russian suppliers of domestic OEMs had to undergo a deep restructuring of production in order to comply with the international manufacturers' requirements. The domestic OEMs' expectations with regard to the quality of supplied parts and the QM methods applied by suppliers started to change in the 2000s as well. Thus, growing competition in the industry made local firms' compliance with international quality standards a precondition for their survival.

This empirical investigation is based on case studies of a Western automobile assembler in Russia (Westauto) and two domestic Russian companies (automobile manufacturer Rusauto and supplier Rusmet) and is complemented by expert interviews in Russia and abroad. The cases allow analysis of diverse processes, determinants and outcomes of change. At Westauto, the persistent path of production work typical for Russian manufacturing enterprises was broken; at Rusmet path dependence was weakened; at Rusauto the change did not lead to either breaking or weakening of the persistent path.

1.3 Theoretical perspective: change in the Russian industrial workplace as breaking path dependence

Most of the existing conceptualisations of continuity and change in Russian industrial enterprises stem from studies conducted in domestic companies,

Introduction 11

where little change in work and management structures was observed. The research addresses causes of persistence in the Russian industrial workplace at the level of the national economy and at the level of management structures on the shop-floor: the lack of impact of radical economic reforms of the 1990s on the industrial workplace (Burawoy 2001; Burawoy and Krotov 1992; Clarke 2007); the inertia of the customary templates, practices and values (Schwartz and McCann 2007; Shershneva and Feldhoff 1999); and interrelatedness of elements constituting the Russian approach to management and work organisation on the shop-floor (Clarke 2007). Integration of Russia's economy into global capitalism is viewed as a force driving change of the persistent practices (see Clarke 2007; Schwartz and McCann 2007), but it happens too slowly to produce observable effects at the national level.

The car industry in Russia provides empirical grounds particularly fitting for studying the effects of internationalisation on the industrial workplace. This is a medium to highly technological industry, which attracted a large inflow of FDI. The car industry was a key empirical context for the international debate about production systems and work. This debate focused in particular on the possibility for convergence of production systems and their elements across borders and the role of national regulatory institutions and culture in this process (e.g. Boyer *et al.* 1998). A recent study on HR policies in car manufacturers' plants in Brazil, Russia, China and India supports the convergence thesis and argues that multinational firms succeed in standardising their HR practices across locations (Jürgens and Krzywdzinski 2016). Personnel management at automobile manufacturers' plants converges towards high-performance work practices (cf. Appelbaum, Bailey and Berg 2001; Guest 1997, on high-performance work practices). The automobile manufacturers, however, bear imprints of their home-country employment systems logics, which surface at a deeper level of personnel management at subsidiaries' plants. The authors conclude that the effects of company-level standards outweigh the influence of the subsidiaries' locations (Jürgens and Krzywdzinski 2016:311).

The research focusing on local Russian firms and the studies on car manufacturers in Russia provide contrasting explanations of continuity and change in the Russian industrial workplace. The former stream of research argues in favour of social structures that are almost impossible to overcome. The latter studies give a picture of nearly unrestricted agency by both multinational and local car manufacturers. A conceptual perspective to continuity and change in the Russian industrial workplace, which would both account for how and why the traditional management structures evolved and explain why agency succeeds or fails to overcome their persistence, is currently missing. The following sections will explain how path dependence theory can fulfil this conceptual gap.

Conceptual toolkit of path dependence theory

The core of path dependence theory lies in the explanation of cases in which actors lose the capability to steer institutional or organisational development.

12 *Introduction*

The concept of path dependence was used in analysis of institutional change in Russia (see, e.g. Hedlund 2000), as well as the political and economic transformation of Central and Eastern Europe (e.g. Stark and Bruszt 1998). However, path dependence in this scholarship is understood rather generically as historical constraints on present choices (cf. Wetzel 2005).

The ideas stemming from path dependence in economics (David 1985; Arthur 1989) were overtaken and developed in historical institutionalism (see, e.g. Mahoney 2000; Mahoney and Thelen 2010b; Pierson 2000; Streeck and Thelen 2005a; Thelen 1999, 2009; Bennett and Elman 2006, for a discussion of the application of path dependence to case studies) and organisation studies (Schreyögg, Sydow and Koch 2003; Sydow, Schreyögg and Koch 2005, 2009). The formation of and changes in the path of industrial work in Russia will be conceptualised with the help of both of these streams of path dependence theory.

The formation of a path starts with a *critical juncture* – a phase in the historical process when the path is set on a trajectory, which it is then difficult to change. In organisation studies, critical juncture can be a decision or a choice that unintentionally sets off self-reinforcing development (Sydow, Schreyögg and Koch 2009:691). In historical institutionalism, critical juncture can be defined not only as a realised choice or an external shock, but also as 'moments of fluidity', when choices are *possible* and decisions *might* have a lasting impact (Capoccia and Kelemen 2007:348). The present study will draw upon this latter definition.

A critical juncture in path dependent processes is followed by a phase when the choices become increasingly constrained, which can eventually lead to the lock-in of an institution or an organisational form. The nature of these constraints plays a central role not only in the analysis of formation of a path dependent process, but also in explanations of deviation from locked-in paths:

> the key to understanding institutional evolution and change lies in specifying more precisely the reproduction and feedback mechanisms on which particular institutions rest.
>
> (Thelen 1999:400)

What is crucial about these constraints is that they give a path a self-reinforcing character: they drive (*antreiben*) the process of path formation "as if they generated a maelstrom that steers actors further and further in a particular direction" (Koch 2007:286, author's translation).

Sydow *et al.* distinguish between four reinforcement mechanisms (Sydow, Schreyögg and Koch 2009). *Coordination effects* develop when more and more actors follow a system of rules. These rules then start gaining support as they help to foresee the reactions of other actors and reduce transaction costs. *Complementary effects* occur as organisational practices are interconnected in a way that creates synergies: 'following a rule becomes more attractive due to its interdependence with other [rules]' (Ackermann 2003:240, author's translation). Therefore, it is attractive to apply clusters or bundles of routines. *Learning effects* develop, as the

Introduction 13

chosen solution becomes more attractive, when actors accumulate the skills required to perform it. Actors are then reluctant to switch to a new solution that would require learning 'from scratch'. *Adaptive expectations effects* result from the need for social belonging and legitimacy. This effect is explained as organisations' "desire to end up on the winning side" (Sydow, Schreyögg and Koch 2009:700).

When a path dependent process becomes *locked-in*, actors' choices are highly restricted and deviation from the path dependent arrangement is very difficult (ibid.:692). Lock-in of an organisational form is conceptualised as a 'core pattern' or actors' logic underlying the action, which remains constant even though some degree of variation might characterise its manifestations (cf. Koch 2007:287). Such understanding of a locked-in path gives space for some diversity as the same organisational principles can be expressed in different organisational settings.

The conceptual tools of path dependence theory discussed above will guide the analysis of the *formation* of the socialist path of industrial work in Russia (see Chapters 2 and 3). The historical account will analyse the choices available at the start of the development of the Russian path of industrial work, identify the self-reinforcement mechanisms that eventually led to a lock-in and question whether the path was unlocked in the 1990s or in the mid-2000s.

Breaking path dependence

Newer developments in path dependence theory call for bringing it closer to real life, which it models. The theory should overcome the deterministic understanding of paths and allow for change in path dependent processes (Thelen 1999:385; Deeg 2001, 2005:170; Sydow, Schreyögg and Koch 2005:19). These developments make path dependence suitable for the study of not only continuity, but also change in the Russian industrial workplace.

The idea of deliberately breaking path dependence is self-contradictory, as lost power to choose among alternatives is the core of the definition of path dependence (Sydow, Schreyögg and Koch 2009:702). Therefore the literature has traditionally followed the punctuated equilibrium model of change, when long periods of stability are interrupted by rare exogenous shocks leading to a radical shift (Pierson 2000; Streeck and Thelen 2005b). Later studies create a dynamic analytical perspective to institutional change, when path reinforcement mechanisms and impulses or mechanisms promoting change can be at work at the same time (Streeck and Thelen 2005b:19). Similarly, Sydow *et al.* argue that actors have to address and interrupt the self-reinforcement dynamics to introduce an alternative solution (Sydow, Schreyögg and Koch 2009).

Conceptual studies on interrupting self-reinforcement dynamics emphasise the cognitive and resource dimensions of change from within (Crouch and Farrell 2004; Sydow, Schreyögg and Koch 2005:19; see also Koch 2007:287). Actors can carry out change if they have access to alternative behaviour (Crouch and Farrell 2004). Such access can come from redundant capacities or include actors'

14 *Introduction*

own dormant resources (e.g. past repertoires of action) and behaviour that exists in other 'fields'. Thus, the impulse to break an institutional path can come both from within the organisation and through actors' insertion into new networks. Two conclusions can be drawn. First, actors can initiate path breaking without an external shock if they gain access to knowledge about alternative behaviour and the resources needed. The second conclusion is a methodological one: the analysis of path breaking processes should carefully distinguish between the old and the new elements in institutions or organisational forms in question.

Summing up, the following definition of path breaking appears plausible. Path breaking is overcoming of the mechanisms reinforcing the old path in order to introduce a new organisational solution. Path dependence can be considered broken when the mechanisms reinforcing the old path are eliminated or significantly weakened and at least some new elements are introduced. A new path is established if the behaviour in question is guided by new principles and mechanisms sustaining the new logic are created.

Outcomes of path breaking

The literature on post-socialist transformation emphasises the coexistence of the old and the new in institutions and organisations (Clarke 2007; Stark 2001; Stark and Bruszt 1998, 2001). Post-socialism scholars apply the concept of 'bricolage' to emphasise the dominance of old elements in the 'institutional materials' used in post-socialist transformation. Path dependence theory also distinguishes between the old and the new elements in institutions and organisational forms. It emphasises, however, that analysis of change in a persistent institution should question to what extent the mechanisms reinforcing the old institution have been weakened (cf. Sydow, Schreyögg and Koch 2009). In this way it offers conceptual tools for a more fine-grained study of continuity and change in the Russian industrial workplace.

The concept of bricolage is understood as institutional innovation that occurs through the creative recombination of several old institutional principles by actors (Campbell 1999:22). Campbell argues that bricolage is a path dependent way of institutional change, as actors choose between the old principles at their disposal, but he does not establish closer conceptual links between bricolage and path dependence theory (Campbell 2004). While bricolage is generally viewed positively by Stark and Bruszt (Stark and Bruszt 2001), Gerber notes that bricolage can also take "a pernicious form" in his study of wage arrears in Russia, due to the negative social and economic consequences of wage arrears (Gerber 2006).

When new ideas are combined with already existing institutions, Campbell uses the term 'translation' to describe the resulting change (Campbell 2004). 'Translation' essentially means adaptation of new ideas to the local institutional context and their combination with the old locally given elements. Despite this distinction between 'bricolage' and 'translation', the concept of bricolage is often used in the literature to signify a mixture of old and new (see, e.g. Boxenbaum

Introduction 15

and Battilana 2005) and change through trial and error, as opposed to purposeful change efforts with clear aims (cf. Stark 2001:70).

Similarly to studies on bricolage, research on breaking path dependence argues that "path breaking can vary in intensity and complexity" (Sydow, Schreyögg and Koch 2009:702). However, the research emphasises that the minimum condition for change is a restoration of a choice situation, when a superior alternative becomes available. Change of a path dependent process requires not only bringing in some new elements, but also interrupting the self-reinforcing dynamics behind the persistent pattern (Sydow, Schreyögg and Koch 2009). Later studies in historical institutionalism call for considering the supporters of and challengers to the institution in question, these groups' capabilities to block the change process and the actors' possibilities to interpret the institutions in question (Mahoney and Thelen 2010a). These elements constitute the rivalling dynamics between the mechanisms reinforcing the old path and the ones stabilising a new institution.

Both the path dependence theory and the concept of 'bricolage' provide important insights for the conceptualisation of breaking the persistent path of industrial work in the present study. They help in focusing attention on the change mechanisms that can be put in place in the course of the change process and on the coexistence and possible contradictions of old and new elements in the change outcome.

The empirical analysis in the following chapters will first retrace the evolution of the socialist path of industrial work in the twentieth century Russia. Then it will concentrate on the period, when the Russian automotive industry was rapidly internationalised. This shift led to establishment of a new 'best way' to manage quality in production: international automotive QM standards, which became recognised and supported by both international and domestic automobile manufacturers. According to the path dependence theory, introduction of the new QM concepts can take place if local managers gain access to new knowledge and resources. These might comprise both the past or 'dormant' repertoires of action, in Crouch and Farrell's terms (Crouch and Farrell 2004), and external resources, which can include interaction with international companies, where the new quality standards are already in place. The rivalling dynamics between the mechanisms reinforcing the socialist path of industrial work and the mechanisms sustaining the new QM standards will determine the outcome of path breaking. It is possible to argue that path dependence was broken, if introduction of new QM concepts led to elimination or significant weakening of the mechanisms reinforcing the old path and a deviation from the punitive principles characteristic for the old path took place.

1.4 Research questions

The study will start by determining persistent characteristics of production work in the Russian automotive industry prior to the start of this industry's internationalisation. Then it will examine the determinants, processes and outcomes of change resulting from the introduction of international QM standards. The study is guided by two starting assumptions. First, it is assumed that the introduction of

16 *Introduction*

international QM standards in the Russian automotive industry has led to breaking the persistent path of industrial work. Second, it is assumed that companies exposed to close collaboration with foreign partners are more likely to break from the socialist path of industrial work.

The study is guided by the following questions:

1. What were the core characteristics of the path of industrial work in the Russian automobile industry prior to the start of its internationalisation? What role did punitive principles play in this path?
2. How did the agency at the industry and company levels shape the introduction of the international QM standards in Russian automotive enterprises? Who were the supporters and challengers of the new QM standards?
3. How did the introduction of international QM standards change the path of industrial work in the Russian automobile industry? Was the punitive path of industrial work broken?

1. The first question addresses the path of industrial work in Russian automotive enterprises prior to the start of the internationalisation of the industry and evaluates the role of punitive elements in it. Multiple studies argue that distinct elements of production work and personnel policies have persisted in Russian industrial enterprises since the planned economy and that these have not been changed by the market reforms of the early 1990s. There is no agreement in the literature, however, with regard to the role that the market reforms played for the whole path of industrial work. The present study will revisit the question of whether the persistent path was broken as a result of the market reforms. The analysis will both retrace the evolution of the main elements of the path of industrial work and study the mechanisms that reinforced the path during the transition to a market economy.

2. The second question will address the role of industry-level (external) and company-level (internal) agency in the processes and outcomes of the introduction of new QM standards at the level of production line. Industry-level agency includes actions of international and domestic Russian automobile assemblers and industrial associations related to the diffusion of the new quality-related requirements in the industry. Company-level agency comprises managers' actions aimed at gaining access to knowledge and other resources needed for carrying out change, as well as their efforts to discontinue the mechanisms reinforcing the persistent path and establish processes sustaining the new QM concepts. The analysis will discuss the supporters and challengers of the new standards at both the industry level and the organisational level.

3. The third question will evaluate the impact that international QM standards have had on the path of industrial work in the Russian automobile industry. Drawing upon the historical analysis, an evaluation will be made as to whether and to what extent the core principles underlying the persistent path of production work were changed by the introduction of new QM standards. This will be followed by a discussion on whether path dependence has been broken following this change.

1.5 Empirical data collection and analysis

The automobile industry in Russia can be considered a typical manufacturing branch, with series production of highly complex products. Yet it represents a unique case due to its rapid internationalisation between the years 2001 and 2007. The core of this research is based upon three case studies of automotive plants in Russia. The case study method allows obtaining "both a holistic view of the story and a detailed view of events", which are important in the study of path dependence (Bennett and Elman 2006:260). The case studies were preceded by extensive preparatory work (see Tables A.3 and A.4 in the Appendix), and were complemented by interviews with representatives of relevant institutions (see Table A.2 in the Appendix).

The case studies followed the 'causes-of-effects' approach (Goertz and Mahoney 2011). The results of case studies were predicted at the outset of the enquiry and cases were then analysed, focusing on how and why the predicted outcome took place (Yin 2009). This approach is in line with Eisenhardt and Stake, who suggest that case studies can be used in both hypothesis testing and theory-generating research (Eisenhardt 1989; Stake 2000). The analysis focused on within-case dynamics in the persistent path of industrial work in Russia and involved causal-process observations or process tracing (Collier 2011; Goertz and Mahoney 2011). Dynamics was mainly traced along research dimensions formulated prior to case studies. Some new categories, however, evolved in the course of research. Thus, the research methodology applied differs from grounded theory, which only develops theoretical assumptions from empirical data (cf. Charmaz 2006). Still, there is some similarity with grounded theory due to a degree of openness in the data collection and analysis.

The selection of cases followed the recommendation to arrive at a 'theoretical' or 'purposive' sample (cf. Eisenhardt 1989:533; Stake 2000:446). In other words, the sample should help to verify the starting assumption of the study. Companies exposed to close collaboration with foreign partners are assumed to be more likely to break from the socialist path of industrial work. Therefore, two of the companies selected were exposed to two different forms of collaboration with foreign partners: Westauto is a greenfield production site of a Western multinational automobile assembler with a European headquarters in Germany; Rusmet is a Russian automotive supplier, which exports a share of its output to a German customer. The third company in the sample, Rusauto, is a long-established indigenous automobile assembler that survived the market reforms.[4]

The three plants are comparable in terms of employee numbers; they employed 2,000–3,000 people at the time of the research and belong to the metal industry (see Table 1.5 for an overview).

This sample of cases is a result of more than a year's effort to get research access to the automotive companies located in Russia. The problem of access is a typical characteristic of empirical research in the industry (see, e.g. Bulmer 1988). Yet, companies in Russia proved to be much more closed than their counterparts in Europe, where some of the expert interviews and pilot case studies were conducted. The access requests, sent by email or fax, had to be followed up

18   *Introduction*

Table 1.5 Case studies conducted in Russia

Company code	Ownership	Product	Employees
Westauto	Western; European Headquarters in Germany	Automobile assembly	Over 2,000
Rusmet	Russian	High-precision metal parts[1]	About 3,000
Rusauto	Russian	Automobile assembly	Over 3,000

Source: Author
Note: 1. The product is not disclosed as the company asked for maximum anonymity

by several phone calls. Then they would slowly travel to the very top of the hier-archical ladder and be rejected. The 'snowball strategy' to contact development (Robson 1993) proved to be the only way to gain access to the Russian compa-nies. Attendance of industry events, such as automobile exhibitions and seminars for industry practitioners, were used to speak to company representatives person-ally. A chain of personal contacts ultimately allowed contacts to be established with representatives of selected companies.

The Russian companies' unwillingness to let a researcher in can be partly explained by the sensitivity of the topic of QM. Companies feared that the study would uncover negative information about the company's quality policies and that the research findings might be communicated to company partners in Russia or abroad. Besides, the very situation of collaboration between production enterprises and a social scientist was new for the companies contacted. Finally, the idea that the research project held no business interest on behalf of a German company or organ-isation was difficult to convey. Russian company managers did not believe in the non-commercial character of the study and suspected industrial spying. Such strug-gle for access might explain the lack of research on Russian industrial enterprises.

The analysis of continuity and change in the Russian industrial workplace encompassed four main dimensions or embedded units of analysis (Yin 2009), described in Table 1.1. Semi-structured interview supported by interview guide-lines was the primary method of data collection (Hopf 1991). The interviewing strategy used in the investigation is referred to as 'expert interviews' (Bogner and Menz 2002; Meuser and Nagel 2002). The chosen interviewing strategy had a strong focus on certain restricted parts of the respondent's experience or knowl-edge that she obtained through her position in an organisational or institutional context. The interview prioritised the *information* provided by the respondent over the *process* of interviewing (cf. Holstein and Gubrium 2002).

Creating an open trustful atmosphere for the conversation proved to be more difficult in Russia than in other countries. Distrust and fear discussed above surfaced in the interview situation as well. The initial interview phase concentrated on overcoming gender-related scepticism from male interviewees (cf. Fontana and Frey 2000). As interviews proceeded, respondents showed signs

Introduction 19

of anxiety. Most of the conversations carried out in Russia have not been recorded, which alleviated the social desirability bias in the answers. Detailed notes were taken during the interviews, instead of recording, and transcribed shortly after. Even so, some respondents asked that some of their statements were not written down.

In total, 62 personal interviews were carried out in the period between 2005 and 2009, when the Russian car industry was promptly opened to international investment and competition (see Table 1.6).

Interviews at the plants lasted between 40 and 60 minutes; some of the interviews with external experts lasted up to 1.5 hours. The interviews were transcribed and a complete data base was created. The transcripts were coded using the software program for qualitative analysis ATLAS.ti (Friese 2014). First, the interview texts were coded on the basis of the research dimensions. Then, new codes were created on the basis of the interviewees' statements, which in some cases delivered new insights for analysis.

Interviewees at the plants typically included managers from three functional areas: QM, production management and personnel management (see Table 1.7). Where possible, interviews with a training manager, a purchasing manager and an employee representative were conducted.

Interviews in the companies were complemented by document analysis, observation, analysis of media publications and industry reports in order to enable the triangulation of data (Flick 2007). Table A.1 in the Appendix gives an overview of the additional sources used. These sources were complemented with interviews with experts in international QM standards, automotive industry, education, vocational training and in-house personnel training. This allowed analysis of the context for the introduction of the international QM standards in Russia.

Table 1.6 Interviews statistics

Type of interviews	Time of interviews	Number of interviews
Interviews with experts in international quality management standards	2006–7	9
Interviews with experts in the automotive industry	2006–8	6
Interviews with experts in education, vocational training and personnel training in the companies	2006–9	8
Pilot interviews at the plants	2005–6	11
Pilot case studies of automotive plants in Germany and Poland	2006–7	8
Case studies of automotive plants in Russia	2007–9	20
Total		62

Source: Author

20　*Introduction*

Table 1.7 Interviews conducted for the case studies of automotive plants in Russia

Plant	Interviewees' positions
Westauto	HR Manager, Quality Manager 1, Purchasing Manager, Production Manager, Supplier Development Specialist, Training Leader, Quality Manager 2,[1] Trade Union Coordinator for Work Safety
Rusauto	Quality Director, Personnel Director, Head of Quality Assurance in Production Department, Quality Manager from a Western partner company, Quality Engineer for Certification, Supplier Quality Assurance Manager at Rusauto JV, Head of Quality of Supplied Parts Department
Rusmet	Plant Director (CEO), Quality Director, Production Director, Chief Auditor and Training Leader, Head of Work Organisation and Pay Department

Source: Author
Note: 1. Quality Manager 2 substituted the Quality Manager 1 interviewed during the first study visit to the plant in 2007

Some of the context interviews, pilot interviews at the plants and a pilot case study were carried out in Germany (see Tables A.2–A.4 in the Appendix). Actors from the German automotive industry played a major role in the establishment of international automotive QM standards. Debate on QM in the German automotive industry peaked in the 1990s and has currently entered the phase of highly specialised discussion, focusing on the needs of the industry. Inclusion of data from Germany allowed for a better understanding of the industry-specific QM standards that are being introduced in Russia and their impact on industrial work. It created a background for comparison between QM in production in the Russian automotive industry and the contemporary approach to quality in a leading automotive nation.

Data from the case studies were complemented by extensive context interviews divided into three groups (see Table A.2 in the Appendix). The first group explored standardisation in the field of QM and the introduction of these standards in Russian industrial companies. It included experts in standardisation and certification in QM, as well as seven management consultants, who consulted Russian companies on QM. The second group concentrated on QM requirements in the automotive industry. It investigated the development and application of automotive QM standards in the international automotive industry, and current requirements for QM in the Russian automotive industry. The third group focused on competencies related to QM provided by public institutions of education and vocational training in Germany and Russia.

Preparation for the case studies in Russia started with pilot interviews at metal industry plants in Russia and at automotive plants in Germany (see Table A.3 in the Appendix). Then two pilot case studies of automotive suppliers were conducted: in a post-socialist country – Poland, and in a developed capitalist economy – Germany (see Table A.4 in the Appendix). Access and geographic proximity were additional criteria for selecting these two plants. The scope of

Introduction 21

enquiry in the pilot case studies was broader than in the actual case studies in Russia, which enabled a narrowing down of the questions for the Russian cases.

The analysis of continuity and change in the main principles of the Russian path of industrial work constitutes the core of the present study. It was based upon a careful historical analysis of the formation of the Soviet path of industrial work performed (see Chapter 2).

1.6 Overview of the chapters

The introduction is followed by four chapters (2–5) and conclusion (6). Chapter 2 describes the formation of the path of industrial work in Russia under a planned economy and identifies its core characteristics. It argues that, by the early 1980s, the industrial workplace in Russia was characterised by a specific pattern of interrelated elements: the separation between direct and indirect functions on the shop-floor, the organisation of group or 'brigade' work, the worker qualification and remuneration systems. The path of industrial work became persistent due to the complementary character of these elements, the high degree of coordination among the state regulatory and research institutions and the system of vocational training that all centred on the Soviet approach to organisation of production and work.

Chapter 3 revisits the question as to whether the Soviet path of industrial work was broken after the market reforms by systematically comparing the characteristics of industrial work before and after the reforms took place. The chapter argues that after the market reforms Russian production enterprises not only recombined the already existing elements constituting industrial work under a planned economy, but they also began to introduce some novel international concepts, primarily in the areas of personnel management and QM. Nevertheless, these new concepts did not challenge the core characteristics of the Soviet path of industrial work.

Chapter 4 opens with a brief discussion of the content of international QM standards and their implications for industrial work in the West. This discussion shows that the two central ideas underlying the new management standards, involvement of shop-floor workers in operational decisions and flexible standardisation, cardinally contradict the Russian path of industrial work characterised by punitive methods and high management discretion. The chapter then analyses the agency aimed at diffusion of international QM standards throughout the Russian car industry and the development of the corresponding institutional infrastructure. It shows that the introduction of new quality standards was met with resistance among domestic firms and analyses the supporters and challengers of the standards at the industry level.

Chapter 5 first analyses how quality assurance in production changed following the introduction of the new QM standards. It discusses the role of Russian managers, expatriates and foreign partners in the change processes and describes the actual management standards introduced at the three plants. It

22 *Introduction*

then investigates how the change influenced the workers' role in quality assurance, managers' attitudes to worker-caused defects and the extent to which the culture of fear regarding the reporting of mistakes was overcome. Second, the chapter analyses the broader implications of the new management standards for the industrial workplace in the plants studied. It discusses whether the plants departed from the Soviet principles of group or 'brigade' work and integrated quality assurance tasks into the brigades' formal functions. Then it investigates if the plants deviated from the narrow technical approach to workers' qualification and trained workers in quality assurance competences. The last section of the chapter addresses remuneration, bonuses and sanctions for performance quality on the shop-floor, which was the key means to discipline workers under the planned economy.

Chapter 6 draws conclusions in the light of the research questions posed in the outset. The empirical study showed that the introduction of international management standards led to different patterns of continuity and change in the three plants studied. The findings suggest that breaking away from path dependence in the Russian industrial workplace is a gradual and lengthy process, and that this is not possible without collaboration with international companies, where alternative solutions to organisation of production, work and quality control are implemented. External pressure and support in learning have to be combined with the enduring presence of managers with personal exposure to international management concepts. This agency should both establish mechanisms stabilising the new QM standards in the Russian industrial workplace and weaken the mechanisms reinforcing the Soviet legacy.

Notes

1 According to the Russian Federal Statistics Service the manufacturing sector in Russia employed 10,281,000 people in 2011 (Federal'naya Sluzhba Statistiki 2012:134).
2 Organisation Internationale des Constructeurs d'Automobiles.
3 It should be noted that low product quality was not the only reason behind the low number of shared suppliers. The Russian automotive industry was still characterised by a high degree of vertical integration. Supplier share in added value in local Russian OEMs in 2007 amounted to about 20–26 per cent compared to 66 per cent in the case of international OEMs (Ernst & Young 2007). Thus, Russian suppliers lacked the expertise in production of more complex and more technically demanding parts for international OEMs.
4 The companies' names were coded. The first part of the code is an abbreviation of a company's location and the second – of its product. In case of automobiles 'auto' was used.

2 Evolving persistence

The socialist path of industrial work in Russia (1920s–80s)

The persistent path of industrial work in Russia was formed in the socialist period of the country's history. The socialist enterprise differed strikingly from the capitalist factory. Due to the centrality of the plan and output targets under the planned economy, most of the conflicts and contradictions elucidated in the literature revolve around the plan and productivity. The role of quality control in the socialist path of industrial work did not receive a lot of attention, apart from brief remarks about the neglect of quality. Nevertheless, the quality of work performance on the shop-floor played an influential role in workers' remuneration and the need to improve product quality motivated development and diffusion of the Complex Systems of production management in the 1950s–70s. The period of the 1970s–80s was particularly significant for the formation of complementary effects between group work, quality control, remuneration and qualification systems at socialist enterprises. The purposeful development of these effects in the Soviet automotive industry is largely underestimated by Western scholarship.

The present chapter will show that the development of the socialist path of industrial work in Russia represented a path dependent process. It will retrace the development of the core principles constituting the socialist path of industrial work and present quality control as one of its integral elements. The analysis will describe the mechanisms reinforcing the path that were in place by the start of the transition to a market economy.

2.1 The 'scientific organisation of labour' in the early twentieth century

The years immediately after the October Socialist revolution were a time of great uncertainty and chaos, but also a time of decisions that shaped the future of the socialist state. This was a critical juncture in the country's developmental path: a short period of 'fluidity', when decisions with a lasting impact were made (cf. Capoccia and Kelemen 2007). Two of the Bolsheviks' decisions taken at that time became very influential for the socialist path of industrial work. One of them had to do with the organisation of production and work in the Soviet state – this was the decision to introduce a narrow technocratic version of Taylor's ideas

24   *Evolving persistence*

about work organisation, authored by Alexei Gastev, and to reject the alternative. The alternative vision demanded modification of Taylorism to bring it into accordance with workers' interests. The other decision was to begin forced industrialisation and to introduce criminal responsibility for work shirking and discipline violation. Forced industrialisation was supported by a number of laws introduced in the 1920s, which gave production work a strongly punitive character in the very early years of the workers' state.

There was some degree of openness with regard to decisions on the organisation of production and work in the early years of the Soviet state. The Bolsheviks were eager to speed up industrialisation and they studied Taylorism's potential to assist in organising work in a socialist state. There were two turning points in the Soviet debate on work organisation at that time. At first, it was discussed whether to adopt Taylorism or to develop an alternative approach, better fitted for a workers' state. Later, when it was accepted that Taylorism could be used to help build socialism, there was still a choice between two Soviet interpretations of Taylorism, which evolved at that time: Gastev's and Kerzhentsev's (Sochor 1981).

Until the 1920s, the Soviet debate about Taylorism remained ambiguous. Lenin spoke positively of Taylorism, arguing that capitalist methods could be employed to increase productivity and efficiency in a socialist state, as workers would be 'working for themselves' (ibid.). However, Alexander Bogdanov,[1] one of the most consistent opponents of Taylorism, argued that "the 'latest achievements of capitalism' were not value-free and required a fundamental alteration before they could serve workers' interests" (ibid.:249). He named several problems that could be not only harmful for the Soviet state, but also counter-productive: a rift between the best workers and less devoted workers, the counter-productivity of repetitive tasks and an increase of managerial personnel due to the need for timekeepers and overseers (ibid.). The discussion ended with the adoption of Taylorism or "the scientific organisation of labour" (or NOT),[2] as the alternatives were less concrete and appeared less feasible.

In the 1920s, two movements within NOT evolved: the 'pragmatists', led by Gastev, and the socially minded 'ideologues', led by Kerzhentsev (Sochor 1981). Gastev studied the works of F.W. Taylor and was in correspondence with Henry Ford; he viewed Taylorism as a purely technical matter and was not concerned with its exploitative character. His ideas were characterised by an individualistic and mechanical view of the worker. Gastev focused on the organisation of a single workplace and wrote poems about 'the mechanical man' (Edelman 2003). 'Ideologues' criticised Gastev's approach for its oversimplification ('narrow base'), its 'militarist drill', low collectivism and mechanical, non-conscious view of work (Edelman 2003; Sochor 1981). The ideologues argued that NOT should attempt to attract workers to its principles through incentives and education, that it should be conceived as a systemic approach and applied to society as a whole. They called for the engagement of the Communist Party in the questions of NOT and had a very humanistic vision of it:

Evolving persistence 25

the point of departure for *NOT* efforts should be the protection of worker interests rather than the intensification of labour. Thus *NOT* should not concentrate on individual exertion but should orient itself toward production processes, efficient utilization of machines, and rationalization of plant. Ultimately, advanced technology and automation would transfer 'slave labour' to machines and liberate man.

(Sochor 1981:253, italics in the original)

Nevertheless, rather than this worker-centred interpretation of Taylorism, Gastev's ideas of mechanical man were supported by Lenin. In 1921, he allocated significant funds to the Central Institute of Labour (or TsIT)[3] headed by Gastev (Edelman 2003).

TsIT took up training peasants for Soviet industry. The simplicity of Gastev's ideas allowed him to quickly advance workers' training, which was a highly pressing task. Training concentrated on precision of physical movement and workers were viewed as 'living machines':

The machine functions properly when its frame and tools are *set* correctly.... It is the same with a man: the *set* of the body and of the nerves defines the movement and the working skill. At first the movement goes with difficulty and then, when the *set* is formed, the movement goes confidently, precisely and fast.... The set is created gradually by training. The training can be precisely *calculated*, made easy. The training can also teach how to switch fast from one set to another.[4]

(Gastev 1973:156, author's translation, italics added)

TsIT complemented training with individual timekeeping: it developed a system of cards for a detailed everyday time record. Remarkably, timekeeping was supposed to include not only employees' working time but also private time. Quoting Ward, "the world envisaged by Frederick Taylor's Soviet disciples makes even Adam Smith's liberal-capitalist prognosis seem positively benign" (Ward 1990). Workers were only trained in a narrowly defined set of direct skills and the organisation of work had a narrow and mechanistic character as well. Mechanistic rhetoric also penetrated private life. The concepts developed by TsIT were later broadly applied in the country in vocational training and the organisation of work, and developed further by research institutes; psychophysiological and 'psycho-technical' laboratories were created at the factories (Kravchenko and Shcherbina 1998).

The Soviet automobile industry became a trial ground for both NOT and Fordism. The manufacture of motor vehicles in Russia started at the end of the nineteenth century; the first Soviet-built motor vehicles were manufactured in Soviet Russia in 1924 (Parker 1980).[5] The automobile industry started to develop rapidly in the 1930s when the first Russian automobile factory, AMO, was reconstructed and the Gorky Automobile Works[6] (GAZ) started mass production of trucks and passenger cars (ibid.). GAZ, which was opened in 1932, was 'the most

26 *Evolving persistence*

up-to-date motor vehicle plant in the world and one of the largest, with a capacity of 100,000 trucks a year' (ibid.:517). Remarkably, mass production of Soviet automobiles at GAZ started with the help of the Ford Motor Company. In 1929 the Supreme Soviet of the National Economy signed an agreement with the Ford Motor Company about technical assistance in the organisation of mass production of passenger vehicles, Ford-A, and lorries, Ford-AA (ibid.). Production technology and parts were provided by Ford and Soviet workers were sent to America for training as foremen. Work organisation at the plant was guided by NOT and a psychophysiological laboratory was created at the plant in the year it was opened (Kravchenko and Shcherbina 1998).

The political support of Gastev's TsIT should be considered within the political context of that time, which was characterised by both openness and experiments with economic policies, and the punitive turn of labour relations. Therefore, the openness of the choice between Gastev's version of NOT and that of Kerzhentsev was rather limited, contrary to the argument of Sochor, who has emphasised the ambiguity and ideological tensions preceding the decision (Sochor 1981). Gastev's Taylorism did have a 'first-mover advantage', as his crude version of Taylorism allowed him to offer the Soviet state training tools that were in high demand in the early stages of industrialisation. Application of Kerzhentsev's sophisticated vision of production organisation would, on the contrary, require time. Nevertheless, the principle reason for adopting Gastev's version of NOT in Russia was its coherence with the intention of the political elite of that time to speed up industrialisation at any human cost. This intention was realised in the punitive labour laws that came into force in the 1920s (Grinberg 1993).

The labour laws introduced criminal responsibility for evading labour and for violation of labour discipline. Moreover, collective criminal responsibility for individual violations of work discipline was introduced. Not only the violator herself, but also managers or colleagues who did not prevent the violation or did not report it could be sentenced or forced into corrective work (ibid.). This blurred the borders between individual and collective responsibility. Pushing workers to report about their peers' misconduct and so to expose them to penalties had a profound impact on social norms in the workplace. On the one hand, this strengthened social control through 'snitches', but, on the other hand, it made concealing mistakes or defects a socially approved action. In this way, penalties had a detrimental effect on individual responsibility in the workplace.

Adoption of Gastev's version of NOT and the introduction of punitive labour laws became the first building blocks in the formation of the socialist path of industrial work. Formal organisation of work concentrated on a single working place and not the production process as a whole. Workers were trained in a narrow set of direct skills. Work execution was separated from control and, just as Bogdanov had warned, a high number of administrative and controlling personnel were needed to keep production going. Socially minded ideology did not constitute the core of the approach to work organisation by, for example, giving workers the right to take decisions about their work. Instead, it became an

Evolving persistence 27

external means of control applied by the state in order to legitimatise the essentially de-humanised character of production work. Socialist ideology was present in production, but detached from formal work organisation, and turned into 'ideological work' kept up by the trade unions.

The decisions to implement Taylor's ideas on scientific management and to carry out intensive industrialisation, neglecting its human cost, did not have a contingent character in the sense of organisational path dependence. They did not represent small events that unintentionally set the socialist path of industrial work on a punitive trajectory (Sydow, Schreyögg and Koch 2009). However, the decisions regarding production work that were taken at that time were contingent in the sense of being a highly unlikely outcome of the historical development of a workers' state (cf. Bennett and Elman 2006, for a discussion of this type of contingency). Adoption of the mechanistic and de-humanising version of scientific management in the socialist state was unexpected and surprising:

> it is almost incredible that not one political leader [in Soviet Russia] tried to articulate a critical sociology of the labour process by developing the libertarian strand in Marxism.
>
> (Ward 1990:142)

Instead of centring on workers' interests, the path of industrial work in Russia attained a punitive character from the very early years.

2.2 Forced-pace industrialisation and worker mobilisation campaigns

The scientific and political debate on work organisation was abandoned as Stalin's forced-pace industrialisation began in the 1930s. In order to speed up the industrialisation, the state began to devise five-year plans for the whole economy. Workers were called to contribute to the industrialisation through worker mobilisation movements, such as shock work, Stakhanovism and socialist competition. Under these rubrics the state attempted to cultivate a certain attitude to work – the eagerness to fulfil work tasks above the formal assignments (Siegelbaum 1988). This had profound implications for the path of industrial work, since the formal regulations in production came under pressure from both within and outside the factory walls. At the same time, Stalin's terror began, which also affected the industrial workplace. The following section will analyse whether the narrow technocratic version of Taylorism and the punitive character of industrial work adopted in the first years of the Soviet state persisted during the 1930s and what new elements were formed.

The formal regulation of production under Stalin came under pressure both from outside the enterprise and from within. On the one hand, the task of devising the detailed five-year plans for the whole economy was highly challenging. The fast-paced industrialisation and limitations of planning led to frequent disruptions in the flow of production. Soviet enterprises had to fulfil growing production

28 *Evolving persistence*

targets while regularly facing supply shortages, low-quality materials and short-age of workers (Christensen 1999; Clarke 2007). All of this made it difficult to follow the technological requirements of production. On the other hand, the rules were undermined furthermore from within the enterprise. Worker mobilisation campaigns supported by the party, such as the shock work movement, Stakhanovism[7] and socialist competition, were aimed at motivating workers to significantly raise their output by applying the available technology or developing new ways to work (Siegelbaum 1988).

Socialist competition called for the introduction of 'progressive' output norms at all levels of the economy: from individual workers and brigades to automobile enterprises that were to compete with each other. The ultimate form of the movement was a nationwide competition:

> 'The Soviet people, in competing with each other, discard everything back-ward and conservative that hinders their progress.' They emulate the experience of the better workers, introduce new techniques and better methods of organizing labour and production. This is manifested in the improvement of the norms of machine utilization, outlay of materials, stocks and fuel, and in the raising of labour norms.
>
> (Wang 1951:407)

In reality, however, these movements led to a divergence between the workers participating in them and the rest of the workforce and they undermined the authority of formal rules governing production work. Siegelbaum quotes Filtzer's argument about the consequences of Stakhanovism:

> Stakhanovism led to serious disruptions of production, a deterioration in quality, an overtaxing of machinery, and increased stoppages and breakdowns.
>
> (Siegelbaum 1988:4)

As Stakhanovites and other shock-workers needed to get all the supplies and machinery necessary for their work, these movements inevitably undermined the formal regulations within the enterprise. Coupled with external disruptions faced by the enterprises, these ideological worker mobilisation movements widened the discrepancy between planned and actual production and work processes, and even inspired falsifications of production results.

Stalin's industrialisation was synonymous with coercion and fear, which applied to managers, engineering personnel and workers. Any manager or engineer who stood in the way of workers adopting Stakhanovist principles or appeared otherwise not safe and unreliable was threatened by the purges (Christensen 1999). Even the ideologists of NOT were subject to repression (Kravchenko and Shcherbina 1998). Reductions in pay, corrective work or imprisonment due to violating labour discipline appeared 'soft' penalties against this background.

Evolving persistence 29

The wage system introduced in Russia in 1931 also served the aim of increasing productivity (Siegelbaum 1988:48). The most important novelty in the new wage system was increased emphasis on individual tasks and individual piece-rates; brigade rates and brigade work in general were criticised and declined. Moreover, progressive piece-rates[8] monitored by the foreman were introduced – that is, wages would rise once the output norm had been reached. Shock-workers and workers participating in other mobilisation campaigns were generously paid and also rewarded by goods. Piece-rates were not an adequate means to motivate workers, as problems with maintenance and supply led to periods of idleness and strongly interfered with workers' productivity (cf. Clarke 1993).

The severity of the penalties aimed at controlling production workers during the time of forced industrialisation did not help to secure discipline. Christensen suggests that the massive numbers of workers violating norms of work at that time was a sign of protest, as work reality was dramatically different from the ideological claims of the regime (Christensen 1999). At the same time, managers had little space for disciplining workers, both during the mass mobilisation campaigns and after them, due to the continuing labour shortage and they were, therefore, reluctant to fire workers. This gave workers the ability to withdraw efficiency. The combination of half-hearted disciplining measures and reluctance to fire resulted in 'punish-but-retain' logic in managing workers. Punish-but-retain logic was combined with workers' 'negative control' on the shop-floor (Clarke 1993). Clarke explains that workers were given a high degree of responsibility over fulfilment of their production tasks and had considerable informal control over the way in which they produced. At the same time, they had very little control over how much to produce or what they were paid for it. The combination of punish-but-retain logic and negative control on the shop-floor made production and work processes unstable and unpredictable and led to a high degree of ad hoc steering and negotiations on the shop-floor.

Production work under Stalin was centred on increasing productivity and output targets, and organisation of quality control on the shop-floor is hardly mentioned, even in thorough historical accounts about production work at that time (see, e.g. Ward 1990; Siegelbaum 1988). However, there is general agreement in the literature that the quantitative production indices were increased at the expense of repair work and of the quality of the finished product,[9] and that there was an enormous rate of wastage (see, e.g. Siegelbaum 1988). The party attempted to address the quality shortage with yet another ideological movement: 'a movement for excellence' (*otlichnichestvo*) was introduced in the mid-1930s (ibid.). Workers with the lowest share of defective articles in their output received individual bonuses. Thus, the regime applied individual material rewards as a means to both increase productivity and improve product quality. These means could not be efficient, as they did not address or question the core contradictions of the socialist path of industrial work.

During the decades of Stalin's leadership, the socialist path of production work maintained the punitive character that was formed in the 1920s, but deviated from the central principle of Taylorism – standardisation of production and work

30   *Evolving persistence*

processes.[10] Work standards were constantly violated due to the bottlenecks of central planning and for the sake of productivity increases. The worker mobilisation campaigns had an ambiguous outcome: they resulted in workers' involvement in the improvement of production technology to some degree, but they also made formal standards and rules in production subject to informal bargaining on the shop-floor.

These specific approaches to work organisation, quality control and the system of remuneration and sanctions became tied together and complementary effects evolved, which meant that application of one of these elements increased the attractiveness of using the others. Three reinforcement mechanisms were shaped at that time; they led to the formation of behavioural patterns on the shop-floor that showed persistence later. The first of them was caused by draconian sanctions that could be arbitrarily applied to everyone in the workplace. The harsh penalties and blurred borders between individual and collective responsibility in determination of these penalties led to the diffusion of fear and attempts to avoid responsibility, which caused non-reporting of defects. The second mechanism that evolved at that time stemmed from the race for productivity growth. This race led to the informal ad hoc organisation of work in production and relativity of work standards and piece-rate wages, as well as sporadic quality control. This, in turn, motivated workers to strive for high output, while paying little attention to quality. The third mechanism arose as a response to the shortage of labour. Lack of labour motivated the management to avoid firing workers and kept the discipline violators at the enterprise. The punish-but-retain approach was applied, even in the time of coercion. This, consequently, led to a selective or arbitrary use of sanctions. These mechanisms contributed to low product quality, but were not its only determinant. Central planning bottlenecks led to widespread shortages of supplies and their low quality, which also affected the quality of the end product.

2.3   The quality turn: Complex Systems of Management of Output Quality in the 1970s and 1980s

Scholarly and political debates on work organisation were interrupted in the 1940s by the war and were revived under Khrushchev at the end of the 1950s. The renewed debates focused on ways to solve problems with quality, which were ubiquitous in Soviet industry. Whereas organisation of quality control had hardly been discussed in the preceding decades, it became the centre of attention of the party and the specialised research institutes. This resulted in the development of Complex Systems of Management of Output Quality (KSUKP), which were diffused in the USSR in the 1970s (Polovikov *et al.* 1977). After decades of disregarding production and work standards, Soviet industry developed elaborate systems of rules in an attempt to strengthen bureaucratic control in production. The KSUKP aimed at improving product quality through applying complementary rules for work organisation, quality control and remuneration, introducing the notion of 'quality of work performance' that started to play a

Evolving persistence 31

central role in the socialist path of industrial work. The following section will trace the development of these systems and analyse their impact on the socialist path of industrial work.

The Saratov System of Defectless Work

The first Soviet management system integrating work organisation and quality control was undertaken at the Saratov Aviation Works in 1955[11] (Egermayer 1979:48A-7). 'The Saratov System of Defectless Work' (BIP) was supposed to help improve the quality of aeroplanes manufactured in Saratov (Basov 2001). This system was based upon the principle of integration of production functions and quality control and was very close to the ideas that were gaining influence in Japan about the same time. This system even attracted attention in the West: Juran, one of the key personalities behind the TQM movement, wrote of it approvingly in one of his articles (Juran 1979).

The Saratov Aviation Works management identified several causes of quality problems, which were characteristic of the Soviet industry at that time (Campbell 1972:591; Goldberg 1992). First of all, responsibility for quality lay only with the Department of Technical Control (OTK). Gross output was the most important success indicator for the plant and production personnel were interested in maximising individual outputs. OTK was under great pressure from production to pass output and agree to departures from established product specifications. There were constraint conflicts between production and OTK, between shops at successive stages and between the shop and the customer.

At the core of the change proposed by the Saratov System was the notion of workers' self-control: the executor of an operation had to be its first controller. Its main principle urged: "Work without defects at each operation and submit the product at the first check" (Krasnyi and Bartseva 1976:5). Goldberg cites Dubovikov, the author of the Saratov System, who preached that "conscience is the best control" (Goldberg 1992:114). However, control through 'conscience' was supplemented with negative monetary incentives. Parts or products with defects were returned to the workers for reworking and they were not paid for such products; when workers presented these products again, they had to provide a statement of the measures that had been taken to eliminate such defects in the future (Belobragin 2003; Campbell 1972). Quality inspectors relied on statistical methods of quality control to check product quality, which was a novelty in the USSR (Goldberg 1992).

The 'quality of work performance' on the shop-floor was measured by the number of products that passed the OTK at the first check on a daily basis, and then summed up for a given time period (shift, week, month). Workers were motivated to participate by a large bonus for a high quality of work performance. Workers, whose percentage of 'right the first time' was high over a long time, received a personal inspection stamp, which authorised them to inspect their own work. Receiving such a stamp was associated with various distinctions and honoured titles.

32 *Evolving persistence*

Along with increased individual responsibility for quality, teams of workers were created to solve quality problems, while a mobile group of foremen and engineers worked on more complex problems. Once a week workers, foremen and engineers gathered for 'days of quality', when they discussed the quality problems the plant was facing. Thus, workers' indirect tasks – that is, tasks going beyond the direct, production responsibilities – were significantly expanded and were linked to a system of material and ideological incentives. However, training for workers in using tools of analysis was not mentioned in the descriptions of the System, which was the case with the Japanese quality control circles (cf. Juran 1979:18–37).

The idea to involve individual workers and teams on the shop-floor in quality control and problem-solving forestalled the future deviation from Taylorism in the West. In the early 1960s, the Saratov System was given attention in the new industrial policy that was discussed in the resolutions of the Central Committee of the Communist Party that decided to diffuse the Saratov System to other Soviet industrial enterprises (Belobragin 2003:28). Nevertheless, the Saratov System did not become the turning point in the evolution of the socialist path of industrial work.

The Saratov System tried to radically change work organisation and involve individual workers and brigades in quality control and problem-solving. However, it represented a missed critical juncture in the socialist path of industrial work as its successors, the KSUKP, developed and disseminated in the 1970s, continued to build on separation between the indirect and direct functions in production. The idea of a 'conscientious worker' did not become the basis for the formal organisation of production, but was turned into a focus of ideological work that started under Khrushchev and continued under Brezhnev and Gorbachev and was carried out by trade unions.

The Complex System of Production Management, Work Organisation and Remuneration at the Volzhsky Automobile Works (KSUP OOT)

In the 1970s, the further search for ways to improve product quality led to the development of the KSUKP (Polovikov *et al.* 1977). These systems built on the Enterprise's Standards (STP) determining functional responsibilities and regulating communication of all units and departments in an enterprise (cf. Krasnyi and Bartseva 1976:6–7). The central idea behind KSUKP was strict separation of indirect and direct production functions. The two novel elements were elaborate standards regulating group work on the shop-floor and remuneration. The Communist Party urged the diffusion of the KSUKP throughout the country in the five-year plan starting in 1976 (Gostev 1980:4).

The Soviet automobile industry designed an industry-specific system of production management, which was a result of collaboration of several research institutes.[12] The system was designed at a brand new automobile plant on the Volga river in Togliatti – Volzhsky Automobile Works (VAZ) (Epochintsev 1980). VAZ grew to a Soviet automobile giant, employing 118,000 people by

Evolving persistence 33

1985 (Sidorskyi 1988:5). The Complex System of Production Management, Work Organisation and Remuneration (KSUP OOT) at VAZ became the role model for production organisation in the Soviet Union not only in the automobile industry, but also in machine building and manufacturing of consumer goods. The Communist Party and the Soviet of Ministers approved the system and, by 1980, the first 20 enterprises of the Soviet automobile industry had implemented it (Epochintsev 1980:4). In the same way, the KSUP OOT was also diffused to other industrial enterprises in the Soviet Union; a list of over 50 enterprises from different branches was created, where the KSUP OOT had to be implemented and adjusted for its subsequent diffusion throughout those industries (ibid.:3). A school for study of the KSUP OOT was founded in Togliatti to facilitate the diffusion of the system throughout the entire Soviet Union. KSUP OOT dominated the discussion on work organisation in the Soviet automobile industry in the 1970s and 1980s.

The system was praised in Soviet research publications for significantly increasing work productivity and decreasing the assembly time per vehicle compared to the average of the Soviet automobile industry. Remarkably, the Soviet standards developed at that time seem to have equated to the technical level of standardisation in production in the West at that period or maybe even exceeded them (Campbell 1972; Hill 1985; Juran 1979). The following section will analyse how the KSUP influenced the socialist path of industrial work and then discuss why they did not solve the quality problems in the Soviet car industry.

Brigade work

The greatest novelty of the KSUP OOT was perhaps its highly elaborate standards for group work. VAZ attempted to solve the problem with the daily fulfilment of output norms, which was common for the Soviet plants, with standardisation of group work. 'Collective forms of work organisation' were standardised and applied in both direct and indirect production shops. Group work or 'brigade work' at VAZ included all workers in direct and indirect production shops by 1980; the share of the total number of workers in brigades to the total number of employees amounted to 0.997 in 1987 (Epochintsev *et al.* 1990:23). However, brigades were viewed as a unit for the standardisation of work organisation and planning output, rather than a social group capable of making decisions concerning work processes.

There were two types of brigades at VAZ: specialised and 'complex' (mixed) (Epochintsev *et al.* 1988). Specialised brigades comprised workers with the same vocation performing similar operations; they worked in assembly operations and machining processes where interchangeability and collaboration between workers was possible. Complex brigades included workers from different vocations, who performed the whole process of manufacturing a part or a fragment of the full process; such brigades worked in all direct and indirect processes.

Brigade work in KSUP OOT was a way to overcome the unevenness of the production process in Soviet industry characterised by periods of idleness and

34 *Evolving persistence*

storming (*avral*). Therefore, brigades were 'penetrating' the shifts: brigades united equal numbers of workers from all three shifts (Epochintsev 1980:22). This explains the high number of people in each brigade – about 25 people (ibid.). The brigade had to fulfil daily 24-hour output norms; all shifts within a brigade had to perform the same tasks in equal volumes; maintenance and supply services and line management were also equal for all shifts of a brigade. The workload in all shifts was levelled and the plant made sure that indirect services were equally available in all shifts. Thus, brigade work was not designed to facilitate workers' interaction in a brigade on a daily basis.

The scope of decisions that workers could take in a brigade was extremely limited: they had to obey the brigade norms. Brigade members received a 'brigade passport' that contained information about brigade work tasks, workplace layout and rotation, and remuneration rules. There were no fixed working places and operations in a brigade, but workers did not choose working places themselves. They rotated within a brigade according to a plan specified in the brigade passport and developed by 'engineers for work organisation'.

Work organisation rules described in a brigade passport were supplemented with internal enterprise norms, describing all indirect operations. Machine service by maintenance workers, transportation of materials and quality control checks were standardised. Soviet scholars report that 'scientific standardisation' of work norms at VAZ in 1988 embraced 100 per cent of direct production workers and 76 per cent of indirect workers; the work of repairmen was the least standardised in the indirect shops (46 per cent of repairmen) and the work of cleaners and quality controllers was the most standardised (100 per cent) (Epochintsev *et al.* 1988:20). Such high standardisation of quality controllers' work was possible due to the character of their work, which was limited to the measurement and inspection of products.

Leadership over brigades was carried out primarily by 'brigade councils' and foremen. Brigade leaders (*brigadiry*) seem not to have played any significant role in work organisation and are not even mentioned in a thorough description of brigade work organisation at VAZ (Epochintsev *et al.* 1988). A brigade council consisted of five to nine people, depending on the size of a brigade; it included 'advanced' leading workers with high authority in the brigade, foremen and 'trade union group organisers' (Epochintsev 1980:22). It was declared in the Soviet era publications that the brigade council was openly elected at the meeting of all brigade members. However, the presence of foremen and trade union representatives at the meetings of brigade councils allowed management and unions to control them and impeded the councils' chances to represent workers' interests.

The brigade councils carried out several functions that all focused on assisting the management. Their primary responsibility was to help assure that the 24-hour output norm was met by the brigade and the individual workers. They also influenced decisions on 'moral and material stimulation' of workers. Finally, brigade councils contributed to work organisation in a brigade (assigning working places, collaboration between the shifts, coaching workers) and coordinated and controlled brigades' and individuals' plans for the 'socialist competition'.

Evolving persistence 35

VAZ tried to safeguard production processes from unexpected shortages in the workforce due to external interferences by developing not just one, but three versions of brigade standards. Workers could be withdrawn from their working places due to 'unexpected (direct and indirect) tasks, construction, assembly and agricultural work' (Epochintsev *et al.* 1988:15). Three types of work intensity were described in the brigade passports: (1) the default one, (2) the 'more progressive' one and (3) work intensity level necessary in a situation when the number of workers was 'less than the optimal but not less than the permissible minimum'.

Such elaborated brigade standards could hardly serve as a solution to the unevenness of production under the planned economy. Along with sudden withdrawals of personnel, there was a continued shortage of labour, and problems with supply and quality of materials persisted even during Gorbachev's reforms (Sidorskyi 1988:62). Therefore, these standards were difficult to fulfil and there were likely to be gaps between them and actual work organisation.

The very idea of group work deviates from the scientific organisation of work adopted in Russia in the early 1920s. Nevertheless, the brigade work in KSUP OOT follows Taylor's principle of separation between execution and control. Brigades appear to have been nominal social groups where all behaviour was subject to regulation by the standards developed by engineers.

Quality control and brigade responsibility for defects

KSUP OOT attempted to improve product quality and increase the efficiency of indirect functions by separating direct production from all indirect functions, including quality control. Management of indirect functions was not subordinate to production management any longer. All indirect functions in production (maintenance, quality control and material supply) became separate and independent from the direct production shops (Epochintsev 1980:5). Large centralised shops with indirect functions were created in direct production areas – for example, shops for current production maintenance. Additionally, all-factory shops with indirect functions were created. This separation was seen as beneficial for both production, as it was 'liberated' from indirect functions, and for indirect shops, as production shops 'lost their patriarchal role' (ibid.:5–6). Collaboration between production and indirect shops took place according to pre-defined procedures (e.g. written orders for indirect services from production), which made it bureaucratised and hampered.

The Soviet publications on KSUKP list a broad range of functions carried out by the "Quality Control Service of Production" at VAZ: quality control of incoming materials and parts, quality control during the process of production, development of technical documents for quality control and quality control of ready-made cars (Polovikov *et al.* 1977:11). The high degree of vertical integration of production at VAZ meant that performing just the entry control of parts was an enormous task.[13] However, the functions of the Quality Control Service were limited to inspection of product quality.

36   *Evolving persistence*

Quality inspection tasks could be integrated, in some cases, into functions of individual direct workers. If a worker had consistently shown high-quality performance, she received a personal stamp, and her output was only subject to sample quality inspection, as in the Saratov System. However, cases of workers' self-control of quality seem rather rare (Epochintsev 1980; Epochintsev *et al.* 1988). Ensuring integration of another indirect task, keeping working places in order, was a continuous challenge reflected in the Soviet rhetoric in support of the 'culture of work'.

Quality control in production relied to a high extent on social pressure for complying with technical product specifications within a brigade. Blurred borders between individual and collective responsibility for the brigade's performance were formally institutionalised at VAZ. Each brigade was collectively responsible for the quality of the output within its 'operation zone'. At the end of an 'operation zone' the quality of every brigade's output was controlled by a quality inspector. The operation zone was also called the 'confines of a brigade's controllability'. Production sections in direct shops could be divided into several operation zones.[14] The operation zone was defined by three operations: the initial, the final and the operation of control and registration of the output. Brigades of direct workers could be responsible either for a closed process (e.g. treatment of engine pistons) or for a stage of a process (e.g. a stage in the general assembly of cars on a conveyer belt). In either case, the quality of a brigade's output was checked by a quality inspector:

> it is necessary to provide conditions for objective estimation of the work results of each brigade and exclude the elements of mutual complaints, particularly in technologically related processes and in neighbouring brigades.
>
> > (Epochintsev *et al.* 1988:6–7)

Therefore, the output quality from a process was checked once if only one brigade was responsible for the whole process, or several times if several brigades participated in the process.

There was an elaborate system of bonuses linked to the quality of workers' performance. The whole brigade and not an individual worker accounted for a product defect in their process:

> In cases, when defects in [a brigade's] operations are found at the registration of ready products, the claim is addressed to this brigade [as a whole]. For example, when defects of a window raiser are found on a ready car, it can be determined, that the brigade responsible for mounting the glass on a car is guilty.
>
> > (Ibid.:7)

The feedback about the defect went to the whole brigade and it was an internal matter for the brigade to find out whose mistake caused the defect. Thus, mistakes were not retraceable to an individual worker. The complaints and conflicts within the brigades, which seemed to be rather frequent, were resolved by the brigades' councils.

Some Soviet publications draw attention to the poor collaboration between brigades in production that was due to brigades' narrow interest in achieving their own output targets and not the performance indicators of the whole plant (Odegov, Freze and Meshkov 1988). Collaboration between brigades in direct and indirect production shops was particularly bad. Odegov *et al.* report that there was frequent idle time due to a delay or the low quality of equipment maintenance. Management attempted to solve this problem not by reconsidering the principle of separation of direct and indirect functions in KSUP OOT but by including some indirect workers into direct brigades. Such organisation of work led to inflated numbers of indirect workers and auxiliary personnel in the Soviet automotive industry. Indirect workers outnumbered direct workers: there were, on average, 1.25–1.4 indirect workers to each direct worker (Tikhonov, Klevlin and Kocharova 1983:12). The ratio of indirect to direct workers at VAZ was lower than the industry average but still amounted to 1:1 (Epochintsev 1980:13). The reported share of 'technical and engineering employees' (employees responsible for organisation and management of production processes) at VAZ was also slightly lower than industry average (14 per cent of the personnel at VAZ and 17–21 per cent in the industry) (Epochintsev *et al.* 1988:12).

The introduction of a strict separation between production and quality control represented a departure from the attempts of the Saratov System to enhance communication between production and indirect functions and involve workers in quality assurance tasks beyond product inspection. Workers' participation in solving quality problems is not mentioned in the descriptions of KSUP OOT; workers were only encouraged to carry out self-control of their output quality, although this rhetoric had little success. The management resorted to social control within brigades as a means to resolve both problems with quality and shortages in the organisation of production.

At the time when KSUP OOT, based on the principle of separation between direct and indirect production areas, was diffused in the Soviet Union, the first studies on Japanese methods of quality control were published in the West. These studies advocated integration of indirect operations into direct workers' tasks. Thus, the path of industrial work in Russia took a direction opposite to these new ideas that started to disseminate in the capitalist economies.

Qualification of industrial workers in the Soviet automobile industry

Training of industrial workers was one of the party's priorities in the 1960s–80s. Vocational training in public schools and enterprises was standardised. The narrow approach to vocational training applied in the scientific organisation of work became the basis for the unified system of vocational qualification described in the *Soviet Wage Rate and Qualification Handbook for Workers* (*ETKS*). Such approach to vocational training represented another mechanism reinforcing the

38 *Evolving persistence*

socialist path of industrial work, as workers were not trained in quality assurance competencies.

The educational level of the Soviet industrial workforce rose rapidly in the 1970s. The state aimed to raise the number of workers with a secondary education and technical vocational training. Pivovar gives an example of ZIL (*Zavod imeni Likhacheva*) as representative of the industry as a whole: the share of workers with completed secondary education or higher rose from 14 per cent in 1965 to 40.5 per cent in 1975 (Pivovar 1983:134). Training in public schools was complemented by various programmes of vocational training and qualification upgrading organised by the enterprises on and off the job. There were 'schools of progressive work method' and 'qualification-raising courses' for technical and production staff (Pivovar 1983). The most highly qualified workers could study in 'schools for foremen' along with engineering personnel. All these programmes were based on the qualification profiles described in the *ETKS*.

The *ETKS* was developed by the Central Bureau of Work Norms as a universal directory of all jobs, applicable in all industries in 1968–9 (Shibaev 2009:3). It was revised but not substantially changed in 1984–6 (ibid.). It contained 72 volumes and each qualification was divided into six grades (ibid.). Each of the volumes listed qualifications for a product group or an industry. Volume 19, for example, was dedicated to electro-technical competences, volume 20 – to electronic and volume 71 – to optical-mechanical competences. The qualifications for metal work were listed in volume 2, which included foundry works, welding and mechanical metal works, among others (2003). There was no separate volume on the automobile industry.

The qualifications were extensively standardised. There were separate job descriptions and skill requirements for each of the six grades within a qualification. It was specified which formal training background a worker should possess to qualify for each grade (some of them required vocational school training, more advanced ones a technical college diploma). The description of each qualification grade contained two sections. The first one was job description – a list of typical operations that a worker should perform and the types of equipment and materials he should be able to use. The second part was the 'must know' – specialised knowledge and knowledge of work methods and instructions. Indirect skills and competencies were not included in the qualifications. Instead, there was a qualification 'controller' in every group of qualifications, such as 'controller of machine and metalworking operations', who focused on product quality inspection, measurement and registration. Thus, product inspection and problem-solving were not a part of direct workers' qualifications, even though brigades bore significant responsibility for quality deficiencies.

The narrow skill profiles were to some degree broadened by ideological work at the plants. It included economic and technical information about production, such as lectures for workers by the enterprise's engineers about introduction of robots, but the central aim of ideological-technical work was shaping the right attitudes in the workplace. The party supported the 'movement of rationalisers and inventors' (*dvizhenie ratsionalizatorov i izobretatelei*). Therefore, workers

Evolving persistence   39

received support in developing and pushing through 'rationalisation suggestions' (Sidorskyi 1988) and were called to show the conscientious attitude to work (*soznatel'nost'*). The emphasis on *soznatel'nost'* did not evolve into inclusion of soft competencies into qualifications but instead inspired some ideologists to add a section on personal characteristics into the *ETKS*. Odegov *et al.* suggest that qualification requirements should be complemented by required physical strength, temperament, capabilities and interests (Odegov, Freze and Meshkov 1988:40).

The use of the *ETKS* and of the corresponding handbook for white-collar employees was obligatory (Gimpelson and Kapelyushnikov 2007). The *ETKS* was utilised by vocational schools and professional colleges for defining training contents and certificates. At the same time, enterprises used the descriptions of jobs and the typical tasks within them from the text for classifying and rating working places, for raising employees' qualification grades or training them in new professions. The state set wage rates corresponding to qualification grades. Therefore, the remuneration systems throughout the industries were bound to the qualifications and wage rates described in the *ETKS*. This led to complementary effects between the remuneration and qualification systems in the Soviet industry.

Development of the *ETKS* allowed the state to unify all forms of training within and outside the enterprise. This unification of training led to development of coordination effects, as the *ETKS* was adopted by more and more actors. Training in elementary vocational schools, secondary technical colleges and at the enterprise took place on the basis of the standards set by the state. Employers had some freedom in developing their incentive systems but the use of the wage rates specified in the book was obligatory. Thus, the obligatory *ETKS* was the basis for coordination effects reinforcing the socialist path of industrial work.

The narrow set of skills that production workers acquired made it difficult to broaden their functions beyond the direct tasks they performed, something which the state later attempted to address under Gorbachev. Thus, learning effects evolved as yet another mechanism reinforcing the socialist path of industrial work.

Remuneration systems in the Soviet automotive industry

After the harsh penalties of Stalin's time were ended by Khrushchev, a combination of material incentives and social control in brigades became a new way to control workers. In the 1970s–80s, the large industrial enterprises attempted to develop effective incentives that would help in resolving the dilemma of both complying with the growing output targets and assuring product quality. A distinct characteristic of remuneration systems at that time was the importance of the notion of 'quality of work performance' on the shop-floor in calculating employees' bonuses. Both piece-rate and time-based remuneration systems were complemented with bonuses for quality of work performance in order to improve the product quality compared to the previous decades.

40 *Evolving persistence*

Workers' wages were defined on the basis of qualification grades and wage rates specified in the *ETKS*. In the 1970s, piece-rate wages prevailed in the automobile industry. The dependence of wages on output was criticised in Soviet publications of that time for reinforcing workers' careless attitude towards output quality:

> In some cases there is insufficient responsibility by employees for the quality of the produced output. In the described conditions, the executors of production operations 'get accustomed' to the presence of an external care, get used to the fact that no matter how good or bad the parts they have produced, these parts will be sorted out after them and will be entirely paid for, without deducting from the wages the costs of sorting that has become a constant necessity as a result of this habit.
>
> (Gostev 1980:6–7)

The enterprises tried to increase workers' attention to quality in two ways. One way was to complement the piece-rate wages with a special bonus for output that passed the Department of Technical Control (*OTK*) at the first check, and 'personal stamps', invented in the Saratov System (Doletskyi 1976; Tikhonov, Klevlin and Kocharova 1983). The other way was to introduce time-based wages. Starting from the late 1970s, VAZ and other enterprises that introduced the KSUP OOT switched to time-based wages linked to the workers' qualifications (1979).

The time-based remuneration systems were supposed to both increase employees' responsibility for quality and motivate them to raise their qualifications. However, fulfilment of the output norm remained a priority; a brigade received a special bonus for the fulfilment of the output norm. This incentive strengthened group pressure on individual workers to reach their output norms. At VAZ the bonus for accomplishment of a brigade's norm was the largest variable share of wages (Epochintsev 1980). Thus, even under time-based wages an individual time-based element was combined with a collective bonus for output.

A variety of individual and collective incentives for both the amount of output ('quantitative side of labour') and quality of work performance ('qualitative side of labour') was characteristic for the Soviet automobile industry at that time (see Table 2.1). In addition, the Coefficient of Labour Participation (*Koeffitsient Trudovogo Uchastia* or *KTU*) was applied. KTU was not a bonus but a way to distribute some of the payment within a brigade; it depended on both the output amount and on the quality of work performance. Remuneration systems included bonuses related to other aspects of work as well – for example, the degree of harmfulness of working conditions (ibid.).[15] This made them quite sophisticated and unclear for the workers.

Incentives for the amount of the output could include a bonus for the whole brigade for accomplishment of a brigade's norm and an individual bonus for increased productivity. Incentives for quality of work performance included a more varied set of tools. Individual bonuses could take three forms:

Evolving persistence 41

Table 2.1 The range of variable incentives used in the Soviet automobile industry

Type of incentives	Individual	Brigade-based	Production-based
Incentives for the amount of output	Bonus for increased productivity	Bonus for accomplishment of the brigade's norm	
Incentives for quality of work performance	1. Bonus for individual output free of defects 2. Bonus for a personal stamp 3. Bonus for craftsmanship	4. Bonus for brigade output free of defects 5. Bonus for 'Brigade of Excellent Quality'	Bonus for output quality to all production workers
Other incentives	KTU – Coefficient of Labour Participation (*Koeffitsient Trudovogo Uchastia*)		

Source: Compilation by author

1. bonus for individual output free of defects was measured as the products or parts that went through the OTK on the first check;
2. bonus for a 'personal stamp' was paid when a worker was authorised to mark her products with a personal quality stamp, which meant that these products were not subject to the 100 per cent control of the OTK and only went through a statistical quality control. For example, the bonus for personal stamp at Avtodizel amounted to 7 per cent of the wage rate (Doletskyi 1976);
3. bonus for craftsmanship, which helped to differentiate the wages of workers who had the same wage rates but different work experience and/or learnt more than one qualification. It was determined on the basis of workers' qualifications and work experience and was defined as a percentage of a worker's wage rate. Mentoring newcomers, submitting 'rationalisation suggestions' and winning in some type of socialist competition made it easier to obtain this bonus (Epochintsev *et al.* 1988:40). The bonus for craftsmanship at VAZ varied between 4 and 22 per cent of the wage rate (Epochintsev 1980:49).

Two more bonuses for quality of work performance could be paid to the whole brigade:

4. a whole brigade could receive a bonus for output free of defects;
5. the title 'Brigade of excellent quality' and a corresponding brigade bonus, if the brigade's output was free of defects over a long time.

In addition, a bonus for output quality could be paid to all production workers.

The KTU was a tool for dividing up the total payment or some or all of the bonuses within a brigade. It represented a multifunctional index that was supposed to help reward both the zeal and diligence of a worker and her actual output.

42 *Evolving persistence*

The KTU represented an individual coefficient ascribed to each worker within a team (or brigade) on a monthly basis. The money was allocated to the whole brigade and then distributed between its members (except for individual payments, such as overtime). It typically varied between 0 and 2 with 1 as the basic. If a worker performed well, she was assigned a KTU of 1; if a worker underperformed then his KTU varied between 0 and 1 and if one over performed – then between 1 and 2. In order for some workers to earn more, others had to lose. In KSUP OOT, the major function of the KTU was to divide the output bonus within a brigade. The individual KTUs could be determined by a foreman, jointly by a foreman and a brigade council or by the brigade itself.

There were no strict criteria for ascribing a KTU to a worker and the distribution of KTUs could cause conflicts within a brigade. According to the former shop manager at the Klimov Aircraft Engines Works in Saint Petersburg, the formal criteria for KTU did not work, and it was divided on the basis of the 'large throat' principle: "The one who had a larger throat got the most" (Interview RET3). According to Clarke, however, workers in Soviet industrial enterprises were almost always ascribed equal KTUs (Clarke 2007:42). Thus, the KTU was not effective as a system of remuneration according to individual results and responsibility, and in some cases it could not help to ensure collective pressure on individuals either.

Introduction of bonuses for the quality of work performance did not eliminate the tensions between the OTK and production workers. The OTKs defining the output quality were under quite strong pressure from production employees. That is why people heading the OTKs were "specialists from the field of product development or production technology with a strong-willed character" (Gostev 1980:187). Remuneration was also viewed as an answer to concealing defects by the OTK. Quality controllers were paid on a time basis, but their wages were linked to the quality of their inspections measured as the number of missed defects in the checked products (Polovikov *et al.* 1977:44; Krasnyi and Bartseva 1976:69). The number of missed defects could be determined at a special quality inspection after the OTK (as at ZIL) or at checks in the subsequent shops or with the customer (as in KSUP OOT). Thus, the controllers' pay also depended on their performance quality, as did the workers' pay.

The high share of variable bonuses within the payments to workers that were calculated monthly and that could be withdrawn at any time substituted the harsh penalties of Stalin's time as a tool of control on the shop-floor. The remuneration systems were characterised by both high sophistication and low formalisation of the evaluation criteria. This led to a high degree of arbitrariness in the determination of bonuses by production management. It was difficult for workers to see how their contribution influenced wages, a fact that was admitted only under Gorbachev (see, e.g. Sidorskyi 1988). Due to the clear distinction between the 'quantitative' and 'qualitative' sides of labour in remuneration, workers could get a bonus for the output (which as a rule was higher than the bonus for the quality) and neglect the quality. High quality of work performance, thus, was not viewed as an inalienable characteristic of work.

Evolving persistence 43

The emphasis on brigade work represented a departure from the individualistic focus of incentives compared to the previous stage of the formation of the socialist path of industrial work. The borders between individual and brigade responsibility for the amount of output and its quality were left purposely blurred in order to strengthen the brigade's pressure on individuals. Nevertheless, borders of responsibility in production became more formalised compared to the period of forced-pace industrialisation. The tight interrelation of the *ETKS*, the remuneration systems and organisation of work in brigades led to formation of strong complementary effects within the socialist path of industrial work.

2.4 Self-financing brigades and workers' self-management under Gorbachev

Gorbachev introduced the first elements of a market economy in the USSR in the late 1980s: he legalised individual entrepreneurship and the creation of cooperatives (Gerber and Hout 1998). At that time the first non-state-owned firms were created, although they were not fully private as they were prohibited from hiring labour or owning the productive assets they used. Gorbachev's industry reforms started with a renewed emphasis on product quality. The slogans and resolutions were already familiar from the previous era: party statements about centrality of product quality and mobilisation, and conscientiousness appeals to production workers (see, e.g. Sidorskyi 1988). The greatest policy innovation with respect to quality at that time was creation of a state institution for the inspection of the quality of industrial products – *Gospriemka* ('State Authorisation') in 1987 (Forker 1991). Gospriemka was supposed to substitute the market competition that was still absent. Change at the enterprise level concentrated on strengthening workers' financial responsibility for output and its quality.

The idea of Gospriemka was to introduce a state quality inspection independent of enterprise management. State inspectors from *Gosstandart* (State Committee for Standards) checked industrial products and were authorised to reject the non-compliant output. Introduction of Gospriemka led to a rejection of 30 per cent of industrial output in 1987, which was an important factor in a 35 per cent shortfall in plan fulfilment for machine building (Forker 1991; Goldberg 1992). According to Forker, the failure to comply with the new quality standards had a complex nature: production equipment was too old, enterprises lacked testing equipment and workers were not familiar with procedures needed to assure high product quality. As a consequence of the output shortfall, workers lost their bonuses, which resulted in a wave of social unrest. This led to loosening of the quality standards at the end of 1987 (Forker 1991; Goldberg 1992). The outcome of Gospriemka showed that problems with quality control could not be resolved by the introduction of yet another product inspection and elucidated the contradictions of the planned economy, which were due to planned output targets.

Other reforms initiated by Gorbachev in the industry did not touch upon the structural problems of a planned economy either but instead concentrated on the level of production. KSUKP were still in effect under Gorbachev but their

44 *Evolving persistence*

application became voluntary in 1988 (Goldberg 1992:117). However, the role of brigades in organisation of production grew. Economic independence of enterprises from the state started at a brigade level (Slider 1987). Self-financing or *khozraschet* brigades were introduced. For example, at AvtoVAZ (formerly VAZ) the changes towards self-accounting and financial independence or "a deepened economic experiment" began in 1985 (Sidorskyi 1988:5). New elements in brigade work included economic accounting ('brigadnyi khozraschet') and brigade order ('brigadnyi podriad'). A brigade could sign a contract with the enterprise management where the production task and brigade's earnings were specified. Brigades were paid for final results and earnings were then distributed by the brigade on the basis of KTU (Epochintsev, Saushkina and Klement'eva 1989). Along with increased financial responsibility, brigades' scope of decisions grew and they could elect brigade leaders.

Diffusion of self-financing brigades in the 1980s met with resistance both from the enterprise managements and workers. Odegov *et al.* report that about 40 per cent of all brigades in the Soviet automotive industry were self-financing by 1986, but point at a pro forma introduction of such brigades at some enterprises (Odegov, Freze and Meshkov 1988:58). According to Slider, enterprise directors faced problems with supplies and lacked incentives to carry out thorough change in work organisation (Slider 1987). At the same time, the Soviet brigade faced contradictory requirements. It was expected to simultaneously "improve efficiency, incentives, discipline, participation, and work attitudes while retaining party control" (ibid.:403).

Gorbachev's reforms of the industrial enterprise did not challenge the persistence of socialist path of industrial work. The two main new policies that were introduced at that time, Gospriemka and self-financing brigades, essentially drew upon the old ideas of independent multi-level product quality inspection and social pressure through monetary incentives in brigades. Brigades did receive some real authority in production process but they could not make use of it, as Gorbachev's policies neither questioned nor weakened the effects reinforcing the socialist path of production work. Workers lacked indirect competencies needed to actually overtake more responsibility for the production process and too many interrelated problems in production were beyond the workers' reach – from shortages with material supplies to equipment maintenance.

2.5 Conclusion: the socialist path of industrial work by the start of the transition to a market economy

The discussion of the formation of the socialist path of industrial work shows that it represented a pattern of mutually reinforcing elements, which became locked in by the early 1980s and largely persisted through Gorbachev's reforms. It was characterised by separation of direct production from quality control and other indirect functions and narrow qualification profiles on the shop-floor. Another important characteristic was a high degree of responsibility of brigades in production. This responsibility was assured by punitive means combining monetary

Evolving persistence 45

incentives that could be withdrawn any time and social pressure within brigades. The pressure within brigades was achieved through blurred borders between individual and brigade responsibility in production. While some principles were formed already in the early 1920s, others were established in the 1970s.

Industrial work in Russia had attained a punitive character in the 1920s, following the decisions to adopt a narrow mechanistic version of Taylorism and to introduce forced industrial work. Two important principles of scientific organisation of work remained in place during the subsequent formation of the path of production work in Russia: separation of direct production from indirect production, including quality control, and the narrow focus of worker qualifications on direct competencies. The socialist enterprise could not fully benefit from the Taylorist focus on standardisation towards the one best way due to the irregularities of production and the relativity of rules governing the workplace. At the same time, the Soviet industry suffered from the major drawbacks of Taylorism: conflicts between production and quality inspectors and inflated numbers of indirect staff.

The narrow qualification profiles remained persistent throughout the era of the planned economy. Their standardisation in the *ETKS* resulted in coordination effects between the industrial enterprises and institutions of vocational training and technical education. Repeated appeals to workers' conscientiousness in order to involve them in increasing productivity and improving product quality were not backed up by workers' formal qualifications. These appeals were to some extent supported by the ideological work, which included a broad range of educational activities in the factories. Yet, this learning was poorly formalised and did not represent a purposeful way to develop the required competencies, and consequently learning effects became one of the stumbling blocks for Gorbachev's reforms on the shop-floor. At the same time, remuneration systems were built on the qualifications and wage rates specified in the *ETKS*. Strong complementarities evolved between the qualification and remuneration systems and work organisation.

Since the 1950s, the Soviet industry had strived to improve product quality by standardising organisation of production and work and purposely establishing coherence between its different elements. The principle of separation between production and indirect functions, including quality assurance, became the central element of the socialist production standards. Following the missed critical juncture of the Saratov System of Defectless Work, which had suggested integrating direct and indirect functions, the socialist enterprise did not question this principle up to Gorbachev's reforms.

The development of the KSUKP marked a change in the Soviet debate about work organisation from an individualistic to a collectivist orientation. After the narrowly individualist focus of the scientific organisation of work, brigade work was applied in both direct and indirect production areas. Brigade work in KSUKP was characterised by a contradiction. Brigades bore high responsibility for output and its quality, but lacked any genuine authority in the production process. Brigades had to assure compliance with output plans and quality standards, while

46 *Evolving persistence*

production equipment was unstable, their communication with the maintenance services was bureaucratised and there were frequent problems with regularity and quality of supplies. This contradiction was not resolved in the elaborate standards for work organisation in KSUKP. Instead, these standards institutionalised collective responsibility for output and quality in brigades. The blurred borders between individual and brigade responsibility became a core element of the socialist path of industrial work, which was further strengthened with the introduction of self-financing brigades under Gorbachev.

Workers' compliance with the rules was reinforced by remuneration systems developed in KSUKP. The high variable share of pay in the Soviet wage system had a double function. It was both an incentive and a sanction, as workers could be deprived of them at any time. Low transparency of remuneration for workers and low formalisation of criteria for bonuses gave space for arbitrary decisions by line management. The combination of these two characteristics gave remuneration systems a punitive character, which significantly shaped the whole path of industrial work due to the complementary effects between remuneration systems and other elements of production work. Thus, the punitive character of industrial work took a more subtle form compared to the early years of the path formation but still remained the core characteristic of the socialist path of industrial work.

The punitive character of industrial work in the 1970s–80s was, however, significantly moderated by the employment guarantee under the planned economy. This guarantee, along with continued labour shortages, led to the punish-but-retain approach to disciplining workers and even the worst discipline violators were kept in the plants. At the same time, guaranteed employment and continued labour shortages reduced the effectiveness of monetary incentives as a means to discipline workers. Some Western scholars even argued that the only effective way 'to break the workers' ability to withhold efficiency' would be the threat of unemployment (cf. Christensen 1999:35). Therefore, even when the brigade assumed complete financial responsibility for the final production results, which was introduced under Gorbachev, discipline in the workplace still remained a challenge for management.

The analysis shows that complementary effects between the elements constituting the path had partly an evolving character but were also purposely cultivated by the Soviet standardised KSUKP of production management. However, the extent of standardisation in production and the degree of diffusion of the KSUKP throughout Soviet industry should be regarded with caution. There had been a long tradition of divergence from formal regulations on the shop-floor under the planned economy and the introduction of KSUKP by enterprises could take place pro forma to comply with pressure from the party (cf. Campbell 1972). Nevertheless, an analysis of practitioners' publications during the Soviet period and of the available empirical accounts carried out by Western scholars indicate that brigade work, quality control, remuneration systems and qualification systems were largely organised in accordance with the principles outlined in the discussion of KSUKP.

Evolving persistence 47

Despite the high technical level of the Soviet production and quality standards (cf. ibid.; Hill 1985; Juran 1979), Soviet enterprises failed to comply with these standards and achieve a level of quality comparable with capitalist enterprises (cf. Gorlin 1981). One explanation is the domination of production by strict production targets and a seller's market (cf. Goldberg 1992). The present chapter showed that inherent contradictions and irregularities of the socialist industrial enterprise made it impossible to comply with extensively elaborate standards. The managers' capability to reflect about these shortages was undermined by the necessity for positive reporting and false accounting that existed under the planned economy (cf. Harrison 2009). Every new party campaign on organisation of work criticised the outcome of the previous ones but did not dare to come up with numbers pinning down the persisting shortcomings in organisation of production and work. Only under Gorbachev did enterprises start to dare openly to state some of the shortfalls in the organisation of production and work and reflect about the ways to overcome them (cf. Sidorskyi 1988).

Notes

1 Bogdanov was a theoretician of proletarian culture and an encyclopaedist who developed a theory of Tectology, wherein he anticipated many ideas of cybernetics and systems theory.
2 In Russian: *Nauchnaya organizatsiya truda* or NOT.
3 In Russian: *Tsentralny Institut Truda* or TsIT.
4 From this point and forward all translations are made by author.
5 At that time, the automobile industry in the USA and Germany was already producing hundreds of cars a year.
6 Gorky was the name of a city that is now called Nizhny Novgorod.
7 Stakhanovism was institutionalised or 'routinised' in Soviet production enterprises in the late 1940s under the name of 'socialist competition' (Siegelbaum 1988).
8 Only about 30 per cent of all workers were paid according to these rates (Siegelbaum 1988:89).
9 Siegelbaum notes that defective articles were even called "Stakhanovite goods" (Siegelbaum 1988:202).
10 Clarke generalises that the Soviet system of production management "was almost the antithesis of the Taylorist system of scientific management that it nominally espoused", but he does not specify when the Soviet enterprise deviated from Taylorism (Clarke 2007:43).
11 According to Basov, the Saratov System was developed in 1956 (Basov 2001:81).
12 Research Institute of Technology of Automobile Industry, Research Institute of Information of Automobile Industry, Research Institute of Information and Technical-Economic Research in the Automobile Industry.
13 For example, for the Zhiguli, the most popular car manufactured at VAZ, the number of materials to be inspected amounted to 600 items (2,000 items of different sizes in total) and 1,897 parts (Polovikov *et al.* 1977:38).
14 Operation zones for brigades in indirect shops could embrace a shop, a building or several buildings (Epochintsev *et al.* 1988).
15 Alternatively, harmful working conditions could be taken into account in a special bonus, which was the case with AvtoVAZ, where the bonus for harmful working conditions varied between 4 and 27 per cent of the tariff rate (Epochintsev 1980: 47–48).

3 Still there

The industrial workplace in Russia after the market reforms[1]

In 1992 a package of radical reforms was introduced in Russia that was designed to rapidly replace the state socialist economy with market institutions and practices (Gerber and Hout 1998). The 'shock therapy' reforms included privatisation[2] of state enterprises, freeing prices from state control, liberalisation of wages and cancellation of many state orders. Most state-owned companies were privatised, new private businesses were established and foreign investors entered the new market. Market conditions started to demand higher productivity and quality than what was necessary under the planned economy. New departments were created in enterprises – marketing, finance and sales – and they began to set the priorities for production. Firms changed their personnel policies as well in an attempt to adjust to the evolving market conditions. The homogeneity of personnel policies under the planned economy gave place to a wide range of practices combining old and new elements.

Despite all these novelties, the prevalent opinion in the literature is that production relations at the shop-floor level remained remarkably persistent in the 1990s. Clarke (2007) and Burawoy and Krotov (1992) even do not view the reforms as an event that changed the trajectory of industrial work. According to Clarke, the economic processes following the implementation of the reforms were just a continuation of the disintegration of the administrative-command system:

> Privatisation did not give enterprises any more rights than they had already appropriated for themselves, while it allowed the state to abdicate all the responsibilities to them which it no longer had the means to fulfil. Thus, the ideology of neo-liberalism and radical reform was little more than a rhetoric to cover what was essentially a bowing to the inevitable.
>
> (Clarke 2007:6–7)

The change in the companies in the 1990s occurred slowly, as they just needed to survive. Burawoy and Krotov argue similarly that supply shortages and unevenness of production technology even intensified after the start of the transition (Burawoy and Krotov 1992). Firms did not introduce any innovative

Still there 49

approaches to organise production and work but continued to rely on a high degree of ad hoc self-organisation on the shop-floor to compensate for them, which the authors refer to as 'worker control over production'. Burawoy even speaks about 'transition without transformation' or 'involution' as taking place in Russia in the 1990s (Burawoy 2001). Clarke argues that a more systemic subordination of the production process to the production of surplus value started in the years following the economic crisis in Russia in 1998 (Clarke 2007).[3] However, the socialist principles of work organisation and quality control have remained remarkably persistent even in the 2000s.

The present chapter will revisit the question of whether the socialist path of industrial work was broken after the market reforms. It will systematically compare the characteristics of production work before and after the reforms. It will discuss the literature on work organisation, employee development and qualification, remuneration and interest representation. Particular attention will be paid to the dissemination of international quality management (QM) concepts and lean production and their impact on work. The changes that took place will be discussed against the background of the analysis of the socialist path of industrial work.

3.1 Compliance with rules and standards in production

The socialist enterprise was characterised by elaborate standards for production and work that answered the technical level of Western standards of that time. However, it was difficult for the firms to live up to these standards due to the irregularities of socialist production. A resulting divergence between rules and standards and actual practices in production was one of the central characteristics of the socialist enterprise. When state regulation weakened in the 1990s, this divergence seems to have grown. Imposing compliance with rules and standards in production was challenging for both local and foreign firms operating in Russia.

Studies on work organisation at Russian enterprises in the early 1990s present a picture of weakly managed or even unpredictable production processes, characterised by frequent equipment breakdowns and very high amounts of slack and waste. Enterprises faced difficulties in coping with workers' lateness, showing up drunk and smoking at the workplace (Clarke 2007). Under these conditions, the Russian management deliberately used workers' ad hoc self-organisation on the shop-floor as a way to assure continual flow of production (Burawoy and Krotov 1992). Indeed, unreliable production equipment and poorly standardised work routines made industrial workers into craftsmen, as work performance required significant tacit knowledge (Alasheev and Romanov 1997). At the shop-floor level, a systematic exchange of favours between production supervisors and workers took place (Alasheev 1995a). Workers could come later than the official shift started and leave before it ended. Production supervisors or 'masters' did not always discipline a worker for misconduct or would not formally register this. In return, the worker would be willing to make concessions to the production supervisor and the management,

50 *Still there*

such as working overtime at the end of the month to catch up with the production targets, known as 'storming' (*avral*) under planned economy, or make other personal favours to production supervisors. According to Alasheev, this system of mutual informal agreements involved not only production processes and work organisation, but also wage systems.

Assuring compliance with formal regulations in production was a central challenge for foreign-owned firms in Russia or Russian firms exposed to international competition. This compliance was typically achieved by tightening of direct control over workers' performance. Lytkina observes that Western acquisition of a major Russian paper and pulp factory was followed by stricter planning in production, weakening of both production supervisors' authority and workers' control on the shop-floor and strengthening their discipline (Lytkina 2008). A new transparent remuneration system, which linked both the fixed share and the variable part of earnings to individual performance, played an important role in this change. Along with new principles in managing human resources, the management kept some of the socialist ideas as well. The new managers revived the Soviet practice of rationalisation suggestions from workers and generously rewarded them. Nevertheless, highly qualified workers still enjoyed a privileged position at the enterprise, as management applied the punish-but-retain disciplining policy in their case (see p. 29).

Ensuring compliance with detailed process standards was difficult at one domestic and two multinational car manufacturers (GAZ, Volkswagen and Toyota) analysed by Jürgens and Krzywdzinski (2016). They attribute this difficulty to the Russian culture and mentality. Compliance with standardised work was a daily concern even several years after the production start at the multinational operations, as the management could not be sure that employees would continue to follow the work standards. This led to tense relations with workers as well. Volkswagen answered this challenge by developing production supervisors from its own employees and establishing communication and collaboration with the unions. Toyota relied on high density of control on the shop-floor and developed a direct communication channel with employees. Employees at GAZ also tended to conceal or supress problems, but overall GAZ did not seem to encounter troubles with discipline. The authors explain this by a recent painful downsizing, a consultation with the trade union when implementing the new production methods and a high share of female workers, who were viewed as more compliant.

In sum, the market reforms did not challenge the domination of informal relations in post-Soviet production, even though these relations had a negative impact on productivity, efficiency and quality. However, foreign acquisition or exposure of a Russian-owned firm to international competition represented a turning point, when assuring compliance with rules and standards in production became a management priority. As the Russian workforce was not socialised into high discipline and formal responsibility in the workplace, new management relied on a combination of dense control and a gradual change of the traditional behavioural patterns. This shift caused tensions on the shop-floor. On the one

Still there 51

hand, arbitrariness and high discretion in managers' behaviour was significantly reduced. On the other hand, workers could no longer enjoy loose rules and non-exhaustive pace of work and had no freedom in disposing of their working time or changing the work practices.

3.2 Quality management and lean production

Formal separation of quality control and other indirect functions from direction production was recognised as the best practice at the socialist enterprise. Quality control was mostly limited to product quality inspection; it had been excluded from direct workers' formal tasks and was carried out by the Department of Technical Control (OTK). Nevertheless, workers bore significant responsibility for quality, which was reinforced through their wages linked to the 'quality of their work performance'. This approach to organisation of production in general and to quality control in particular was costly due to the inflated numbers of quality inspectors and other indirect employees in production. It did not allow manufacturing of high-quality products either. The old approach to organisation of production and quality control did not seem to be questioned in the 1990s. In the 2000s, Russian companies began to show interest in international standards and concepts governing production. Certification of the QM system for compliance with ISO 9000 became popular, but few domestic companies aimed at adopting lean production or related concepts. Multinational car manufacturers transferred lean production to their Russian operations.

There is a general agreement in the literature that the way quality control was performed had not changed significantly in the decade after the start of the transition (Clarke 1995; Clarke 1996; Clarke 1998; Kabalina 2005, among others). Quality inspectors from the OTK performed multiple checks and visual control of the products and these tasks were not formally integrated into the tasks of direct workers (Alasheev 1995b; Alasheev 1995c). However, workers had a high degree of discretion within their working area, as discussed in the previous section. The shop-floor relations were characterised by frequent conflicts between production workers and the OTK over acceptable product quality and fulfilment of the process requirements (Alasheev 1995c).

Despite some signs of change in the 2000s, it still went very slowly and unevenly. According to Schwartz and McCann, all types of Russian firms (holding companies, formerly state-owned firms and SMEs established after the start of the transition to a market economy) answered the new market requirements by work intensification and strengthening work discipline (Schwartz and McCann 2007). This resulted in a 'punitive quality regime': Russian firms used fines as the major means to discipline workers. Workers were fined even though a lot of the causes of quality problems were beyond their influence, as even skilful and experienced workers could not solve the problems caused by ageing equipment and low-grade components and raw materials.

Some Russian firms started to show interest in internationally established concepts and standards of quality and production management. The pace of diffusion of these standards was not high though. The major change efforts were aimed at improving quality control.

A survey of 732 Russian manufacturing enterprises by Kononova, with about 288 of them from machine building, shows that about 32 per cent of enterprises introduced some principles related to lean manufacturing (Kononova 2006:124). Of these enterprises, 23 per cent improved their production systems on the basis of their own ideas and 45 per cent of the enterprises did not modernise their production systems at all. Only 5 per cent of all enterprises surveyed reported that they aimed at improving the organisation of production processes systematically and consistently (ibid.:122). Most of the enterprises that did use lean manufacturing ideas implemented only one or two tools (134 and 63 enterprises respectively) (ibid.:125). Of all firms questioned, 5 per cent introduced three to six management instruments (ibid.). Total quality management (TQM) was by far the most popular management tool: about one fifth of all companies surveyed reported implementing it (Figure 3.1). 5S[4] was the second most popular practice implemented by the firms. The survey shows that Russian manufacturing enterprises were in the very early stage of introducing lean manufacturing methods in 2006.

Increased attention to quality control in the 2000s was caused by stricter quality requirements in supply chains. Both foreign and local customers started to require certification of their Russian suppliers' QM systems for compliance with ISO 9000 (Burnyshev, Vandyshev and Priamikova 2006). The popularity of this certification was growing in the 2000s (Burnyshev 2001; Burnyshev and Donova 2007; Burnyshev and Zubaidulina 2000; Burnyshev, Vandyshev and Priamikova 2006).

Studies on the impact of the certification on the industrial workplace do not present conclusive evidence of its effects. In some cases, the certification helped the firms to assure greater compliance of production processes to the formal regulations (Burnyshev and Donova 2007). Such were the changes observed at a formerly state-owned metal construction plant (Burnyshev and Zubaidulina

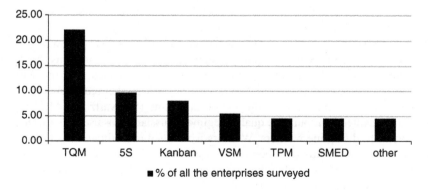

Figure 3.1 Lean manufacturing tools applied at Russian enterprises

Source: Figure by author on the basis of data from (Kononova 2006)

2000). The plant used its Complex System of Management of Output Quality (KSUKP) that had been in place since the planned economy as the basis of the standardised QM system. However, all work and production processes had to be described anew and requirements and responsibilities regarding quality control had to be redefined. It should be noted, however, that such transition was a lengthy process, taking up to two years (Dickenson and Blundell 2000). In other cases, though, the ISO certification did not lead to elimination of discrepancies between formal procedures and actual processes. The quality inspections by line management still had a sporadic character and were determined rather by the relationship between the line manager and the workers than by the formal procedures. The line manager could omit the checks if he thought he could trust the worker (Burnyshev, Vandyshev and Priamikova 2006).

The available studies agree that certification for compliance with ISO 9000 did not seem to lead to overcoming of the separation of quality control from the functions of production workers. Multiple levels of quality inspection through OTK or production supervisors persisted even after certification:

> Supplied parts are not used for manufacturing before the entry check is carried out... The product is not passed to the next operation before the checks and trials of the previous operation are completed. An OTK stamp is put on the accepted product and a corresponding OTK note is made in the technological passport. Non-compliant products are marked and placed into the 'isolator' of defective parts. The products are not sent to the customer without their final check and until they receive the documents confirming their compliance to the defined requirements. The approved products receive a document with an OTK stamp and a signature.
>
> (Burnyshev and Zubaidulina 2000:7–8)

Nevertheless, certification led to improvement of the status of the quality control units and their greater respect by the production.

In general, it appears that changes to quality control rarely reached the level of the shop-floor or were not sustainable, as in the case of a Russian supplier of a British aerospace company (Dickenson and Blundell 2000). This was due not only to obsolete production equipment, a factor already mentioned above, but also to the fact that development of employees' competencies and skills was not a part of firms' efforts to introduce new approaches to QM (Clarke 2007:210; Burnyshev and Donova 2007; Burnyshev, Vandyshev and Priamikova 2006; Dickenson and Blundell 2000). According to Dickenson and Blundell, senior Russian management was not able to pass the knowledge from the top down through the organisation. Both Russian managers and employees lacked knowledge and skills in the international QM requirements. They were unwilling to take personal responsibility and lacked incentives to change their attitudes to work.

Recent studies on automobile manufacturers in Russia stand out from the rest of the literature (Jürgens and Krzywdzinski 2013, 2016). The authors argue that

54 *Still there*

the companies they studied succeeded in aligning their manufacturing with the principles of the Toyota Production System and modelling their human resource (HR) policies on high-performance workplaces. This was possible due to extensive employee training programmes and careful selection of production supervisors. High density of control was still needed in order to assure workers' compliance with the standards on the shop-floor, as discussed in the previous section. The management of these plants did not intend to integrate quality-related tasks, such as problem-solving or process improvement activities, into workers' functions.

Summing up, QM in production in Russian firms was mostly limited to product quality inspection in the first decade of the 2000s. There had been no shift to viewing quality as a characteristic that originates in production processes, which require consistent audits, and even adherence to standardised process descriptions remained problematic. Certification for compliance with ISO 9000 did not have a strong impact on organisation of production and quality assurance.

Diffusion of lean production was at a nascent phase in the 2000s. Research on automobile manufacturers pioneering this development in Russia shows that introduction of lean production required consistent change in HR policies.

3.3 Group work and employee empowerment

Collective group (*brigade*) responsibility for output and its quality played a central role in the Soviet enterprise and persisted after the market reforms. While a low degree of formalisation of brigade work persisted, Russian industrial enterprises seem to have given the brigades even more responsibility for organisation of production processes. Contrary to this approach to work organisation, foreign-owned firms in Russia attempted to introduce individual responsibility for performance results, which was met with resistance both by Russian managers and employees.

Brigade work at Russian industrial enterprises in the 1990s was still characterised by a high degree of self-organisation. Workers and brigade leaders themselves could decide about production tasks or about issues related to discipline. This authority, however, was not always formally registered and evolved in the spaces not covered by the existing formal regulations – or contradicted them. Burawoy and Krotov observe that brigades could autonomously decide about work organisation and even had the authority to discipline their members:

> Management deliberately undermined the positions of master [the foreman] and *nachal'nik* [the shop manager]. They were sacrificial lambs, punished for not maintaining discipline on the shop floor, but at the same time denied the support and resources to maintain that discipline. Rather than agents of higher management in the exercise of control over the shop floor, supervisors were forced to cede power to the brigades in the hope that peace would prevail while management got on with the task of providing the materials of production. As one chief engineer said, "We are frightened of workers.

Still there 55

At any time they can stop work and we can do nothing." To give more support to *nachal'niki* and *mastera* would be to risk rebellion from the shop floor.

(Burawoy and Krotov 1992:27)

The authors conclude that management abdicated control over production; management set output plans and the brigades were, to a large extent, self-regulating as to how to fulfil the plan.

There was little novelty in work organisation in Russian factories in the 2000s. As Schwartz and McCann note:

> there have been substantial changes to the ownership and strategies of many of the firms in our sample, limited changes to management structures and systems of control of the enterprise, and very few changes to work organisation.
>
> (Schwartz and McCann 2007:1543)

The reliance of management on self-organisation in brigades was in some cases formally embraced by the management. Plotnikova notes that production tasks were formulated in a way that left some space for brigades to decide about how to perform them (Plotnikova 2005). Workers had a say regarding the time given for the production tasks and about the process design for performing the tasks. Moreover, in 'non-standard' situations, workers within a brigade would search for solutions themselves; the managers would not interfere in the process of 'solving a production problem' and only 'control the results'. Plotnikova underlines the importance of the brigade's bonus in reinforcing collective responsibility for fulfilling the production tasks. If one brigade member had not fulfilled a task or did not fill out the documents correctly, the whole brigade was deprived of a part of a bonus or a whole bonus.

The high degree of workers' self-organisation at Russian enterprises contrasts with problems with employee participation in decision-making at foreign firms in Russia discussed in the English-language literature (Fey 2008; Fey, Nordahl and Zätterström 1998; Jürgens and Krzywdzinski 2016; Michailova 2002). As Western companies attempted to shift from collective responsibility for performance results to individual responsibility, they met a lot of resistance from both Russian managers and employees. While some scholars observe that 'moderate' employee empowerment was optimal in Russia (Fey, Nordahl and Zätterström 1998:12), others note that it was regarded as "highly problematic or even impossible" by Western managers (Michailova 2002:186).

The obstacles to employee participation in decisions had to do primarily with the Russian employees' unwillingness to take responsibility (Fey, Nordahl and Zätterström 1998:12) and show initiative (Michailova 2002). At the same time, Russian managers were unwilling to empower and to share knowledge with employees as they perceived it as a loss of power (ibid.). They preferred to maintain their formal status and top-down communication. This led to contradictory requirements and expectations from Russian and Western managers. Fey *et al.* also note, however, that expatriates or even local managers did not empower

56 *Still there*

Russian employees as they did not believe that employees were competent enough (Fey, Nordahl and Zätterström 1998). Changing such patterns of thinking was difficult. Fey stresses the importance of strong leadership, which, however, should be based on competence rather than formal status (Fey 2008). He also notes that personnel policies should include providing information to all, not punishing mistakes; training management in listening skills; and providing rewards and quick feedback for useful suggestions.

The recent analysis of work organisation at multinational car manufacturers' plants in Russia shows that self-organisation in teams on the shop-floor had low management priority (Jürgens and Krzywdzinski 2016). Although the self-organisation played an important role at the multinationals' headquarters, they did not transfer such approaches to the Russian operations. Controlling compliance with process standards was a part of team leaders' daily responsibilities, as workers attempted to change the work procedures. Improving communication with team members and maintaining trust between management and workers were viewed as crucial for releasing the tensions on the shop-floor.

Summing up, the local Russian enterprises competing in the internal market continued to follow the socialist principles of work organisation. They still resorted to highly autonomous brigades as a way to compensate for the obsoleteness or absence of detailed work instructions and action plans, and the instability of production equipment. Brigades seem to have been given a better opportunity to decide about work processes than under the planned economy. However, brigades appear to be left on their own with these challenges without possessing the competencies and qualifications needed to find and remove the root causes of problems in production. Although workers in a brigade took a broad range of decisions, they were not 'empowered' in the Western sense of this term. Rather, it was a weakly standardised work pattern, in which management demonstrated a laissez faire attitude and avoided responsibility for rendering production and work processes more measurable and predictable.

Foreign companies are attempting to deviate from this work pattern by introducing individual responsibility for performance results among Russian employees and highly formalised team work on the shop-floor. These companies have to adopt complex measures in order to break away from the blurred borders of responsibility. These measures address not only local employees' but also managers' behaviour and include changing the traditional authoritarian communication style, competence development and non-punitive remuneration systems.

3.4 Worker qualification and development

The Soviet Union undertook significant efforts to educate and train a labour force for the needs of its growing industrial manufacturing. Vocational training followed the narrow technisist approach going back to the 1920s, which excluded indirect competencies from workers' qualifications. This approach became the basis of the *Soviet Wage Rate and Qualification Handbook for Workers* (*ETKS*) used both in the public institutions of vocational training and at technical colleges

Still there 57

and for in-house training. Vocational training curricula had not been updated after the market reforms. This raised the importance of in-house training at both local and foreign companies. While the latter developed new employee competence profiles, there is no evidence showing that Russian industrial enterprises moved away from the traditional narrow qualifications.

Worker qualification system

Universal use of the *ETKS* had been one of the mechanisms that reinforced the socialist path of production work under the planned economy. The qualification descriptions had only been slightly revised after the reforms and were still in use in vocational schools and technical colleges (see Shulzhenko 2012 for an overview of education and vocational training system in Russia). The outdated curricula, obsolete equipment and poor quality of teaching made state vocational qualification insufficient for manufacturing conditions at a contemporary foreign company (Jürgens and Krzywdzinski 2016).

Since 1992, the application of the *ETKS* was no longer mandatory for private enterprises (Gontmacher 2007). Nevertheless, many enterprises continued to adhere to it in the 1990s and 2000s (Donova 2005; Gimpelson and Kapelyushnikov 2007; Gontmacher 2007; Vedeneeva 1995). The available research provides little detail either on how exactly Russian firms used the book or on other approaches to wage differentiation that were used by industrial enterprises in the 2000s. Donova observes that less than one third of over 50 industrial enterprises she had studied stopped using the 'traditional' system of wage differentiation completely (Donova 2005). The rest of the firms used the old wage rate schemes; some of them applied the *ETKS* unmodified, others used it 'as guidelines' (ibid.:119). According to Kapelyushnikov, different versions of the book were applied at 45 per cent of his sample enterprises; 12 per cent of them still used the *ETKS* and 29 per cent adjusted it to the enterprise's characteristics (Kapelyushnikov 2007:126–127). Only about every second enterprise set the level of wages and salaries independently from the one recommended therein.

In sum, vocational qualification in post-Soviet Russia was still characterised by a significant degree of coordination due to the use of *ETKS* by vocational training institutions. Even though Russian companies had the freedom to develop their own systems of qualifications and competencies, only about half of them did so. There is no research about what qualification profiles Russian companies developed if they did not base them on *ETKS* or whether they departed from the old qualification descriptions, which strictly separated direct and indirect qualifications in production.

The shortage of qualified labour

In the early 1990s, a sharp decrease in industrial production took place in Russia, resulting in a significant reduction of employment at manufacturing enterprises (Breev 2003). However, shortage of qualified labour had been one of the major

58   *Still there*

challenges for post-Soviet production enterprises from the late 1990s onwards. Under the planned economy, it had been caused by the growth of industrial manufacturing. After the market reforms, young and highly qualified people were the first to leave the enterprises and look for new jobs. This contributed to an ageing workforce and scarcity of labour after the market reforms: companies lacked both qualified workers and engineers (Ryvkina and Kolennikova 2007). Other factors behind the labour shortage included massive wage arrears, disorganisation of the work processes at the plants and an unwillingness of young people to work in production after completing their studies (ibid.).

In the 2000s, labour shortages affected both local and foreign industrial firms in Russia. Paradoxically, Russian companies reported labour shortages but still had excessive numbers of employees, who they were unwilling to fire even though workers did not have an employment guarantee any longer (Gimpelson 2010; Ryvkina and Kolennikova 2007). The managers surveyed by Ryvkina and Kolennikova pointed to higher pay and employee training and retraining as measures that should be taken to attract employees. Despite acknowledging this, local enterprises were unwilling to train or retrain their excess employees (Gimpelson 2010). Foreign companies in Russia faced a different challenge. High employee turnover in production raised the effort and resources that companies had to invest in qualification and training needs (Jürgens and Krzywdzinski 2016).

Thus, industrial enterprises in Russia had difficulties with hiring and retaining sufficient numbers of qualified industrial workers. This made in-house training programmes crucial for smooth flow of manufacturing.

In-house training at Russian and foreign enterprises

Due to the obsoleteness of the state system of vocational training, upgrading of employees' qualification and skills was a necessary condition for breaking away from the socialist path of industrial work. While some in-house training programmes existed at both domestic and foreign firms, the latter seem to have had more extensive training programmes based on competence profiles developed by the companies specifically for the needs of their production.

The organisation of training at Russian enterprises did not change much after the start of the transition. Employee training still concentrated on technical competencies, and enterprises used mentorship as a means to raise the competence level of less experienced workers. According to Bizyukov, there was a well-developed system of personnel training at most of the over 50 enterprises that took part in the study, particularly at large ones (Bizyukov 2005). Training included a start-up programme for newcomers and 'further training courses'. Start-up training comprised work safety and technical skills training at a specific working place (ibid.). 'Further training courses' (*kursy povysheniya kvalifikatsii*) for blue- and particularly for white-collar employees varied a lot. In some cases, white-collar employees could search for further training opportunities themselves; in others this was subject to strict planning by management.

Still there 59

Some Russian firms started to use 'employee assessments' to confirm workers' qualification grades and to assess managers and white-collar staff (ibid.). The assessment procedure was quite elaborate: an assessment committee was created and a variety of assessment tools were applied, which could include interviews, questionnaires, exams and tests. However, assessments often had a ritual character and their results were not used for further decisions and action. Additionally, there were frequent cases when management purposely developed strict assessment criteria that would allow for reducing workers' qualification grades. Bizyukov also notes that many firms had a training programme, which was supposed to help in fulfilling the 'future development plans' of the enterprises. The recent results from a major Russian car manufacturer GAZ show a combination of continuity in the use of *ETKS* for the blue-collar staff, with efforts to shift to a meritocratic appraisal of production supervisors (Jürgens and Krzywdzinski 2016).

Foreign companies located in Russia found personnel development crucial for their Russian operations (ibid.; Fey and Björkman 1999; Fey, Engström and Björkman 1998; Shekshnia 1998). According to Fey *et al.*, 65 per cent of the firms in their sample carried out a complete analysis of the competencies needed for their Russian operations and developed training programmes specifically for these Russian subsidiaries (Fey, Engström and Björkman 1998:8). The programmes applied in other emerging markets were not suitable due to the high diversity of Russian employees' backgrounds and their generally high education. At the same time, the programmes used in the Western countries did not fit either, as many Russian employees lacked understanding of the basic concepts of a market economy, such as customer focus and competition. Training was a necessary means by which to provide them with this background.

Multinational car manufacturers that standardise their production systems across locations transferred their approaches to employee training to their Russian operations (Jürgens and Krzywdzinski 2016). Both Volkswagen and Toyota developed new qualification profiles for their Russian plants independently from the *ETKS*. Volkswagen transferred the dual vocational training model to the region, where the plant is located. Seven qualifications taught in the new college follow the German standards. Toyota relied on extensive on-the-job training at its Russian operation, with communication and problem-solving skills included in blue-collar workers' training.

The majority of foreign companies also trained Russian managers (Fey, Engström and Björkman 1998:8; Fey, Nordahl and Zätterström 1998). According to Fey, Engström and Björkman (1998:8), 65 per cent of the firms considered sent them to study abroad, which helped Russian managers to understand their employer's organisational culture. Jürgens and Krzywdzinski underline that lengthy and carefully designed development and appraisal procedures for managerial personnel, starting from the production supervisor level, was crucial for both Volkswagen and Toyota (Jürgens and Krzywdzinski 2016). Production supervisors were promoted internally and both of these companies paid a lot of attention to developing their communication and leadership skills.

60 *Still there*

Summing up, Russian industrial firms did not deviate from the narrow qualification profiles characteristic of the socialist path of industrial work. They experienced difficulties in developing formalised and transparent systems of employee training and appraisal. Foreign companies seem to base their personnel development on systemic analysis of the required and available competencies. Multinational car manufacturers in Russia follow their global standards both with regard to organisation of employee development and the content.

3.5 Remuneration systems

Remuneration systems represented a key means to discipline workers and assure their compliance with the production and work rules in a Soviet enterprise. The system of remuneration[5] in post-socialist Russia was still characterised by a combination of a low share of fixed pay and a high variable share of pay, and high managerial discretion in determination of the variable share (Clarke 1998). However, since the 1990s, employers have begun to unilaterally change remuneration systems (Gimpelson and Kapelyushnikov 2007). Formalised personnel appraisal systems were not the basis for these changes and were rarely applied at Russian firms. However, foreign companies operating in Russia seemed to rely considerably on personnel appraisals.

Unilateral change of remuneration systems by employers

A central characteristic of the remuneration systems in post-socialist Russia was a combination of relative stability of employment with remarkable changeability of wages. No rapid reduction of employment at privatised enterprises took place in Russia in the early 1990s; instead, employment was reduced gradually throughout the 1990s and the first half of the 2000s (ibid.). Enterprises did not lay off employees but frequently *unilaterally* changed criteria for personnel remuneration, which applied to both white- and blue-collar employees (see Figure 3.2).

Employers could also cut wages and salaries or delay payments. Reduction of wages might be followed by an increase, when the enterprise's situation improved; this, however, would be at the discretion of management. Employees were forced to accept the new conditions or quit their jobs; in some cases they could also be required to sign a paper consenting to the unilaterally changed conditions of pay. As Gimpelson and Kapelyushnikov observe, wages varied, depending on the economic situation of the enterprise:

> As a matter of fact, this is specifically a scheme of employees' participation in the firm's losses as opposed to a scheme of employees' participation in profits.
> (Gimpelson and Kapelyushnikov 2007:58)

Practices used by employers to reduce remuneration included temporary lay-offs, delays of the payment of wages and salaries ('wage arrears') and limited compensation for inflation in the wages, which had very tangible effects on employees

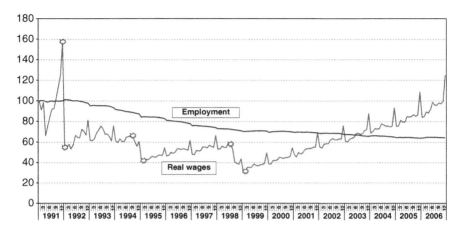

Figure 3.2 Dynamics of employment and real wages at medium and large enterprises in 1991–2006 (January 1991 = 100%)
Source: Gimpelson and Kapelyushnikov 2007:124

due to very high rates of inflation in Russia, and change in the variable share of pay (Gerber 2006; Gimpelson and Kapelyushnikov 2007:61; Sobolev 2008; Donova 2005). The choice of practices varied depending on the economic situation in the country. For example, wage arrears peaked in 1998, when employers were saving 15–20 per cent of the total 'contract' costs of the labour force (Gimpelson and Kapelyushnikov 2007:61). They decreased throughout the 2000s, but reappeared in the financial crisis in 2008, when delays in payment started to grow once again (Shcheglov and Sergeev 2008).

The use of unilateral change of remuneration was possible due to the absence of sanctions against employers from the state and trade unions. Anisimova and Sobolev confirm the extremely poor enforcement of work contracts in Russia on the basis of a large employee survey:

> Only 7 per cent of employed in the private sector... consider that the contract conditions are decisive for determination of their pay.
> (Anisimova and Sobolev 2010:32–33)

Gimpelson and Kapelyushnikov (2007) observe that the low mobility of the labour force was another reason making the unilateral change of remuneration possible.

Determination of the variable share of remuneration

Under the planned economy, the variable share of remuneration was a key lever used to assure employees' productivity and quality of work performance. It allowed the enterprises to punish-but-retain workers due to the scarcity of labour

62   *Still there*

and the employment guarantee. The variable share of pay was linked to group or brigade responsibility. After the market reforms, Russian enterprises further increased their reliance on a variable share of remuneration. Only a minority of Russian firms introduced formal personnel appraisal systems based on measurement of individual performance. Foreign companies in Russia seemed to rely more frequently on individual performance appraisals.

Russian enterprises answered market reforms by drastically decreasing the 'guaranteed share' of pay (Sobolev 2008; Donova 2005). Instead, a higher share of wages was determined monthly and could vary. Donova (2005) notes that managers tended to think that the higher the 'non-guaranteed share of pay', the better it was for the enterprise. According to Andreeva, changes in payment systems were one of the most frequently used HR measures during organisational change (Andreeva 2006).

Estimates of the variable share of pay differ. According to Sobolev, it amounted to 15–30 per cent of the total pay on average (Sobolev 2008:101). Donova reports that the variable share of pay amounted to 40 per cent of total pay at the companies she studied (Donova 2005:130). Gimpelson and Kapelyushnikov found that the variable share of pay amounted to at least 25–30 per cent (Gimpelson and Kapelyushnikov 2007:76). This way, enterprises could change the cost of wages without having to revise the wage system that they had adopted.

A low share of fixed pay made it easier for the management to use 'grey', 'shadow' or 'envelope' salary payments. Sobolev quotes survey data showing that 32 per cent of employees in Russia received 'shadow' salary payments in 2005 (Sobolev 2008:133).

Notably, foreign companies in Russia seemed to rely on a variable share of remuneration as much as domestic companies. Fey *et al.* found that about 80 per cent of firms had some kind of bonus system (Fey, Engström and Björkman 1998:11). In most cases bonuses varied between 20 and 40 per cent of total salary (ibid.), however the size and type of bonus differed significantly among companies and across departments. Contrary to these findings, Jürgens and Krzywdzinski (2016) observe that the multinational companies they studied did not introduce individual bonuses accounting for a large share of remuneration.

The criteria for determination of such high variable share of pay were generally weakly formalised and the use of performance appraisals was rare. Gurkov *et al.* (2009) observe, on the basis of a survey of personnel managers in 32 countries, that the use of formalised appraisal systems by Russian enterprises was the lowest among all the countries. According to their results, 40 per cent of Russian companies reported that they applied formalised personnel assessment systems for workers and 21 per cent for white-collar employees in the late 2000s (see Table 3.1).

Results from qualitative case studies show that Russian industrial companies hardly used personnel appraisals for assessment of employees' performance:

> The routine evaluation of an employee... is made mainly on the basis of data on the employee's discipline (misconduct, penalties, incentives etc.), on

Table 3.1 Application of personnel appraisal systems at Russian firms

Employee category	Share of studied firms (%)
Managers	38
Specialists (highly educated professionals)	43
White collar employees	21
Workers	40

Source: Adapted from Gurkov *et al.* 2009:145

> fulfilment of work tasks that are registered in the wages and on the basis of informal relations (relations with the colleagues, the management etc.). This system can hardly be considered sufficient in order to objectively evaluate an employee's performance, to say nothing of obtaining a general evaluation of the use of the workforce at the enterprise as a whole.
>
> (Bizyukov 2005:48)

Bizyukov notes that there were no centrally set rules or standards with regard to discipline in most of the cases. Instead, there was an informal agreement between the employees and line management on acceptable behaviour.

Foreign companies seemed to use personnel appraisal systems far more frequently than domestic firms. Fey *et al.* found that about 75 per cent of foreign firms studied used a formal appraisal system (Fey, Engström and Björkman 1998:10); 23 per cent of the firms applied an 'up-and-down evaluation system' – whereby not only superiors evaluated their employees, but also a reciprocal process took place (ibid.). Jürgens and Krzywdzinski (2016) observe that formalised performance assessment was applied at both Volkswagen and Toyota, where it was used in connection with promotion to a higher pay grade. The criteria at Volkswagen focused on the demands of the job performed by workers and included attendance, quality, flexibility, initiative, good teamwork and discipline. At Toyota, criteria were based on workers' competencies – for example, teamwork, self-development and continuous improvement.

A low rate of application of formalised personnel appraisals at Russian firms strengthened the discretion and subjectivity of line management in decisions on remuneration. According to the employees' survey conducted as part of the case studies by Donova (2005), only 14.1 per cent of workers thought that their wages depended on their own behaviour at work (see Table 3.2).

About 80 per cent of employees viewed their wages as dependent on the managers' will. Donova emphasises two characteristics of bonus systems introduced at the enterprises. First, these systems did not differentiate workers on the basis of their performance. Second, they were, in most cases, linked to fulfilment of output plans by the enterprise or by the shop – that is, not directly linked to an employee's productivity. She concludes that the new bonus systems ultimately contributed to demotivation of employees.

64 *Still there*

Table 3.2 "On whom does the size of your wage depend mostly?"

Possible answers	% of respondents
Management of the enterprise	56.2
Shop or unit management	20.4
Production supervisor or brigade (team) leader	5.5
Me myself	14.1
Hard to answer	3.7

Source: Donova 2005:127

Survey data from Gurkov *et al.* (2009) confirms the high discretion of line management in decisions on bonuses. In 46 per cent of the companies, these decisions were taken solely by line management, in 20 per cent of the cases predominantly by line management, in 22 per cent predominantly by the personnel department and in only 11 per cent solely by the personnel department (ibid.:139). Donova found that at about half of the enterprises she studied the line management disposed of a wage fund that they distributed on the shop-floor (Donova 2005).

Data from an employee survey by Anisimova and Sobolev (2010) and case study evidence by Bizyukov (2005) emphasise the importance of employees' behaviour that could not be measured, such as loyalty to the firm or to the line manager or avoiding conflicts. Jürgens and Krzywdzinski (2016) describe how Volkswagen first introduced an individual bonus based on performance appraisal by production supervisor and then incorporated the bonus into basic pay due to complaints about cronyism from employees and trade unions. Remarkably, Toyota, where no bonuses were in place, observed high expectations for an individual bonus among their Russian employees (ibid.).

Some studies report that Russian firms continued to use the Coefficient of Labour Participation (KTU) (see Section 2.3) to distribute wages or a variable share of pay (Donova 2005; Posadskov 2002). In Donova's study KTU was not used by the brigade itself but by production management: it helped the management to allocate the payments that were a part of the overall earnings. Posadskov (2002) reports on dozens of KTUs, which were in use in Sibir, one of the largest Russian airlines. Both Donova and Posadskov argue that as the payments allocated by KTU could be withheld by management at any time, they played the role of sanctions rather than incentives.

One more type of bonus in use was payment linked to company's or department's performance. The most common type of bonus at foreign firms in Russia was the payment of a 13th month of salary if firms met their objectives (Fey, Engström and Björkman 1998:11). Jürgens and Krzywdzinski (2016) note that the Russian car manufacturer GAZ paid a company bonus of 5–10 per cent of the total – the same for all employees – and a variable bonus linked to criteria set at the plant level and specific for manufacturing areas, amounting to 20 per cent of the total remuneration (ibid.:202).

Summing up the overview of the remuneration systems in the post-socialist era in Russia, their most striking characteristic was their high changeability. Pay systems were linked to the enterprise's economic situation, which was possible due to greater freedom from state regulation following the reforms and the poor enforcement of labour rights in Russia. Although remuneration systems at Russian industrial enterprises varied a lot and were frequently changed, these changes seem to largely follow the principles inherited from the past. The variable share of remuneration became even larger than in the past and management discretion in its determination grew as well. Measurable individual performance did not become the central determinant of remuneration at Russian industrial enterprises. As in the past, the variable share of pay was used to compensate for ad hoc work processes (cf. Donova 2005). The available research on foreign companies in Russia shows that they seemed to use formalised personnel appraisals more frequently than domestic firms. While some relied on individual bonuses, others did not use variable share of pay.

3.6 Representation of employees' interests

The two main functions of the unions under the planned economy were to assist management in meeting production targets and to administer social benefits. Unions participated in organisation of the socialist labour competition and supported other forms of ideological work in production. Representing the members' interests took up least of the unions' time and was limited to activities that did not challenge consensus with management and the political authorities (cf. Clarke 1993; Mandel 2004). The post-socialist period is characterised by withdrawal of the employment guarantee and of the state benefits that used to be distributed by the unions. At the same time, violation of labour rights by employers became ubiquitous (Zaslavskaya and Shabanova 2002b, 2002a). While the successor of the communist union, Federation of Independent Trade Unions (FNPR), followed the 'traditional' role of the unions, 'new' or 'independent' unions established in some enterprises broke with the loyal relationship to the management and attempted to genuinely represent employees' interests.

The post-soviet workplace was characterised by violations of labour rights, on the one hand, and by the lack of employee protection by either the state or the trade unions, on the other hand. Zaslavskaya and Shabanova argue that illegal labour practices became the norm in industrial relations in Russia (Zaslavskaya and Shabanova 2002a, 2002b). According to them about 60–65 per cent of employees encountered violation of their labour rights. Remarkably, only 35 per cent were aware of such violations, while the rest interpreted them as 'life troubles', were not informed about their rights, or agreed to illegal conditions when they entered the company. Borisov and Clarke (2001) note that employees organised by the 'traditional' unions also showed remarkable tolerance to their labour right violations.

The FNPR – the largest trade union association in Russia, organising over 90 per cent of all union members (Krzywdzinski 2011) – did not switch from the 'service

66 *Still there*

model' to the 'organisational model' (Borisov and Clarke 2001; Plotnikova, Germanov and Plotnikova 2005). Borisov and Clarke observe that the unions in the FNPR did not attempt to organise employees for collective protection of labour rights. They still attempted to offer services to the individual members, even though their traditional distribution functions weakened. Ordinary union members had little information about the union and were very passive. Plotnikova *et al.* observe significant differences between the way the management and unions perceive the unions' functions and the way employees think about them. Employees were much more sceptical than the management and the unions about the unions' engagement in all questions regarding labour rights, from work safety to observing employees' rights during staff reductions (Plotnikova, Germanov and Plotnikova 2005:24). The issues of increased wages and job security received the lowest scores by all three groups of respondents. Thus in the late 2000s, the FNPR continued the tradition of loyalty to the state. It has been in official partnership with the United Russia party since 2004 (Clarke and Pringle 2009:88).

The new labour law that came into force in 2002 improved the position of the FNPR and made it more difficult to establish independent new unions at the companies (Klimova and Clement 2004; Shulzhenko 2012). Although trade unions received significant rights to information and consultation, the employers are only required to recognise the unions, if at least 50 per cent of employees are organised in one or more unions (Jürgens and Krzywdzinski 2016). Despite these barriers, new independent unions were established and merged to form the Confederation of Labour of Russia, which remains weak overall (ibid.). These new unions started to compete for influence in the Russian industrial workplace with the 'traditional' unions.

Establishment of production locations in Russia by international automobile manufacturers gave new opportunities for independent trade unions (Clarke and Pringle 2011; Krzywdzinski 2011). A trade union established at Ford's plant in 2003 succeeded in some of its demands to the management after a number of strikes (Clarke and Pringle 2011). Ford's trade union joined with a number of other workplace unions to establish the Interregional Trade Union of Automobile Workers of Russia (MPRA) in 2007. In 2008 an MPRA organisation was established at Volkswagen, which was, however, followed by setting up of two 'traditional' workplace unions at the plant with the help of the local government in order to weaken the independent union (Jürgens and Krzywdzinski 2016).

Jürgens and Krzywdzinski (ibid.) observe that Volkswagen took important steps to transfer the global standards for industrial relations to the Russian operation. The MPRA union was recognised at Volkswagen even though this meant exceeding the requirements of the Russian labour law. Amid the competition between the MPRA and the 'traditional' union, the Automobile and Agricultural Machinery Workers' Union (ASM), Volkswagen also attempted to establish a single channel for employee voice by setting up a Works Council at its Russian plant in accordance with industrial relations at Volkswagen Group. This attempt failed even though Volkswagen provided the resources for this arrangement. Jürgens and Krzywdzinski explain this as caused by the prevalence of a culture

Still there 67

of mistrust and conflict and the competition between 'old' and 'new' unions that weakens the attention that both of them pay to employee interest representation.

The overview of the employee interest representation in Russia shows that employees' interests and labour rights were not protected by the traditional unions, which still mainly concentrated on the distribution of benefits allocated by the employers. Establishment of multinational companies in Russia and transfer of global standards of industrial relations represented a window of opportunity for switching to a model of interest representation closer to the values of industrial democracy. However, steps towards these values met with obstacles from the state and were impeded by the lack of trust in the possibility of a genuine dialogue with the management on the side of the 'new' unions.

3.7 Conclusion: industrial work in Russia after the market reforms

The Russian industrial workplace did not undergo a rapid revolutionary shift after the radical reforms of the early 1990s. The path of industrial work at domestic firms did not remain static, but the pattern of change can best be characterised as loosening of the old principles, while very few novel ideas were introduced. The mechanisms reinforcing the old path remained largely in place. Foreign firms set up in Russia seem to differ significantly from domestic firms with regard to work organisation and personnel policies, but there is little research on them. Their attempts to deviate from the 'traditional' practices appear to be successful, despite the resistance they meet both from Russian employees and management. The few studies available on change efforts and outcomes at local firms operating in internationalised industries or supplying to foreign customers present rather contradictory evidence.

The domestic firms do not seem to have challenged the core characteristics of the socialist path of industrial work: a high degree of arbitrariness in management decisions on the shop-floor and reliance upon immediate control and punitive means to discipline workers. Withdrawal of state regulation, poor enforcement of labour law and weakness of employees' interest representation made it possible for firms to compensate for their economic shortcomings by cutting labour costs, even with violations of labour rights. This only sharpened the punitive character of the path of industrial work in Russian firms in the decades following the market reforms.

Russian enterprises did not either develop the Soviet time production standards further or adjust them to the new market conditions. The technical level of the standards, which used to be high in the Soviet time, were lost and gaps between formal procedures and actual production and work processes even widened. The firms did not overcome the separation between direct production and indirect functions, such as quality control. Production was still characterised by a high degree of control or 'overseeing'. Group work was characterised by blurred borders between individual and collective responsibility and ad hoc steering. A narrow approach to qualifications of production workers continued to prevail

68   *Still there*

and firms did not undertake systematic attempts to train new competencies in quality assurance or group work. Remuneration systems were frequently changed, but local firms did not turn away from relying on a high variable share of pay as a means to discipline workers. Personnel appraisals came into use in some firms, but formalised assessment of individual performance did not become the basis for determination of pay.

In the 2000s, certification of QM systems for compliance with the international standard ISO 9000 became popular. Still, the certification did not question the separation between production and quality control. In some cases, the certification increased the degree of formalisation of production and work processes, but the evidence about this is ambiguous. Quality assurance still focused on product quality and little attention was paid to the quality of processes or the company as a whole. Some Russian firms showed interest in lean production but did not carry out systemic reorganisation of production in accordance with its principles.

The strongest of the mechanisms reinforcing the persistent path of industrial work even after the reforms stems from complementarity between the elements constituting the path: group work, quality control and systems of employee qualification and remuneration. Despite the particularity of each of these elements they complement each other, so that altering one of these elements is impeded by the continued presence of all the others. Learning effects caused by the continued reliance of the vocational training system and companies' in-house training on the socialist approach to workers' qualification hinder introduction of novel management principles that employees have no competencies for.

Literature on foreign firms in Russia shows that they significantly deviate from the traditional practices, even though research results differ in some respects. Foreign firms decrease the gap between the process standards and actual production and work processes. They deviate from the blurred borders between individual and collective responsibility characteristic of the socialist path of industrial work and foster individual responsibility and individual performance appraisal. Nevertheless, there is no research that consistently compares old and new principles governing the industrial workplace in Russia and explains how and why some firms succeed in overcoming the self-reinforcing mechanisms perpetuating the old path of industrial work.

Notes

1 Some parts of this chapter draw upon my review of the research literature on labour relations and HR management in post-socialist Russia (Shulzhenko 2012).
2 As a result of the privatisation, the majority of Russian enterprises were sold to their managers and employees by 1996. The Russian privatisation left workers with one of the highest rates of ownership of their enterprises in the world (Russell 2002:555). Despite employees' participation in the firm's ownership, researchers report that the privatisation left workers with less power than before, giving managers more autonomy than before (Borisov and Kozina 1994; Russell 2002; Temnitsky 2007). Employees' ownership after privatisation rapidly declined and by the end of the 1990s the enterprises were again largely under the control of the people who had been in power before the start of the market reforms.

3 The financial crisis in 1998 that was caused by government default on its internal and international debts (McCarthy, Puffer and Naumov 2000). The rouble was devalued precipitously, which had both negative and positive consequences for Russian production enterprises. On the one hand, the devaluation of the rouble made it difficult for the firms to fulfil their contract obligations with foreign suppliers in foreign currency. On the other hand, the conditions created by the crisis stimulated the development of domestic companies that started to establish supply chains within the country and to 'optimise' production (Gurkov 2003). After the crisis industrial manufacturing in Russia grew steadily until 2008, although it did not reach the level of 1990 (Golikova *et al.* 2007:12; Rosstat 2012).
4 5S is a Japanese workplace organisation method, which includes five terms: sorting, streamlining, systematic cleaning, standardising and sustaining.
5 There is no linguistic difference between 'wage' and 'salary' in Russian; both of them are mostly referred to as 'pay for work' (*zarabotnaya plata*).

4 The new times

International quality management standards in the Russian car industry

The international quality management (QM) standards that Russian automotive enterprises started to introduce in the 2000s have more than 20 years' history in developed capitalist economies. The dissemination of these concepts, known as the total quality management (TQM) movement, became the second important shift in the path of industrial work in the West after the establishment of Taylorism. This shift started from the transfer of the Japanese idea of quality circles to the West. Later Western automobile manufacturers developed standardised production systems based on the Toyota Production System, where QM was integrated with other elements of production. This shift marked a deviation from Taylorism and had a profound impact on production work. In contrast to the exclusion of initiative on the shop-floor characteristic of scientific management, TQM and lean production called for workers' involvement in quality control and decision-making within their work area. Some of the ideas of TQM were institutionalised in the form of international QM standards.

The present chapter will, first, provide background information on the origins and content of international QM concepts and will outline how they changed industrial work in Western enterprises. Then the chapter will analyse the diffusion of the international QM standards in the Russian automotive industry during the period of its internationalisation. The analysis will concentrate on key actors supporting the introduction of the new standards and the mechanisms they employed in order to foster the introduction of the new standards by the local enterprises.

4.1 The origins of international quality management standards: from Taylorism to total quality management

Standardisation of work operations and separation of direct work from indirect functions, including quality control – the two ideas at the core of Taylorism – played a key role in the early development of industrial management in the West, just as in Soviet Russia. The later trajectories of these two paths of industrial work, however, differed. Soviet industrial enterprises faced difficulty in assuring compliance with the standards in production but continued to adhere to the separation of direct work from indirect functions. Capitalist enterprises, on the contrary, kept the standardisation of work operations but questioned the

The new times 71

separation of control from execution in production following the dissemination of TQM ideas. This shift had broad implications for the industrial workplace in the developed capitalist economies.

Taylorism in the West: the turn away from initiative on the shop-floor

The strict separation between the execution of tasks in production and the 'science of labouring' was adopted in both the capitalist and the socialist regimes. Craftsmanship or management by 'initiative and incentive' (Taylor 1911) was eradicated in production. Workers were compelled to follow the standard established for the operation through direct control and individual piece-rate pay. By the 1920s elements of Taylorism (piece-rate pay and time-motion studies) became widely accepted, and in the 1930s they became considerably diffused in the USA (Barley and Kunda 1992; Strang and Kim 2005). Taylorism soon became part of the Fordist model of mass production; Ford further simplified work operations by introducing automation and then shortened the transit time of work pieces from machine to machine by introducing the moving assembly line (Sabel 1982:33). It is widely argued that Taylorism led to the simplification of work on the shop-floor, de-qualification and demotivation of production workers (see, e.g. Jürgens, Malsch and Dohse 1993). Taylorism considerably changed the distribution of power in a firm: workers' decision-making abilities were constrained, whereas engineering and managerial personnel obtained much more authority than in the past (Strang and Kim 2005).

The idea of establishing 'one best way' to perform every production operation, creating a standard and diffusing it throughout production fascinated industrial engineers in both capitalist economies and the Soviet state. Yet, it gave stronger roots in the West, where formal control based on standards became the foundation of the subsequent development of mass production. Both workers' initiative and management discretion were subordinated to the primacy of standards. In Soviet Russia, on the contrary, standards in production became of secondary importance shortly after the adoption of Taylorism. The imperative of increasing output gave the right to both workers and managers to compromise with 'one best way'; the draconian penalties of the decades of forced industrialisation further relativised the rational basis of power in production.

The principles of scientific management in the West were first questioned in the middle of the twentieth century in what came to be called the 'human relations movement'. In particular, the lack of attention to the social aspects of work and non-economic motivation factors was re-evaluated (Barley and Kunda 1992:375). In the 1950s firms started to introduce innovative remuneration systems, schemes for participatory decision-making and job enrichment on the shop-floor. While work organisation and personnel management were rapidly transformed, the separation of control from execution was left intact and it was mostly the technical aspects of quality control that were changing. Technical innovations in quality control at that time were associated with the introduction

72   *The new times*

of statistical methods (Walgenbach 2001; Tuckman 1995). These activities were performed by technical staff or newly created quality control departments without the involvement of other employees in the company. This innovation, therefore, remained a purely technical matter that did not challenge the general organisation of quality control in a firm.

Total quality management movement: bringing workers back in

The transfer of Japanese ideas on organisation of quality control to the USA became the starting point for change in the whole path of industrial work in the capitalist economies. This change, which began with the involvement of workers in quality control through quality circles, developed into what became known as the TQM movement and international QM standards. The change of quality assurance at automobile manufacturers' plants became the first step towards development of integrated production systems based on principles of lean manufacturing. The present section will describe the evolution of these new ideas on QM and their impact on industrial work.

The impulse to question the organisation of quality control in Western industry came from post-war Japan. The Japanese Union of Scientists and Engineers (JUSE) promoted 'quality control circles' – small groups of foremen and workers who studied and applied quality control methods (Strang and Kim 2005). The first circle was registered in 1962; by 1980 their number exceeded 100,000 (ibid.:184). Japanese companies put considerable efforts into teaching foremen how to apply statistical quality control (Cole 1979:137). Foremen then taught workers the methods of quality control at the meetings of the quality control circles. The tools of analysis studied at the meetings included not only statistical diagrams and charts, but also cause-and-effect diagrams (ibid.:138). Workers thus learnt skills that allowed them not only to register quality problems, but also to look for their causes and implement improvement projects on the shop-floor. Quality control circles were a part of companies' complex efforts aimed at saving the costs of quality inspection, as shop-floor workers would take over detection of defects (Tuckman 1995). Kaoru Ishikawa, one of the most prominent figures in the development of quality control in Japan, argued about the economic rationale behind employee involvement in quality control:

> If defective products are produced at different stages of the manufacturing process, even strict inspection cannot eliminate them. If instead of relying on inspection, we produce no defective products from the very beginning – in other words, if we control the factors in a particular process which cause defective products – we can spare a lot of money that is expended for inspections.
>
> (Ibid.:62)

The process that started as dissemination of Western statistical quality control methods became more than a technical change in the field of quality control in

The new times 73

Japan. It initiated a process of eliminating hierarchical inspection and integrating quality inspection and problem-solving tasks into shop-floor employees' functions.

The departure from traditional inspection-based notions of quality control became integrated with other principles of quality control. The ideas and supporting practices of quality control in Japan evolved into 'a new quality model', which later became known as 'company-wide quality control' (Cole 1999; Strang and Kim 2005:188). The new quality model included three dimensions (Cole 1999:26). The first dimension was the increased significance of product quality and quality control activities for the company, which led to re-evaluation of customer orientation. Customer needs had to be not only satisfied, but also anticipated; improved quality became a competitive strategy. The second was functional changes in the organisation of quality control, as a focus on top-down product inspection and defect detection was complemented with an emphasis on bottom-up prevention activities, problem-solving and continuous quality improvement. Prevention meant focusing on processes in organisation ('process orientation') and their improvement. The third was the focus on all-employee participation in quality-related activities. Quality control expanded across the hierarchical levels to involve shop-floor workers and across functional boarders to achieve firm-level quality goals.

Dissemination of the Japanese principles of company-wide quality control in the USA started with quality circles. In the late 1970s ideas on quality control were spread in the West, mostly through contributions from single personalities, referred to as 'gurus' in the QM debate (see Table 4.1). The most active personalities included E.W. Deming, J. Juran, A.V. Feigenbaum and P.B. Crosby, and Japanese experts Ishikawa and Taguchi.

Western companies introducing quality circles were confronted with the necessity to adjust their personnel practices. Borrowing from Japan was impeded by the differences in systems of work organisation and labour relations between the USA and Japan (Cole 1979). Cole argues that quality circles could not be transferred one to one as an independent practice and the transfer should run parallel with readjusting other elements of work relations. According to him, two strategies were possible due to the absence of permanent employment in the USA. First, firms could make arrangements complementary with quality circles, such as introduce worker rewards and recognition oriented to financial benefits. Second, firms could introduce career paths and make resources available for training for all employees, including blue-collars, striving for lifelong employment, like in Japan.

Quality circles were spreading in the USA and Western Europe fastest in the industries most exposed to competition with Japanese manufacturers: the automobile, electronics and computer hardware industries. The first wave of their adoption, however, had a 'faddish' character. Firms followed normative expectations rather than taking conscious choices befitting their company situation (Cole 1979). Quality circles were viewed by companies as a 'packaged solution' that could be applied without changing other practices or power relationships in an organisation. Their role changed to "voluntary groups that made recommendations to management" (Strang

74   *The new times*

Table 4.1 Prominent personalities in the debate on quality management

'Gurus' and their principle books	*Central ideas*
Deming, Edwards W. 1982. *Quality, Productivity, and Competitive Position.* Cambridge, MA: MIT Press. — 1986. *Out of the Crisis.* Cambridge, MA: MIT, Center for Advanced Engineering Study.	• 14 points of management programme; • systematic problem-solving or plan-do-check-act (PDCA); • principle of continuous improvement process (CIP)
Juran, Joseph M., Frank M. Gryna and R.S. Bingham, Jr, eds. 1979. *Quality Control Handbook.* New York: McGraw-Hill. Juran, Joseph M. 1988. *Juran on Planning for Quality.* New York: Free Press.	• quality trilogy – quality planning, quality control and quality improvement; • Pareto principle – roughly 80% of the effects come from 20% of the causes; • cultural resistance of managers to change
Feigenbaum, A.V. 1961. *Total Quality Control Engineering and Management.* New York: McGraw-Hill.	• total quality control; • starting quality control with product design; • simultaneous engineering – a workflow that instead of working sequentially through stages, carries out a number of tasks in parallel
Crosby, Philip B. 1979. *Quality is Free: The Art of Making Quality Certain.* New York: The New American Library.	• defects, their causes and costs; • do it right the first time principle; • zero defect programme
Ishikawa, Kaoru. 1985. *What is Total Quality Control? The Japanese Way.* New York: Prentice-Hall.	• quality circles; • control over processes in which defective products are manufactured; • cause and effect diagram; • company-wide quality control (CWQC)
Taguchi, Genichi. 1986. *Introduction to Quality Engineering: Designing Quality into Products and Processes.* Tokyo: Asian Productivity Organization.	• 'quality loss function' – definition of quality as a financial loss or cost caused by undesired variance in the product quality; • design of experiments (DOE) to provide near-optimal quality performance; • design of robust products that are insensitive to variations in environmental conditions

Sources: Own compilation based on Kamiske and Brauer 2003; Martinez-Lorente, Dewhurst and Dale 1998; Tuckman 1995 and others

and Kim 2005:193). Cole argues that the attempt to implement this single Japanese quality tool, taking it out of context, was largely a failure (see also Hill 1995 for the case of the UK). In Japan, the circles were one part of the complex efforts aimed at quality improvement at an organisational level; moreover, introduction of the quality circles was supported at the national level through cross-company information sharing, selecting the best circles etc. In the USA, the 'national infrastructure for quality' (a term coined by Cole) had just started to evolve in the 1980s.

Thus, two issues became prominent in the early debate on the transfer of quality control concepts from Japan to the West. The first is the complex character of the change that would have to take place to allow reproduction of the original function of quality circles. The second is the industry- and national-level contexts shaping the change in quality control at the company level. Apart from the national infrastructures for quality control or coordination between industrial actors, important national determinants for the effective diffusion of quality innovation include the labour–management power balance and the prevailing principles of work organisation.

Impact of total quality management on production work

The next phase of development of QM in the West is associated with the TQM movement (cf. Hackman and Wageman 1995). Western companies aimed at introducing the system known in Japan as company-wide quality control. Firms that already had some experiences with quality circles started to focus more consistently on changing the organisation of quality control and job profiles in production. Shop-floor employees received more responsibility in solving problems in production (Cole 1999). Such focus on quality throughout the organisation as a whole was reflected in the gradual change from the term 'quality control' to 'quality assurance' and then 'quality management' in the management debate.

The company's success in moving from the old to the new 'quality model' depended on the type of motivation for TQM adoption (ibid.). Competition and pressure from OEMs could lead to a 'mechanistic' or 'ritualised' adoption of TQM activities; if these external pressures were internalised, internally driven motivation for adoption could be generated (ibid.). Barley and Kunda stress the centrality of internalisation of new quality rules in the organisation as well (Barley and Kunda 1992). They argue that management emphasis on normative control in an organisation and on employee commitment to the employer was central to the management discourse in the 1980s–early 1990s (ibid.). They call the 1980s the time of "organisational culture and quality" and state that it was dominated by quality that could only be achieved through cultural change in organisations:

> Quality was seen as the product of a state of mind that required a revolution in the way both managers and workers viewed their jobs.
>
> (Ibid.:381)

The new "state of mind" implied the identification of workers and management with their enterprises and internalisation of new organisational values, such as customer orientation and continuous improvement.

Critical management studies drew attention to the limited character of employees' participation in decision-making under total quality initiatives and to the impact of internalised management control on shop-floor interest representation. Wilkinson *et al.* argue that employee involvement under quality initiatives had a

76 The new times

very limited character: the scope of their decisions was very narrow and they could not influence the ultimate goals of the enterprise:

> It is a form of involvement in which the agenda is said to be dictated by customer requirements. Therefore, employees are immersed in the 'logic' of the market and are thus more likely to be convinced of the legitimacy of company decisions.
>
> (Wilkinson, Allen and Snape 1991:)

This conceived legitimacy of the company's decisions could thus undermine employees' willingness to protect their interests. McCabe argues similarly that TQM did not question the distribution of power in the studied enterprise but rather reinforced it (McCabe 1999). The 'task-based involvement' of employees under TQM also legitimised this logic for employees and encouraged the trade unions to buy into the management agenda. Yet, the quality initiative could also provide a channel for unions' influence on management innovations.

The introduction of self-managed teams on the shop-floor facilitated the internalisation of control by employees (Barker 1993). Barker argues that a specific form of management control evolved – 'concertive' control, which complements Edwards's typology of three control forms in an organisation – simple, technical and bureaucratic (Edwards 1979):

> a key shift in the locus of control from management to the workers themselves, who collaborate to develop the means of their own control.
>
> (Barker 1993:411)

Self-managing teams gradually developed their own system of value-based rules that were more powerful than the previous forms of control, while at the same time being less apparent. Concertive control thus did not free workers from the 'iron cage' of rational rules but rather strengthened the cage through workers' identification with the system.

The implications of TQM for remuneration and training systems commanded less attention in the research. An important aspect of remuneration under total quality is the sharing of economic benefits arising from employees' efforts with employees themselves (e.g. Griffin 1988; Coyle-Shapiro 1999). Coyle-Shapiro found a positive relationship between profit sharing and employees' orientation towards continuous improvement (Coyle-Shapiro 1999:453). Köper and Zaremba found that the implementation of the ideas of the TQM in Europe led to changed requirements with regards to personnel qualification (Köper and Zaremba 2000). Along with technical or specialist skills, relevant for QM (e.g. knowledge of quality-critical points in products) new categories of competencies became important for companies. These included knowledge of QM systems (process competence and customer orientation) and the general skills (e.g. information management and social skills) necessary for running problem-solving and improvement projects in an organisation. Köper and Zaremba point to the

The new times   77

reciprocal influence between the QM system and personnel qualification: a QM system may be used to organise and improve personnel development and, vice versa, employee training enables the functioning of the QM system.

The existing literature on the impact of TQM on work in developed capitalist economies shows that the primary change was associated with internalisation of market values and TQM principles by employees. There is also limited evidence of change in work organisation, remuneration and training systems. The broader impact of 'quality initiatives' on organisation of quality assurance and work was, however, undermined if their implementation had a 'ritualised' character and companies lacked internally driven motivation for adoption.

4.2 Lean production and standardised production systems in the international automotive industry

The Western automotive industry was particularly strongly exposed to competition with Japanese manufacturers and it was among the first to start to explore the Japanese approach to organisation of production and quality control systematically (Jürgens, Malsch and Dohse 1993). Toyota Company became a role model for Western automobile manufactures due to an innovative way to manage a mass-production enterprise that it conceived and perfected – lean production. The 'lean revolution' in the West began with reorganisation of quality control and resulted in deviation from the Taylorist division of tasks in production.

The development of lean production at Toyota attracted the attention of the Western automotive industry due to the superior quality of its vehicles. In the early 1980s, the first detailed accounts of the Toyota Production System were published (cf. Monden 1983). At the same time, the first study of the Western automotive industry in the face of the Japanese development originated from the international programme "The Future of the Automobile" coordinated by the Massachusetts Institute of Technology (MIT) (Altshuler and Roos 1984; Jürgens, Malsch and Dohse 1989). The conclusion of the research programme was that,

> the auto industries of North America and Europe were relying on techniques little changed from Henry Ford's mass-production system and that these techniques were simply not competitive with a new set of ideas pioneered by the Japanese companies, methods for which we did not even have a name.
> (Womack, Jones and Roos 1990:3)

Lean manufacturing, which was pioneered by Toyota, was seen as a superior alternative to mass production as it allowed for combining the advantages of craft and mass production by achieving both low vehicle cost and flexible production. This was achieved through consistent and systematic elimination of 'muda' – that is, wasted effort, materials and time. The struggle to eliminate 'muda' led to development of new principles for the organisation of production and work. The first was the transfer of responsibilities and tasks to shop-floor workers, who actually performed value-adding activities. The second was thorough

78 *The new times*

problem-solving, when the root cause of a problem was investigated and removed so that striving for continuous perfection of the production process penetrated the enterprise (ibid.:55–58). These principles were realised through a set of practices that gradually became known in the West: Just-in-Time,[1] poka-yoke,[2] kaizen,[3] to name just a few of the most influential Japanese concepts.

'The Japanese threat' caused a departure from Taylorism at American, British and German assembly plants (Jürgens, Malsch and Dohse 1993). Reorganisation of quality control was one of the key elements in firms' restructuring efforts. It was supposed to both improve product quality and increase the efficiency of production work. The efficiency drive started to penetrate not only direct production work, but also indirect processes and was directed against the inflation of supervisory and control functions:

> A vicious circle arose: the less the direct workers were responsible for quality, the more elaborate the policing apparatus of quality control had to be, the more narrowly the tasks in direct production were defined, so as to achieve the highest possible efficiency there, the more the inherently unproductive area of control grew.
>
> (Ibid.:127)

In the 1980s, companies attempted to integrate the indirect tasks of quality control into direct production tasks. Simple checking operations were reduced and workers used stickers to mark defects or certify that the operation was performed according to the description. Companies also experimented with repair tasks, trying to merge them with quality inspection in some cases. Involvement of production personnel into problem-solving activities proceeded more slowly than integration of checking tasks into workers' functions. A study by MacDuffie on problem-solving based on data from three automobile assembly plants in the USA served as the empirical foundation for Deming's imperative about the importance of eliminating fear in production (cf. Deming 1986):

> when problems are framed as opportunities for learning and not liabilities to be avoided, problem-solving will benefit from the combination of positive attributions that boost motivation and the suppression of threat effects that can lead to reduced search and reflexive routine responses.
>
> (MacDuffie 1997:501)

Quality assurance functions also changed and demanded higher qualifications than before. Another trend discussed by Jürgens *et al.* is the introduction of computer-aided quality control, which served to provide workers with feedback on defect rates and other indicators of quality, and also contributed to stronger involvement of workers in quality control (Jürgens, Malsch and Dohse 1993).

Within the general trends outlined above, the changes in quality control at vehicle assembly factories in different countries varied in content and speed. The character of change in the field of quality control was significantly shaped by national systems of industrial relations. Job losses resulting from the integration of indirect functions into direct workers' tasks was a big concern for trade unions and work councils. In Germany, works councils pursued a compensation-centred strategy, which included some compensation or social protection for employees losing their jobs as a result of reorganisation and, in one case, an 'integration allowance' for direct workers integrating indirect tasks to a major extent. The German system, on that basis, could better accommodate change than the American and British systems of industrial relations. Additionally, the change in quality control depended on the existing pattern of power distribution, as in some cases the quality control department insisted on keeping its policing role.

Diffusion of lean production and other Japanese management and production concepts gave rise to the 'Japanisation' and 'hybridisation' debates in the Western literature (Bacon and Blyton 2000; Boyer *et al.* 1998; Brunsson and Jacobsson 2002a, 2002b; Freyssenet *et al.* 1998; Institut kompleksnykh strategicheskikh issledovaniy 2005). The seminal work on hybridisation by the international group of scholars GERPISA[4] challenged the postulate of Womack, Jones, and Roos (cf. 1990) about the universal superiority and applicability of lean production in the automobile industry and beyond (Boyer *et al.* 1998; Freyssenet *et al.* 1998). The central argument of their study of the transfer of production models across national contexts was that hybridisation of productive models was inevitable. The outcomes of the hybridisation are shaped not only by the initial productive systems, but also by institutional and national contexts and strategic choices.[5] Therefore, the same organisational systems might have varying effects in different contexts (cf. Tolliday *et al.* 1998:2). Instead of sharing the normative stance of Womack *et al.*, this group of scholars argued that hybridisation "should be seen not simply as a process of compromise and retreat but also as an important dynamic innovation and learning" (ibid.).

The case of the introduction of lean production into the German automotive industry illustrates the central argument of the hybridisation debate about the impact of institutional context on productive models that emerged in the course of the introduction of lean production. In the early 1990s, a deep restructuring process started in the German automotive industry, aimed at the implementation of lean production. The first step taken by the automobile manufacturers was the introduction of group or team work (Jürgens 1997). From the beginning of the introduction of team work, the concept developed by IG Metall was taken as a basis by many firms. This concept emphasised the need to elect a team spokesperson as well as the sociotechnical requirements of group work. Later management started to emphasise kaizen activities and groups' contribution to performance targets (ibid.). Thus, the introduction of group work and other elements of lean production and of new QM concepts in Germany was significantly shaped by the German system of co-determination (see also Hancké and Casper 1996; Jürgens 1995). The measures taken by management were negotiated with the unions, and works councils influenced company-level patterns of change.

The next stage in the change of the organisation of production and work in Germany focused on development of standardised production systems

80   *The new times*

('*ganzheitliche Produktionssysteme*') at the company level (see, e.g. Clarke 2005 for the case of Mercedes-Benz). Standardised production systems unite technologies and the organisation of production and work in a coherent way to maximise efficiency and quality. The standards regulating production and work are subject to continuous development. Therefore, improvisation in production gave place to variability reduction and process stability (Springer 1999). Development of holistic production systems by German automakers motivated discussion about the skills that the Facharbeiter actually need for working in standardised production systems (Clement and Lacher 2006; Lacher and Vollmer 2007). The character of work in the holistic production systems combines performance of routine tasks with activities related to organisation of the work process. Therefore, according to Clement and Lacher, employees should both accept the high degree of routine work with short cycle times and learn to critically review the standards regulating their work and be able to improve them (Clement and Lacher 2006). Hence, workers have to possess much more knowledge than in the past about the principles underlying production and QM. In this way, the impact of lean production and standardised production systems on work in Germany was significantly shaped by the German institutional system. At the same time, the introduction of lean production created an impulse for the national system of vocational training to question the existing competencies of industrial workers.

The debate on lean production in the West evolved from the transfer and implementation of single Japanese concepts – for example, quality circles – to development of highly complex but still flexible systems of coherent standards regulating technical, organisational and social aspects of production. Lean production transformed industrial work by altering work organisation and content of work on the shop-floor, and by changing requirements towards workers' competencies.

4.3 International quality management standards ISO 9000 and ISO/TS 16949

The diffusion of lean production in the automotive industry ran parallel to the development of an international QM standard ISO/TS 16949 specifically for the automotive industry. In 1987 the International Standards Organization formulated and published the first QM standard ISO 9000 applicable in any industry (Cole 1999; Hancké and Casper 1996). In 1999, special requirements for QM in the automotive industry were developed on the basis of this standard – ISO/TS 16949 (Raack 2008). These standards have been diffused in the Russian automotive industry, along with lean manufacturing.

The ISO 9000 family of standards

The ISO 9000 family of standards (henceforth 'ISO 9000') aims to serve as systemic guidelines on how to manage an organisation in order to achieve sustainable customer satisfaction. This standard embraces the core management

The new times 81

functions in a company and goes beyond quality assurance. The standard also provides a set of criteria for the evaluation (or audit) of the company's QM system. The audit can be performed by the company itself (first-party audit), by the customer (second-party audit) or by a recognised independent certification body (third-party audit). By 2010 over 1.1 million companies complied with ISO 9001 (in 178 countries) (International Standards Organization 2010).

The core requirement of ISO 9000 is a documented QM system. The purpose of the standard is, however, to register the work practices that exist in a company rather than prescribing what they should look like. Walgenbach argues, therefore, that ISO 9000 standard only represents a company's first step towards TQM (Walgenbach 2000). Yet, the standard plays a normative role as it prescribes which elements a QM system should contain (ibid.). These include not only quality assurance elements (e.g. inspection and testing), but also general management elements (e.g. responsibility of top management for quality) and personnel management (employee training).

Customer expectation from suppliers, competition and marketing purposes played a significant role in companies' decisions to implement ISO 9000 standards and obtain a corresponding certificate (Hancké and Casper 1996; Walgenbach 2000; Beck and Walgenbach 2005). In the German automotive industry, ISO 9000 was introduced after the OEMs implemented Just-in-Time and rid themselves of the entry inspection of supply parts. ISO 9000 became an instrument for "making new supplier relationships tolerable within German liability law" (Hancké and Casper 1996:15). In a cross-industry study of German firms, Walgenbach argues that companies implemented ISO 9000 due to three main reasons: a trend in the organisation's environment, marketing purposes and competition (Walgenbach 2000:294). Certification was, thus, rather a signal to the firm's environment than an attempt to improve internal processes.

Since ISO 9000 is a rather broad standard, its impact on work may vary across organisations. Hancké and Casper argue that its implications for work depend on the way firms interpret and implement it (Hancké and Casper 1996). In the German automotive supply industry, the workers' views on how the standard should be implemented shaped the outcome of the ISO 9000 certification. The certification led to the broadening of skilled workers' functions to include additional responsibilities for quality control:

> workers incorporated most quality control duties into their work and had a large voice in negotiations with industrial engineers and the quality control manager on how this was to be done.
>
> (Ibid.:19)

In the German automotive industry, ISO 9000 norms reinforced workers' high level of autonomy within a new, more formalised framework.

A cross-industry study shows that German companies did not have to change their processes significantly in order to certify for compliance with ISO 9000 (Walgenbach 2000). Instead, they started to look for ways to improve their

82 *The new times*

processes on the basis of the standard only after the certification. These included optimisation and standardisation of work processes, increasing transparency, optimisation of interdepartmental relations and increased productivity and reduced costs (ibid.:310). Only six out of 37 firms studied by Walgenbach attempted to improve the quality of products or services (having already received the certificate). This resulted in increased management control and the standardisation of the jobs, both of employees and middle, sometimes even top, managers (ibid.:376).

Thus, the introduction of the ISO 9000 led to higher formalisation of management control in the organisation as a whole. Yet, its other implications depended on the interpretation of the standard by the actors in charge of its implementation.

The automotive quality management standard ISO/TS 16949

Leading Western automobile manufacturers did not view the standard ISO 9000 as meeting the needs of the industry with its highly complex products and global supply chains. Each OEM developed its own quality-related requirements for supply chains. This led to a variety of quality-related regulations in international supply chains and a growing need for harmonisation of OEM-specific quality requirements. The International Automotive Task Force (IATF)[6] was established to develop a standard that was supposed to harmonise different OEMs' quality-related requirements of suppliers and to reduce the number of second-party audits in global supply chains (Raack 2008). The IATF took ISO 9000 as a basis and developed an international automotive QM standard ISO/TS 16949 (ibid.). The new standard contained tighter requirements for QM than the ISO 9000 and left less scope for interpretation by the enterprises that certified their QM systems for compliance with it. IATF also established overseeing procedures to verify suppliers' compliance with ISO/TS 16949.

The ISO/TS 16949 QM standard expands and details requirements contained in the ISO 9000 standard. It demands measurable evidence of process orientation in all firms' activities and continuous improvement of product and process quality (Interviews GBQ1, GBQ2 and GQC6). This standard puts a strong emphasis on senior management involvement "through setting and communicating quality objectives, allocating resources and integrating these into business plans" and requires demonstration of a commitment to improving the supplier base (Kartha 2004:339). In this way, the automotive QM standard requires and measures actual implementation of some of the key TQM principles by the enterprises.

The automotive QM standard was meant to be applied throughout the automotive supply chain, not only in production, but also in design and development, and, when relevant, installation and service of automotive-related products (International Standards Organization 2009). IATF organised its own control over independent certification and third-party audits through 'oversight offices' (Raack 2008). The offices got the authority to appoint certification bodies and to oversee their activities, including training of auditors. The suppliers' audits

The new times 83

carried out by the certification bodies (third-party audits) were to be recognised by all OEMs internationally.

Worldwide certification started in 1999 and the standard has enjoyed rapid global diffusion since then. The number of certificates granted for compliance with ISO/TS 16949 worldwide grew from 347 in 2002 to 27,999 in 2006 and 43,946 in 2010 (Interview GAV1; International Standards Organization 2010:5, 2006:33). In Germany alone there were 3,178 certified companies in 2010 (International Standards Organization 2010:6).

Thus, ISO/TS 16949 leaves less space for interpretation by the enterprises that implement it. There are two preconditions for the effectiveness of ISO/TS 16949 in inducing and verifying suppliers' compliance with the principles of process orientation and continuous improvement. The first was due to the content of the requirements, and the second due to the procedures and mechanisms for overseeing certification bodies and their auditors. A stronger impact on production and work organisation, compared to ISO 9000, can be expected, but there have been no empirical studies exploring this question so far.

The new QM principles changed industrial work in the West in three ways: they strengthened the market-related orientation of production through increased customer-focus, changed the workers' role in the production process, and caused renewed focus on the role of standards in an enterprise. While market relations had long been governing production in developed capitalist economies, the total quality revolution urged companies to orient all their value-adding and non-value-adding activities to serve customer interests. One of the means to achieve this was through greater internalisation of market-related values by employees. A shift of forms of management control over workers' performance took place. Whereas simple hierarchical control prevailed under Taylorism, the quality movement contributed to application of a broad range of forms of control, starting from the late 1980s. The use of simple hierarchical control lessened; management control became more formalised and individualised, and the role of social control in workers' groups rose. The new QM principles challenged the Taylorist principle of excluding workers from decision-making and 'brought workers back in'. Workers took over some tasks of quality control, problem-solving and improvements in their immediate working area. At the same time, management attention to standards was renewed. The change in production work built upon formal control in production based on standards, but standards became more holistic, embracing the whole organisation, and more flexible – that is, regularly reviewed in such a way that the users of the standards had a say on their content.

QM frameworks and instruments have moved towards standardisation and internationalisation during the two decades of their development in the West. Japanese concepts were standardised and international QM certifications were established. The leading automobile manufacturers developed international industry-specific QM requirements. Yet, the impact of these standards on the workplace depends on both the institutional conditions at the national level and on personnel policies in the company where they are introduced.

84 *The new times*

The two central ideas underlying the new QM standards – worker involvement and flexible standardisation – contradict the core principles of the persistent path of industrial work in Russia. The complementary principles comprising this persistent path revolved around informal or arbitrary forms of management control in production, separation of direct production operations from indirect functions, including quality control, and punitive means of control over workers. These contradictions point to the complex character of change needed for the introduction of these standards in Russian automotive industry.

4.4 Quality management in the Russian automobile industry during the first decade after the market reforms

The collapse of the Soviet Union and the radical market reforms led to weakening of the coordination effects reinforcing the socialist approach to the organisation of production and work in the Russian automotive industry. The reforms dealt a severe blow to the Russian automobile industry's capability to develop new approaches to management fitting for the new conditions. At the same time, international competition in the industry was too weak to motivate the local enterprises to introduce international management standards.

The market reforms ruptured the communication and collaboration structures between manufacturers, suppliers, state organisations and research institutions that had evolved under the planned economy. The state withdrew its control over the automotive industry and reduced the financing of the research institutes that had supported it. The automotive companies had to adjust to the new conditions with fewer resources, including knowledge-based resources:

> The functions of the [research] institutes of the [automotive] industry, which had been carrying out centralised scientific and technical propaganda and information support of the industry's professionals, were weakened or lost; the activities of various scientific and technical councils of the industry and conferences, where professionals could communicate with each other, virtually ceased.
>
> (Association of Automotive Engineers 2010)

These institutes had supported and advanced the socialist path of production work through research, evaluation and diffusion of the enterprises' best practices. New initiatives, such as a new networking platform for professionals, the Association of Automotive Engineers, which was established in 1991, could not compensate for the lost functions that had been fulfilled by the all-union institutions.

In the first decade after the market reforms, the competition was not a tangible factor for the local automotive firms' approach to the organisation of production and quality control. Foreign brands were increasingly present in the local market already in the 1990s, but the share of imported automobiles grew very gradually in the first decade after the start of the transition. Local manufacturers remained

The new times 85

protected from international competition by import duties even after market reforms came into force. Soviet import duties for cars were lifted for only about half a year between 1991 and 1992 and then introduced again (Kozichev 2009).[7] Consumers started to prefer foreign brands to local Russian cars, and the share of imported cars gradually grew throughout the 1990s due to the import of used and new cars, although this was a slow process. At the same time, Russia faced difficulties with the enforcement of a new market legislation, including the protection of consumers' rights. A buyer's market, thus, had not yet been introduced in the first post-transitional decade.

While the invisible hand of the market remained weak, the institutions of state control over product quality were largely eliminated. Due to these factors, the market reforms actually led to lower attention to quality than before. Manufacturers attempted to make fast profits by selling extremely low-quality goods:

> De facto there was a vacuum, when the state already did not control the quality and there was no market [regulation] yet. Rubber parts for brake systems, which were dissolvable in the braking fluid, came onto the market... Such was the situation from the early 1990s until about 1995.
>
> (Interview RAV2)

Thus, market reforms did not provide incentives to Russian automobile enterprises to change the way they managed quality. On the contrary, a lower degree of government intervention and coordination in the automobile industry led to a loosening of the quality control structures that existed in the Soviet automotive industry.

In 2001, competition with foreign brands in the internal market for cars was intensified by the start of foreign direct investment into the Russian automotive industry. The reaction of the Russian automakers to growing competition with international brands was not to try to modernise their production processes but to attempt to keep or strengthen protectionist industrial policies.

The first response of Russian automobile enterprises was to establish domestic industrial associations of automakers and suppliers. The National Association of Automotive Component Manufacturers (NAPAK), founded in 2001, attempted to serve the interests of local enterprises by lobbying for protective industrial policies. As late as 2003, the head of NAPAK advocated customs duties and quotas for imported parts for the automotive industry for at least five more years (Sharonov 2003).[8] At the same time, supporting internal modernisation efforts by suppliers, including updating their approach to QM, was beyond the remit of NAPAK.

In 2003, the Association of Russian Automobile Manufacturers (OAR) was established. OAR also attempted to strengthen the competitiveness of the domestic OEMs primarily by lobbying within government structures for protectionist industrial policies for the domestic segment in the government structures:

> When the concept of the Association was developed, the purpose was to preserve the automotive industry as a branch of machine building [in Russia]...

86 *The new times*

> I mean the enterprises, the set of the enterprises.... Our first-priority area of activities is legislation. Lobbying the interests of the automotive industry, making [the legislation] 'digestible' to the automotive industry. [We deal with] tax, customs, technical legislation.... 100 per cent is devoted to the legislation, as, in the end, the enterprises' economy depends on how the legislation is organised.
>
> (Interview RAV1)

Improvement in the quality of domestic brands also deserved some attention at OAR and a Working Group for Quality Management (WG) was established by the Association. However, the WG's activities did not have a high priority among the Association's goals (this is discussed in more detail in the next section).

Thus, the market reforms did not result in the modernisation of approaches to quality control in the Russian automotive industry. Domestic automakers lacked incentives for change during the first post-socialist decade, as market competition was low. They did not react to the gradually growing share of foreign brands in the internal market for cars in the 1990s by reconsidering their approach to quality control, even though the low quality of domestic cars was one of the determinants of their loss of market. However, even when competition in the internal market started to grow in the early 2000s, the domestic automakers' reaction was not directed towards the internal modernisation of local enterprises but rather towards maintaining protective industrial policies. As a consequence, local suppliers did not receive any impulses to change their approach to quality control in the first ten to 13 years after the start of the transition to a market economy. The socialist approach to quality control dominated the Russian automotive industry until about 2005.

4.5 Dissemination of the 'local' and the international versions of ISO/TS 16949 in Russia

In 2005, the local automakers lost over half of the market share to foreign brands. Another important event that took place this year was the significant reduction of customs duties on car components imported to Russia for industrial assembly. Around this time, the domestic automakers started to introduce some measures aimed at improving the quality of domestic brands. Their first step was to change the quality required of their suppliers. International manufacturers that established production in Russia began to support modernisation of quality control at Russian suppliers as well, as they had to increase the share of locally purchased parts according to the industrial policies introduced. The dissemination of international QM standards and concepts among Russian suppliers became the focus of attention for both international and domestic automakers in Russia. Yet, international OEMs demanded only an internationally recognised certification for compliance with ISO/TS 16949. Russian automakers established a local version of the international automotive standard and recognised both the international and the local certificates.

The new times 87

From about 2004, two versions of the automotive QM standard began to be diffused throughout Russia: the international and the 'local'. The international version was established and overseen by IATF. The 'local' version was established and diffused by the WG[9] for QM in OAR. The WG focused narrowly on supporting the diffusion of the automotive quality standard ISO/TS 16949 in Russia. While the content of the Russian standard did not differ from that of the international standard, Russian certification bodies were not authorised by IATF and not recognised internationally.

The WG for QM was established as collaboration between the leading Russian automakers and the Research Institute for Automobiles and Automotive Engines (NAMI) (Interview RAV1). NAMI is an organisation that has survived since the early years of the planned economy; it is a state organisation that was founded in 1920. At the time of the interviews, NAMI was affiliated with the national suppliers' association NAPAK through its General Director, who was, at the same time, the President of NAPAK. The Head of the Department for the Certification of Quality Management Systems of NAMI became the head of the WG. Most of the members of the WG came from AvtoVAZ and other national OEMs and organisations, and there were no foreign experts in the group.

The WG established a Russian-language version of the ISO/TS 16949 standard – GOST 51814.1. The international standard was translated and adapted by the All-Russian Research Institute of Certification (VNIIS) and approved by the Federal Agency for Technical Regulation and Metrology (former State Standard or GOST). The translation and adjustment of international concepts into Russian opened the possibility for some discrepancies between ISO/TS 16949 and GOST 51814.1 (Interview GQC6). Nevertheless, GOST 51814.1 did not establish an alternative set of requirements compared to the original international standard. Yet, there was a major problem with the enforcement of the requirements in the case of the local certificates.

In 2003, OAR founded a Coordination Council that obtained the right to appoint audit and certification bodies in Russia. The members of the WG became the members of the Coordination Council for Voluntary Certification of Quality Management Systems of Suppliers' Enterprises for the Automotive Industry. The CEO of OAR became the Head of the Coordination Council. The Coordination Council was registered in the Russian Federal Agency for Technical Regulation and Metrology (at that time – still GOST)[10] and it started to accredit certification bodies to certify for compliance with GOST 51814.1 in Russia. These certificates, however, were not recognised by IATF:

NAMI organised a certification authority for ISO/TS 16949. We are a legal body but the Russian system is not harmonised with IATF. NAMI registered the [Coordination] Council in 2003, and it started to develop in 2006–7. The Coordination Council consists of [automobile] manufacturers, some institutes and public organisations, about 16 members in total. This is a Russian alternative to IATF – GOST 51814.1.

(Interview RAV2)

88 *The new times*

In this way, OAR initiated the diffusion of the local standard, which was based upon ISO/TS 16949 but was not internationally recognised and overseen. Certification bodies were selected by the Russian OEMs and included NAMI itself. None of the Russian certification authorities received an accreditation from IATF. Only foreign certifiers were allowed to grant international ISO/TS 16949 certificates in Russia (Interview GAV1).

Both the international and the Russian versions of the ISO/TS 16949 standard began to be diffused throughout the Russian automotive supplier industry in the mid-2000s. In 2005, AvtoVAZ, the leading domestic automaker, mentioned the introduction of a QM certification requirement of suppliers for the first time in its annual report. That year, 21 per cent (out of 758 suppliers) of its suppliers were officially labelled 'unreliable' (OAO AvtoVAZ 2008). AvtoVAZ reported decreasing the share of such suppliers to 12 per cent (out of 927 suppliers) in 2007 and excluding unreliable suppliers from purchasing for new models (ibid.). In 2007 AvtoVAZ, together with GM-AvtoVAZ, established an internal Centre for Automotive Certification and introduced a complex quantitative evaluation of suppliers (ibid.). GAZ, the second-largest local automaker, demanded that its suppliers certified for compliance with ISO 9001:2000 by 2005 and with ISO/TS 16949:2002 by 2006 (Semkina 2005). According to the CEO of OAR, 'about five or six' suppliers obtained a so-called 'local' certificate (i.e. GOST 51814.1.) by 2007 (Interview RAV1) (see Table 4.2).

In 2008, there were already about 20 suppliers who received the 'internal' certificates (Interview RAV2).

The reliability of 'local' certificates in the industry was low due to the absence of international control over the certifying bodies that were authorised by the Coordination Council. The bodies authorised to grant the international certificate ISO/TS 16949 were subject to surveillance by IATF. No such surveillance mechanisms were designed to control the Russian bodies accredited to grant the Russian 'internal' ISO/TS 16949 certificate:

> The certification market [in the Russian automotive industry] is very disorderly. Certification bodies certify everything, from automobiles to toothpaste. But this does not depend on us. The regulation of the certification market is not our activity.
>
> (Interview RAV1)

Table 4.2 Diffusion of the ISO/TS 16949 standard in Russia

Year	ISO/TS 16949	GOST 51814.1 (Russian version of ISO/TS 16949)
2004	5	
2005	16	
2006	42	
2007	78	5–6
2008	106	about 20

Sources: International Standards Organization 2008; interviews by author

The new times 89

OAR and NAMI took a rather passive position with regard to the regulation of the certification services that they initiated. The absence of such regulation led to problems with the recognition of the national GOST 51814.1 certificates by OEMs. Even Russian OEMs, which supported the establishment of GOST 51814.1 and appointed certification bodies, preferred that suppliers were audited by bodies accredited by IATF:

> There is a clash now [with regard to recognition of the domestic Russian certificates]. Our automobile manufacturers want that certification is carried out by bodies accredited by IATF. At the same time, our enterprises do not have the money to be certified in the West. There is a mess now – everyone does what he finds profitable. A lot of enterprises consider this [certification in GOST 51814.1] as the first preparatory step [towards certification in ISO/TS 16949]. At the same time, a lot of enterprises haven't got even the ISO 9000 certificate [which describes the basic requirements towards QM].
>
> (Interview RAV2)

Thus, domestic suppliers had an opportunity to choose between the Russian and the international versions of the standard and could opt for the former one to save certification costs. Russian OEMs were 'in a trap': having themselves appointed and accredited the certification bodies, they could not reject their certificates. In this way, obtaining a GOST 51814.1 certificate became a way to gain legitimacy for suppliers vis-à-vis their customers, domestic OEMs, rather than an internationally recognised compliance with the requirements of the standard.

The certification of enterprises' QM systems for compliance with the international standards became a major mechanism for imposing change on Russian automotive suppliers. Yet, the low reliability of QM certification in Russia has been a subject of lively debate in practitioners' journals since the mid-2000s. The debate targets ISO 9000 certificates in particular: frequently, cases are reported where these certificates are sold to the firms by the auditors (see, e.g. Novitskiy 2005). Not only was the reliability of the domestic certification bodies disputed, but also the activities of the international certification firms in Russia. There were cases in which the certification firms did not fulfil the requirement that consulting and audits were to be performed by two different parties:

> In Europe there are strict requirements towards all [certification] bodies: those who help [to create a QM system] are prohibited from auditing it. In Russia this is not fulfilled. It does not matter there, who will audit. In Russia and the Ukraine the same bodies have consulting in their left hand and auditing and certification in their right hand.
>
> (Interview GQC6)

> There are six to eight affiliate certification bodies in Russia, among others TÜV and DQS. The Russian TÜV is very aggressive. The same people

90   *The new times*

> consult today and certify the day after [for compliance with ISO 9000] and they have very high market shares.
>
> (Interview GQC2)

In some cases, the reliability of ISO/TS 16949 certificates issued in Russia by international bodies was also doubted:

> I was at a conference in Russia dedicated to quality at suppliers' plants. AvtoVAZ stated that 30 per cent of its suppliers who received ISO/TS 16949 certificates do not fulfil requirements towards the product quality.
>
> (Interview GQC6)

> It was pointed out at a seminar dedicated to the international recognition of the Russian suppliers organised by AFNOR[11] yesterday that Veritas[12] and TÜV deserved an ambiguous assessment. They've had failures [related to certification of suppliers' QM systems in Russia].
>
> (Interview RAV2)

Thus, there were cases where the certification of Russian suppliers' QM systems did not guarantee that the principles and procedures required by the standards were in place, and that these were yielding results with regard to product quality.

Actual compliance with the requirements of either the local or the international automotive QM standard had a strong potential to challenge the old approach to quality control in Russia. Both of these versions of the standard require introduction of TQM principles of process orientation and continuous improvement. Yet, the use of QM certification as a mechanism for enforcing compliance with the standards showed significant weaknesses in Russia. Third-party audits were particularly unreliable in the case of the local ISO/TS 16949 standard, as Russian certification bodies were not overseen by IATF and no local controlling procedures were established.

The attempts of the WG and OAR to diffuse QM certification among Russian suppliers were not complemented with initiatives to collect and generalise the experiences of single companies that tried to introduce the new QM concepts and tools. The Russian Association of Automakers did not establish mechanisms other than certification to support the complex change demanded from suppliers. This role was, to some extent, taken over by Western automotive associations and management consultants. Russian firms shared their experiences at conferences organised for practitioners by management consulting companies or Western automotive associations, such as the German VDA-QMC in Moscow or the French AFNOR. In this way, Russian companies received some support in their efforts at change outside the traditional local networks from consulting firms and Western automotive associations. Nevertheless, the diffusion of the international QM standard in the Russian automotive industry and its support by OAR further weakened the coordination effects reinforcing the old principles of quality control in the industry. The internationally established concepts and tools included into

The new times 91

ISO/TS 16949 were gradually becoming the new reference model for QM in the Russian automotive industry of the 2000s.

4.6 Enforcing new quality management requirements through supply chains

Supply chains became an important channel for enforcement of new QM requirements in the Russian automotive industry after its internationalisation. Local Russian automakers mostly concentrated on certification for compliance with ISO/TS 16949 and did not rely much on their immediate interaction with suppliers to facilitate change. Western automakers viewed certification of suppliers' QM systems as the first step in the suppliers' change process. They used their globally applicable suppliers' evaluation guidelines that allowed them to both control and support suppliers' change efforts. Yet, the pace of change among local suppliers collaborating with Western OEMs was rather slow. Few suppliers began to introduce international QM concepts, and the ones who did could still discontinue their efforts towards change. The following section will analyse the agency of local and foreign OEMs in diffusing the new QM concepts through supply chains and discuss the causes of suppliers' resistance to change.

The section will be based upon four cases: Westauto (a Western OEM), Rusauto (a Russian OEM), Rusauto JV (a Western–Russian joint venture; Rusauto and Rusauto JV belong to the same corporation) and Rusmet (a Russian supplier exporting to Germany). Westauto was one of the first foreign OEMs to establish manufacturing in Russia and to sign an agreement on increasing the share of locally purchased parts with the Russian government. Rusauto JV was founded in order to select and evaluate suppliers for a new production line, Car2, based on a platform purchased from a Western OEM, and it planned to localise its production. JV was not bound to already existing suppliers when it came to supplier selection. The Rusauto plant, a Russian OEM, was trying to change its quality requirements for existing suppliers. Rusmet succeeded in complying with the requirements of a German OEM and two more Western tier-one suppliers.

Automakers' quality management requirements of suppliers

Western OEMs' requirements of Russian suppliers were much broader than the local automakers' expectations. Domestic OEMs' requirements were limited to certification for compliance with ISO/TS 16949 because of their lack of knowledge of the international QM concepts.

Requirements that Western OEMs presented to their suppliers were standardised for application in their global supply chains. In case of Westauto, Russia became yet one more location to which Westauto's global requirements of suppliers, and their evaluation and development practices, were transferred. Suppliers' evaluation guidelines were a part of Westauto's internal quality

92   *The new times*

system that it had implemented at its own plants globally and that was integrated with the Westauto Production System. The Westauto quality system included both requirements for prospective suppliers and practices for suppliers' evaluation and development:

> Practices [for suppliers' evaluation and training] that we conduct here are equivalent globally... Our people participate in the same programmes here and elsewhere in the world.
>
> (Interview WAS1)

This meant that Russian companies that attained Westauto's supplier status could supply to other locations of Westauto outside Russia also.

Certification for compliance with the ISO/TS 16949 standard was the foundation for all Westauto's other requirements. As a rule, certification had to take place in the pre-series phase. Westauto required a general shift of emphasis in the suppliers' QM efforts towards process development:

> We demand a shift towards the process, i.e. [introduction of] poka-yoke and engineering expertise in organisation of production processes and quality assurance, contribution of experts. [We require] organising the work in such a way that a worker hasn't got a chance to make a mistake or that he can see it.
>
> (Interview WAS2)

These requirements covered both process development and work organisation, and implied that change should reach the shop-floor level. Other criteria included statistical process control (SPC), Six Sigma, lean management, problem-solving and a continuous improvement process (CIP).

According to the Purchasing Engineer, the Westauto quality system was a very broad system that could be understood as a 'balanced score card', as it represented a matrix of key objectives for an enterprise and its separate units. Westauto's requirements of suppliers embraced not only quality-related issues, but also production and logistics. In order to start supplying to Westauto, the whole enterprise should comply in all of these fields and not only in the production unit, where the parts for Westauto were manufactured:

> We expect that suppliers who have Russian orders [orders from local Russian OEMs] comply with our requirements. We check the production as a whole and not just the business unit. One may, of course, build the Greek Hall,[13] but we demand that the whole plant, the whole enterprise be certified, up to the level of administrative departments. Pulling the rug from one place in favour of another is not the right approach. Suppliers can be compared with footballers. There are people [players] who are not in shape; they play in the Champions' League once a month and play in secondary matches the rest of the time. In this case, a failure happens immediately. This is why we demand a holistic approach. This is the most difficult approach. It is the most

difficult to restructure the whole company but we don't have any unfeasible expectations [of suppliers] to do it within two months.

(Interview WAS2)

Westauto required large scale change from its prospective suppliers and gave them one and a half to two years to carry it out. During this time Westauto conducted regular audits of the supplier and provided expertise and assistance in questions of production organisation and QM.

Rusmet faced the same quality-related requirements from its Western European customers while it was preparing to qualify for exporting its products. The German OEM's terms for collaboration with suppliers started with certification for compliance with ISO/TS 16949 or VDA 6.3. The auditors from the German OEM regularly examined the whole production process, not only the production line where the parts for this OEM were to be manufactured. That production line, however, was given particular attention and was only used for these products.

Requirements of suppliers set by Rusauto JV also centred on the tools of the ISO/TS 16949, particularly on the pre-series evaluation tool 'PPAP'.[14] Russian-owned suppliers willing to collaborate with Rusauto JV faced difficulties even at the stage of calculation of quality costs for the prospective production projects. According to the Manager for Suppliers' Quality Assurance at Rusauto JV, quality was the major reason why Russian suppliers' products were often too expensive. The 'burden'[15] of large Russian enterprises could amount to hundreds of times the direct production costs. Management at Russian enterprises was unwilling to make a calculation of 'burden' for the Rusauto JV production project separately, as it would reveal unprofitable contracts:

This comes from the planned economy, when nobody counted money. This psychology is still present. They [the managers at Russian enterprises] still do not calculate how much their conveyer's idle time costs. All these costs accumulate and increase the price for parts for the OEM.

(Interview RAQ1)

Russian suppliers were used to collaborating with domestic OEMs and therefore faced difficulties in starting up a new production project, which demanded more transparency and stricter accountability of production and quality costs.

The Rusauto plant attempted to change its requirements for its existing suppliers as well. However, these efforts at change were impeded by the complexity of its purchasing structure and the presence of an intermediary. The purchasing structure at Rusauto was rather complex. Supplier selection and purchasing were managed by an internal purchasing company. It was an independent company within the Rusauto Corporation that was positioned in the corporate hierarchy at a higher level than the Rusauto plant where interviews were conducted. It selected suppliers for all the plants of Rusauto Corporation, had the authority to

94   *The new times*

set quality-related requirements of suppliers and participated in all interactions between Rusauto and the supplier:

> We have hundreds of internal and external suppliers. I cannot tell you how many precisely. For us [the management at Rusauto plant], there are just three [suppliers]: the purchasing company is one of them, and it really has hundreds [of suppliers].
>
> (Interview RAS2)

The purchasing company introduced a QM certification requirement of suppliers in 2005. They required that suppliers obtain an ISO 9000 or ISO/TS 16949 certificate within a year and that all the suppliers receive an ISO/TS 16949 certificate in three years' time. At the end of 2007 about 40 per cent of Rusauto's suppliers already had an ISO/TS 16949 certificate (ibid.). This high share of certified suppliers contradicted with the frequency and deep rootedness of the quality-related problems encountered by management at the Rusauto plant. The quality managers at Rusauto found it difficult to make suppliers comply with the product quality requirements specified in contracts:

> Suppliers had not even heard that these are defects. For example, the fog lights, namely, the clearance between the light and the bumper, exceeds the norms. We controlled 50 per cent of them. When we addressed the supplier [with this], he told us: "What is the matter with you? You haven't put any questions to us for so many years, and now, all of a sudden..."
>
> (Interview RAS2)

Until the introduction of new QM concepts began at Rusauto in the beginning of 2007, there were cases where deviation from the product quality norms specified in suppliers' contracts was considered acceptable. This connivance had gained legitimacy over time, so that the suppliers perceived the change in Rusauto's demands as inconsistence.

According to the managers at Rusauto, the purchasing company gave priority to the price of the purchased parts, even though it included QM certification in the requirements of suppliers:

> As an intermediary, it does not particularly bother the suppliers... One of the challenges [related to quality assurance in supplier relationships] is that when the purchasing company selects a supplier, it makes the choice in favour of a cheaper product.
>
> (Interview RAS2)

Therefore, the presence of an intermediary impeded the efforts of the Rusauto plant to change the quality-related requirements for its 'old' suppliers, as the requirements of the plant management diverged from those of the purchasing company. The purchasing company's low prioritisation of part quality undermined the power of the quality managers at plant level to impose change on suppliers.

The new times   95

Another significant factor that impeded change in Rusauto's quality requirements was the monopolist position of the old suppliers. The company wanted to avoid the investment needed for finding new suppliers for the model it assembled (Car1), as it was planned to stop manufacturing it in a mid-term perspective.

According to the Russian supplier Rusmet, the only new requirement that Russian customers of Rusmet introduced into the supply contracts was ISO/TS 16949 certification. The introduction of this requirement was not based upon prior audits of Rusmet by OEMs and they did not support Rusmet in carrying out the change needed for the certification. One of the reasons for this was that Russian OEMs lacked knowledge of the standard and its tools at the time when they started to require it from their suppliers:

> The only change that took place [in domestic OEMs' quality requirements] is that a certification requirement for compliance with ISO/TS 16949 was introduced into the contract. But the automobile manufacturers did not quite understand what they required. We told them that we cannot [certify the QM system] this year, gave them the reasons, and that was it. They did not come here with the [second-party] audits. Rusauto Corporation, for example, demanded that we send them a PPAP. We asked them at what level[16] [PPAP should be made]. They did not understand what the question was about. At that moment we were already more advanced than them. Now there is no work either [regarding QM with Rusauto Corporation].
>
> (Interview RMQ)

> Suppliers call AvtoVAZ and ask for help [with implementation of the quality concepts that it required]. They reply that they do not know what that is.
>
> (Interview GQC6)

The change that Rusmet underwent with support from its Western customers allowed it to have more knowledge of the QM tools included in the ISO/TS 16949 standard than its Russian customers had at that time.

Local automakers' requirements were limited to QM certification as late as 2008. The major cause of this was the delayed start of change in QM at the OEMs' own plants, which had not allowed them to accumulate enough expertise to assist their suppliers in their efforts at change. That is why the local automakers underestimated the time that the suppliers would require to actually introduce the new QM standards, and in this way they pushed the suppliers to a pro forma certification. This kind of certification would not challenge the mechanisms reinforcing the old principles of quality control in production.

In contrast, the Western automakers and the joint ventures viewed QM certification as the beginning only of the local suppliers' change efforts. Their requirements embraced not only QM, but also other functions in the production system, and demanded change in the organisation as a whole and not at a single production line. The fulfilment of these requirements was controlled in a tight interaction between the supplier and the automaker, which allowed the Western automakers to verify that change actually took place.

96 *The new times*

Suppliers' audits and training opportunities provided by Western automakers

Western automakers' QM requirements for Russian suppliers were complemented by direct audits of prospective suppliers and significant support for their learning (see also Shulzhenko 2009). These audits and training opportunities had a strong potential to impose change in quality assurance at the level of suppliers' production lines.

Supplier audits by Westauto fulfilled two functions. Westauto collected evidence that the procedures described on paper had been really introduced, and demanded an action plan when needed. Supplier audits by Westauto included an evaluation of suppliers' competencies in an internal questionnaire, where suppliers' activities were ascribed red/yellow/green ratings:

> Audit is not a check-list, it's an action plan, and it's coaching. They can call us and ask questions and we help them.... We visit the site to make assessment, review, talk to people. We ask suppliers to produce evidence of the written procedures and ascribe them green/yellow/red. For the fields marked with red we require an action plan with the responsible people and date.
>
> (Interview WAS1)

Thus, Westauto viewed audits as an opportunity for the supplier to learn in direct interaction with representatives from the OEM.

Supplier evaluation started at the pre-series phase of manufacturing. The frequency of supplier audits by Westauto depended on the 'maturity' of a supplier and its managers' ability to keep promises. Before they got the required quality status, Westauto audited them every six months; after that – once a year.

New QM concepts had to be introduced several months to a year before the planned start of production of parts for Westauto. During this preparation, suppliers were given check-lists, forms etc. Besides working with suppliers individually, Westauto organised training programmes for several suppliers. These programmes were standardised and conducted in English. Russian suppliers lacked English-language skills, but, nonetheless, Westauto did not translate the terms into Russian, which made language a serious barrier to communication.

When new concepts were implemented, auditors from Westauto posed 'challenging questions' to the experts at the supplier's plant. The purpose of the questions was to make sure that new procedures were not randomly designed but were thought through:

> Why this way? [and not another]. For example, certain parameters are specified. They were written theoretically [without empirical evidence] and the engineer signed them.
>
> (Interview WAS2)

As the next step, test manufacturing was carried out, during which all the conditions and the production rate were the same as for series production. This allowed for discovering all shortages and 'escape points'. At this stage, the auditors spoke to production managers and employees 'down to the level of an operator or tool setter' (Interview WAS2). The talks had the explicit purpose of finding out 'systemic matters' and not to allocate blame. Westauto made sure that the employees at the supplier's plant possessed the necessary skills and measurement tools to assure stable quality.

Suppliers' evaluation by Westauto went beyond QM and included, among other questions, the sufficiency of employees' skills. Suppliers had to develop a responsibility matrix for key functions at different organisational levels, and a competence matrix where the responsibilities and necessary skills were listed. The earlier in the process of preparation for series manufacturing, the more frequently this was evaluated:

> Our questionnaire is divided into sections, and personnel department is one of them. The supplier gives us a folder with plans and a package of documents for a period of time. Every position is substituted with a list of requirements. These things should also be detailed in internal procedures and standards. The supplier decides, itself, what the list of requirements [for every position] should consist of. We do not necessarily demand raising employees' skills. The most important is that the person has the tools to solve his task, including competencies and skills.
>
> (Interview WAS2)

Thus, the supplier had to formalise the descriptions of employees' skills and assure coherence between the newly introduced QM concepts and available skills and competencies.

Westauto had to make particularly strong efforts to train Russian suppliers to search for the root causes of problems, as this contradicted the prevailing culture of finding someone to blame:

> If one asks the question why, then one stops at a certain person. If one goes deeper, then one comes to one of other causes, e.g. part design or mismatch related to our equipment. Workers – yes, at first sight they look guilty but in the end we expect [from supplier] introduction of visualisation and poka-yoke.... The worker is a hired comrade. The main thing is the framework, although formal training also plays a role.
>
> (Interview WAS2)

The implementation of specific problem-solving tools required suppliers to question the predominant pattern of the superficial attribution of guilt to executors on the shop-floor.

The German OEM purchasing from Rusmet also combined audits and training when it took the decision to purchase parts. Rusmet had been audited several times before the decision to train it as a prospective supplier was taken. Audits went beyond QM to embrace production processes and finance:

98   *The new times*

> Six people came to us every three to four months and conducted audits. They checked everything: quality as a system, production processes, financial issues. Then they gradually decided and told us "We will train you as suppliers." There was about a year more work after that. Once a month we had telephone conferences and discussed our work plans for the preparation for their [qualification] audit.
>
> (Interview RMQ)

Rusmet hired a German QM consulting company in order to prepare for the qualification audit. The consultants assisted Rusmet in complying with the ISO/TS 16949 standard and implementing the principles of lean production.

After the German OEM took the decision to prepare Rusmet as a supplier, it started a large training programme at the plant. The programme was centred on the '5M': 'method' – production process and technology, 'machines' – production equipment, 'materials' – agreement with the customers on sub-suppliers, 'man' – skills and competencies of both direct and indirect workers and 'mir' (Russian for 'environment') – 'production culture' (i.e. order and cleanliness at the working station). Thus, the German OEM assisted Rusmet in complying with its requirements by offering an original training programme including all aspects of the production system. Preparation for the qualification audit took Rusmet about two to two and a half years. As already mentioned in the previous section, Rusmet's interaction with its Russian customer OEMs differed significantly from its interaction with its German customer. The Russian costumers did not carry out direct supplier audits and did not offer any support in the implementation of the new quality requirements.

The discussion of the audits and training opportunities, which Western OEMs offered to their prospective Russian suppliers, shows that audits and training represented mechanisms that supported a systemic change in the organisation of production, QM and personnel training at Russian plants. Supplier evaluation by automakers allowed for discovery of the gaps between the written procedures and actual production routines, and to reduce them. This challenged one of the principles of the old path of industrial work, which was characterised by significant divergence between formal rules and actual production and work processes. The Western OEMs' requirements for presentation of evidence of problem-solving aimed at finding the root causes of problems in production. This, and requirements of coherence between the necessary and available employees' competences, contradicted the principles of the punitive path of production work as well. Either workers had to be provided with the problem-solving competencies that they did not have in the past, or responsibility for quality within an employee's process area should be withdrawn from her tasks. Thus, the audits and training provided to Russian suppliers were likely to weaken the complementary effects between quality control and personnel policies that reinforced the punitive path of industrial work.

Suppliers' resistance to change

In all three of the cases discussed above, OEMs encountered strong resistance to change from Russian suppliers. Resistance to change manifested itself both at the

The new times 99

stage when the decision to try to comply with new quality requirements was made and at the stage when the collaboration with an OEM had already started.

The rate of the dissemination of the international QM standards among Russian suppliers in the late 2000s was very low, despite the significant support that Western OEMs offered. Westauto had about 22–3 tier-one suppliers in Russia after about four years. However, among these there were only seven to eight local Russian-owned firms without a foreign partner. Most parts purchased locally were simple components, so that most of the tier-one suppliers did not require tier-two suppliers. Westauto took over the investment in retooling that a supplier had to make, but only if the purchased volume was large enough to make collaboration profitable for Westauto.

> We would make the investment the supplier needs to make. We try to find the equation: the more complex the product is, the more capital investment we need to make. To make it profitable, suppliers have to produce millions of units, not thousands of units that we have. If we happen to share this volume with a local OEM – great. But unfortunately there is not a lot of similarity between the product complexities. For example, local OEMs do not need the parts for air conditioning that we need. Here there is a difference in the technology. When we look at local suppliers they don't have the equipment. We speak to other Western OEMs (which are in the same situation and have to increase the localisation) – it's the same. Therefore most localisation is low-complexity products.
>
> (Interview WAS1)

Westauto's low production volumes represented another problem for localising production. Due to the gap between the technological levels of local OEMs and Western OEMs, there were very few local suppliers that had the equipment and experience in manufacturing high-complexity parts.

Rusauto JV had pre-selected about 200 suppliers at the time of the study, but had not started purchasing. Only about 12 of them were located in Russia and there were no Russian-owned enterprises among them:

> Among the alternatives [during the suppliers' selection process] there always appear some purely Russian enterprises, but they cannot qualify either due to the price, or due to the quality, or due to the technical level.
>
> (Interview RAQ1)

According to the Quality Director at Rusauto, Russian-owned enterprises without foreign participation were unable to introduce the change that Rusauto JV required for its new production line (Car2).

Westauto encountered a lack of willingness from Russian suppliers to try to comply with its quality requirements when it tried to establish collaboration with them. This attitude was particularly pronounced in the case of suppliers who worked with the leading Russian OEM AvtoVAZ:

100 *The new times*

Some suppliers, especially the ones working with AvtoVAZ, consider that they do not need to be taught, as they are leaders already.

(Interview WAS2)

This unwillingness to change had two reasons. On the one hand, suppliers still perceived the domestic automaker AvtoVAZ as a leader in the internal market, at least until 2008, which reinforced the legitimacy of the old approach to QM that it represented. On the other hand, the discrepancy between the current state of QM and the new requirements were so high that implementing them would entail a significant effort from suppliers' management:

First, the general level of quality systems Russian suppliers have is low. Second, their management commitment [to change] is not always demonstrable. If we can fix the former, the latter is more difficult to fix. If they don't have it, we can do nothing.

(Interview WAS1)

The top managers of the Russian suppliers were unwilling to talk to the representatives of Westauto, if they had a lower hierarchical status:

We are looking for suppliers who it is possible to talk to. Who can listen without pomposity and excessive ambitions... If the management considers that it needs only management for a talk, it is difficult to talk to such suppliers. We have highly qualified non-managerial specialists who can very well communicate the systemic things. It is important for us that it is possible to talk to a supplier, irrespective of the hierarchy. There are cases when we come and he [the Russian manager] says "From Westauto? No, I'm busy."

(Interview WAS2)

As this manager pointed out, in order to start the process of change, Russian managers' commitment should be high enough to help them overcome the hierarchical communication traditions common at Russian enterprises.

Even when Russian suppliers had already started the change process, they still did not take a proactive position and showed lack of responsibility in relations with Westauto:

This [the challenge in working with Russian suppliers] is the psychology of relations between the supplier and the customer, i.e. that the customer is paying the money [which the Russian suppliers do not realise]. The typical attitude [of Russian suppliers] is 'tell me what to do and I will do it. If it went out wrong, then you told me [to do it this way] yourself.' We make it differently. You get a list of 'to do' as requirements. Then you have to come and discuss it yourself. Russian suppliers are used to working on the basis of the documents developed by the OEM.

(Interview WAS2)

The new times   101

Russian firms supplying to a Western OEM had to learn to take a more empowered and responsible role in developing production processes than was the case when supplying to the traditional OEMs.

Rusauto JV also encountered the problem that Russian suppliers were unwilling to even try to change their quality control practices:

> Russian suppliers reason this way: it would be good to get the contract but it requires serious efforts, which they do not want to apply. Working with foreign customers requires the destruction of the [old] system. A strong will of the management and the owner is needed.
>
> (Interview RAS1)

The experiences of Rusauto JV are similar to those of Westauto: Russian suppliers were unwilling to change their existing approach to quality control even for the sake of obtaining a new supply contract and despite the declining position of the local OEMs in the market.

Management at the Rusauto plant did not require complex restructuring from its suppliers, but even requests for stricter product quality standards were met with strong resistance:

> He [the supplier] argues: "That will do, it is not visible and does not cause problems. The chief thing is to assemble a certain number of automobiles."
>
> (Interview RAS2)

> Suppliers are so insolent here! I don't think I've seen such ones anywhere else. You tell them: that that won't do, and they get indignant: why was it normal [accepted] before and now, suddenly, not?
>
> (Interview RAQ1)

Some deviation from product norms had been accepted by Rusauto in the past. The new managers had to start by clarifying the very notion of 'defect' with suppliers.

The analysis of suppliers' resistance to changing their approach to QM shows that, despite the growing pressure of competition, most suppliers avoided even starting a process of change. The support offered to them by Western OEMs did not suffice to motivate Russian managers to begin introducing the international QM standards. Rather they postponed the implementation of these standards, as it required reconsideration of not only QM, but also their approach to the organisation of production and work, and related personnel policies. Thus, they preferred to decline the chance to obtain international supply contracts rather than to question the complementary mechanisms reinforcing the old path of industrial work.

4.7 Conclusion: international quality management standards in the Russian automotive industry

The chapter analysed the change in QM in the Russian automotive industry focusing on two critical junctures: the market reforms and the internationalisation

102 *The new times*

of the industry. The market reforms led to a weakening of the coordination mechanisms reinforcing the old approach to quality control in the automotive industry. But they did not motivate the local enterprises to reconsider their approaches to quality control. Local automobile manufacturers remained protected from international competition throughout the 1990s and did not take any steps to anticipate the growing competition. This explanation of the lack of change in quality control complements the findings of the literature review on quality control and production work in post-socialist Russia (see Section 3.2).

The internationalisation of the industry did affect local firms' approaches to QM. Change, however, began only around 2005, when the local car makers were exposed to a rapid increase of competition with international companies in the local market. Russian plants of international OEMs were the first to introduce the international QM standards. These companies became also the key actors supporting the introduction of international QM standards in the Russian automotive supplier industry. The domestic OEMs took only hesitant steps, starting with new QM requirements for their supplied parts. The diffusion of the international QM standards took place differently within two segments of the industry – the domestic and the international.

The international and the local OEMs adopted different strategies aimed at changing their suppliers' approaches to QM. Local OEMs had not yet implemented the new standards at their own plants when they began to demand their introduction by suppliers and did not possess thorough knowledge of these standards and tools. The agency of both the individual OEMs and of OAR focused on new QM certification requirements of suppliers. QM certification represented a weak mechanism for imposing change in QM on local suppliers in Russia. Yet, OAR established a local version of the international automotive QM standard ISO/TS 16949, not supported by overseeing certification bodies and not recognised outside the domestic segment of the industry. This undermined the effectiveness of the local standard in challenging the old approach to quality control in production and reinforced the separation between the domestic and the international segments of the industry.

The international OEMs trying to increase the share of locally purchased parts differed in their change agency from the local car makers. While domestic automakers tended to see quality certification as the ultimate goal of suppliers, this was only a step in the process of suppliers' development by the Western OEMs. They interacted with prospective suppliers over an extended period of time and both audited and supported suppliers' change efforts. The examples of Westauto and a German OEM analysed above show that their requirements for suppliers went beyond QM and included some aspects of organisation of production and personnel policies. Suppliers received assistance in both learning the new QM standards and establishing mechanisms stabilising these standards in production.

International OEMs met with the unwillingness of Russian suppliers to even try to comply with the new QM requirements, also when offered significant support. The new QM standards seriously contradicted to the old approach to quality control. They required reduction of divergence between formal standards in production and actual processes, which was characteristic for the old path of industrial work. Suppliers also had to reduce the extremely high indirect production costs and to calculate them for every customer OEM separately. Later in the change process, suppliers needed to update and formalise employee training and depart from attributing guilt for product and process quality to production workers. Instead, they had to learn to look for the root causes of process disturbances and product defects. This indicates that the introduction of international QM standards was not possible as a substitution of the old approach to quality control, but it challenged the punitive path of industrial work in the Russian automotive industry.

Notes

1 Just-in-Time – central logistic concept in production aimed at flexibility and reduction of in-process inventory; material delivery to every operation in production takes place by order.
2 Poka-yoke – mechanisms that help an equipment operator to avoid mistakes by drawing attention to human errors as they occur.
3 Kaizen – striving for continuous improvement.
4 Groupe d'Etudes et de Recherches Permanent sur l'Industrie et les Salariés de l'Automobile.
5 A related debate analyses whether Western companies establishing subsidiaries in Central and Eastern Europe transfer their labour and industrial relations policies to the new locations (see, e.g. Bluhm 2001; Jürgens and Krzywdzinski 2009, for the case of German firms).
6 IATF encompassed the OEMs from the leading Western automotive states (France, Germany, Italy, the UK and the USA): BMW Group, Chrysler Group, Daimler AG, Fiat Group Automobile, Ford Motor Company, General Motors Company, PSA Peugeot Citroen, Renault SA, Volkswagen AG and the vehicle manufacturers respective trade associations – AIAG (US), ANFIA (Italy), FIEV (France), SMMT (UK) and VDA (Germany).
7 The size of import duties has varied, but they remain in force until the present time Ernst & Young 2013.
8 Customs duties on car components imported by OEMs for 'industrial assembly' in Russia were reduced in 2005.
9 The full name of the group: Working Group 'for quality management system complying with the ISO/TU 16949 standard'. In Russian: *'Rabochaya gruppa po sisteme menedzhmenta kachestva na sootvetstvie standartu ISO/TU 16949'*.
10 The CEO of the OAR was the Deputy Head of GOST in 2003, and he signed the registration himself.
11 AFNOR – French Association for Standardisation (Association Française de Normalisation).
12 Bureau Veritas is an international certification agency with headquarters in France.
13 The Greek Hall – a richly decorated hall for gala receptions and balls in Pavlovsk Palace near Saint Petersburg.
14 PPAP – Production Part Approval Process.
15 'Burden' (overhead costs) – costs not directly related to production, e.g. management, organisation, equipment maintenance and idle time that are calculated as percentage of direct production costs or labour costs.
16 The PPAP submission levels define what kind of evidence about the part production process the supplier should provide to the customer.

5 What about the workers?

Impact of international quality management standards on the Russian industrial workplace

The question about Russian workers in the title of this chapter was first posed by Simon Clarke, Peter Fairbrother, Michael Burawoy and Pavel Krotov in the early 1990s (Clarke *et al.* 1993). In their book they looked for signs of transformation of social relations in production in Russian enterprises after the liberal market reforms of the late 1980s–early 1990s. They did not find any. The present chapter will pose this question again, this time focusing on one Russian industry – the automobile – about 15 years later. It will analyse whether the industrial workplace was transformed following the internationalisation of this industry that began in the second half of the 2000s. The chapter will investigate whether the principles constituting the socialist path of industrial work in Russia were affected by the international quality management (QM) standards that gained popularity due to growing competition with international carmakers.

Section 5.1 will provide basic information about plants, production processes and employees. Sections 5.2–5.5 will analyse change in the four dimensions of industrial work. Section 5.2 will discuss the reorganisation of quality assurance. It will start with the role of local managers and Western partners in the change process and will give an overview of the management standards introduced at the enterprises. Then it will discuss whether new quality assurance responsibilities were integrated into workers' functions. The next section will discuss how the new QM standards influenced work organisation and whether they led to change in groups' tasks (Section 5.3). The section that follows will investigate the impact of new QM standards on personnel development and will focus on the integration of quality-related competencies in workers' qualification profiles (Section 5.4). The ensuing section will analyse whether the introduction of international QM standards resulted in weakening of the punitive character of remuneration systems (Section 5.5). The conclusion to the chapter (Section 5.6) will summarise the change found and will then discuss the patterns of change to the path of industrial work found in the three cases analysed. The section will conclude by stating that path dependence was broken in the case of Westauto, weakened in the case of Rusmet and persisted in the case of Rusauto.

5.1 Production processes and workers in the plants under study

The following section will provide context information necessary for the analysis of the introduction of international QM standards. It will briefly describe ownership, products and production processes at the plants studied and then characterise workers employed in production at the three plants and affected by the change processes.

Ownership, products and production processes

The studied plants include two automobile manufacturers (Westauto and Rusauto) and a supplier (Rusmet). They are comparable with regard to employee numbers (see Table 5.1).

Westauto is one of the world's largest automobile manufacturers. It established a greenfield production site in Russia in the early 2000s and enjoyed considerable growth in employee numbers and production volume until the financial crisis in 2008. Production technology was transferred to the Westauto plant in Russia from the European headquarters and the plant in Russia received the imported stamped panels. There were three production areas at the factory: body shop, paint shop and trim and final assembly area, along with several sub-assembly stations in the final assembly (e.g. doors).

Rusauto Holding is one of the largest formerly state-owned domestic Russian automobile manufacturers. The plant where the study took place was a financially autonomous production unit within the holding. At the time of the interviews, Rusauto was producing a Russian-brand passenger car, Car1, and was preparing for production of a Western-brand passenger car, Car2. The production equipment in the Car1 shop was outdated; there had been no large investment into Car1 production and only some minor improvements were implemented in the early 2000s. Most production operations at Car1 were performed manually; the degree of automation in the body shop was about 30 per cent. The Car2 vehicle platform

Table 5.1 Basic data about the enterprises studied in Russia

Factory name	Ownership	Product	Annual production volume	Employee number
Westauto	Western automotive multinational	Passenger cars	Several tens of thousands units	Several thousand people
Rusauto	Russian automotive corporation	- Russian-brand passenger car Car1 - Western-brand passenger car Car2		
Rusmet	Russian supplier holding	High-precision metal parts		

Source: Data compiled by author

106 *What about the workers?*

had been acquired by Rusauto from a Western OEM. The complete production line for this vehicle was transported to Russia as well. The new production line was characterised by a high degree of automation, with hundreds of robots transported to the plant. Rusauto planned to perform welding, paint and assembly operations. At the time of the study the production of Car2 had not started, but Rusauto was already recruiting employees for this new production line.

Rusmet is a fully Russian-owned automotive supplier, which supplies high-precision metal parts to Russian OEMs, to joint ventures (JVs) in the CIS and exports a share of its output to Germany and other Western European customers. It is a formerly state-owned enterprise that was privatised, becoming part of a large Russian holding, which has one of the biggest shares in its product market in the post-socialist countries.

Production at Rusmet takes place in four shops: turning, thermal treatment, grinding and assembly. There was a large investment into the renewal of production equipment and renovation of plant facilities at Rusmet in 2006. The renewal of machines and production sections at Rusmet took place in stages, which lent the production equipment a patchwork character, with very different age and origins of the machines. Production equipment was purchased from different countries: Ukraine, Poland and China, among others.

In all three cases, foreign partners in Germany and/or North America supported the enterprises' efforts to introduce new QM standards. In the case of Westauto this was the company's headquarters. In Rusauto's case this was the Western OEM that previously owned the Car2 platform and another large automotive multinational. For Rusmet this role was played by the German customer OEM.

The different ownership structures and histories of Westauto, Rusauto and Rusmet made starting conditions for the introduction of international QM standards rather different. Westauto differs considerably from the two Russian plants in its degree of internationalisation: it is present in multiple locations abroad. In Russia it had to deal with only a few of the challenges faced by the other two companies studied. It imported machinery and hired new managers and employees that mostly had not had experience in the Russian automotive industry before. Still, it faced a shortage of skills and competencies in QM both on the shop-floor and among the Russian managers. Rusauto and Rusmet were introducing new QM concepts in old production shops with employees and management that mostly had been employed for a long time. The differences between the cases offer the opportunity to compare the attempts of Rusauto and Rusmet to introduce new QM standards with the case of the multinational Westauto.

Employees' classification

The plants used different employees' classifications in their statistics. Westauto classified its Russian employees by applying the scheme it uses at its other locations. The Russian plants Rusauto and Rusmet adhered to the socialist classification of employees.

What about the workers? 107

All employees at Westauto were divided into three categories: salaried employees, 'hourly' (paid) employees (or production operators) and contract (or agency) employees, although there is no contractual difference in Russia between salaried and 'hourly' employees (see Figure 5.1).

There was a rather low share of salaried employees at Westauto (only 7 per cent), which contrasts to that at the Russian plants discussed below (cf. Figure 5.2). The rest of the personnel were direct and indirect workers, including the agency employees. Agency employees were working mainly in material planning and logistics. About 20 per cent of agency workers came from outside Russia (from the former Soviet Union) and some of them could not write Russian well.

The personnel at both Rusauto and Rusmet were divided into two basic categories inherited from the Soviet era: '*rukovoditeli, spetsialisty, sluzhashchie*' or RSS ('managers, specialists and office employees') and workers. 'Workers' at Rusauto and Rusmet were divided into two groups: 'production workers' (direct workers) and 'workers for the preparation of production' or 'auxiliary workers' (indirect workers). The share of RSS in the total employment at Rusauto in December 2007 equalled about one third (see Figure 5.2). For Rusmet this share amounted to 16 per cent. The Personnel Manager at Rusauto explained the high share of managers and white collars by the fact that a lot of these specialists needed for the Car2 production line had already been hired, whereas the recruitment of workers was still under way.

A striking characteristic of the staff at both Rusauto and Rusmet is that the share of direct workers makes up less than 50 per cent of the total in employment (43 per cent and 47 per cent, respectively). At Rusauto the personnel composition was not stable, as hiring of direct and indirect workers continued at the time of the study. At Rusmet the ratio of direct to indirect workers was quite stable. The plant's adjustment to a market economy and introduction of new QM standards did not lead to a reduction in the share of non-value-adding workers compared to

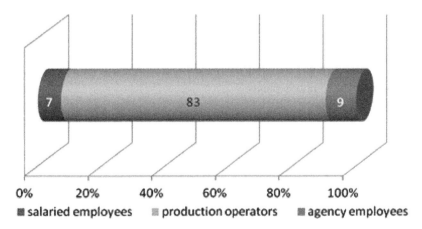

Figure 5.1 The composition of personnel at Westauto.
Source: Interviews at Westauto

108 *What about the workers?*

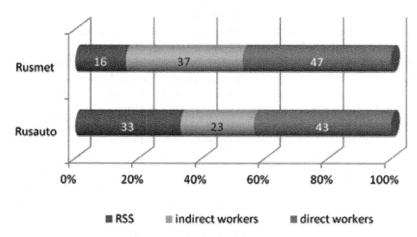

Figure 5.2 The share of different categories of employees at Rusauto and Rusmet.
Source: Calculation by author on the basis of interviews and internal company data

the Soviet enterprises. As discussed in Section 2.3, Soviet automotive enterprises were characterised by very high ratios of direct to indirect workers (1:1 in the case of VAZ and 1:1.25–1.4 at other Soviet automotive enterprises). Several explanations for such a high proportion of indirect workers are possible. Indirect workers helped assuring compliance with process and product standards in production. The need to maintain and repair the old production equipment could be another reason. The old production and storage halls might need a large internal logistic system. Finally, the management could be unwilling to fire the unnecessary staff in an attempt to preserve employment.

Another essential aspect of formal organisation at the plants for the subsequent analysis is organisational hierarchy. Organisational hierarchies at Westauto and Rusauto were identical and included seven levels (see Table 5.2). There had been eight hierarchical levels at Rusauto before it started to introduce lean and QM standards. In course of the change, the hierarchy was made flatter and more similar to the Western automotive plants.

The hierarchy at Rusmet differed from the other two plants and included nine levels. There were no shift manager positions, as only 5 per cent of the personnel worked on a second shift. Instead, there were more levels within the line management (positions of deputy shop managers and senior production supervisors) and brigades were larger and were divided into smaller groups (*zveno*) with group leaders.

Workers' age and earnings at the studied plants

The employees at Westauto were rather young: the average age was 28 years. The employees at the Russian plants were significantly older. About 90 per cent of

What about the workers? 109

Table 5.2 Organisational hierarchies in production at the studied plants in Russia

Westauto	Rusauto	Rusmet
1. Plant manager 2. Production manager 3. Area (or shop) managers 4. Shift managers 5. Production supervisors (heads of line sections) 6. Brigade leaders 7. Production operators (workers)	1. Plant director 2. Production director 3. Shop managers 4. Shift managers 5. Heads of production sections (*mastera*) 6. Brigade leaders (*brigadiry*) 7. Workers	1. Plant director (Executive Director of Rusmet Holding at the plant) 2. Production director 3. Shop managers 4. Deputy shop managers 5. Heads of production sections (*nachal'niki uchastkov*) – senior production supervisors (*starshie mastera*) 6. Production supervisors (*mastera*) 7. Brigade leaders (*brigadiry*) 8. Group leaders (*zven'evye*) 9. Workers

Source: Interviews by author

workers in the assembly shop at Rusauto were between 35 and 40 years old. The plant experienced a particular shortage of young people in the repair areas, where the average age of employees was 45 years. At Rusmet, more than half of the employees were over 40 years old (see Figure 5.3).

The plants had a small pool of young people to recruit from. The birth rate in Russia decreased throughout the 1990s and less numerous generation born during that period started to enter the labour market around 2007 (Shulzhenko 2012:66). At the same time, an increasing share of the number of young people decided in favour of an academic education rather than technical colleges or vocational schools. The

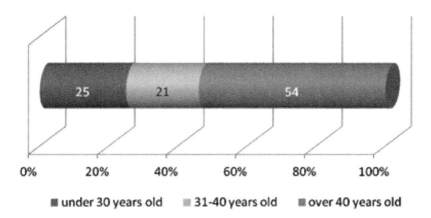

Figure 5.3 Average age of employees at Rusmet.
Source: Company internal data provided to the author

110 *What about the workers?*

number of university graduates more than tripled from 1990 to 2009, from 401,000 to 1,442,000 (ibid.: 70).

Under such labour conditions, production enterprises must offer attractive wages in order to attract young people, and young men in particular. While Westauto paid almost 500 euros, on average, to the production workers, the Russian plants paid significantly less. Wages at Rusmet were almost two times lower than at Westauto (see Table 5.3).

It should be mentioned that Westauto and Rusauto were located in larger cities than Rusmet, with higher living costs, which slightly levels the differences in wages. Still, the main explanation that was expressed by the interviewees was that production jobs at Rusauto and Rusmet were not attractive for young people.

Gender composition

Gender composition of production personnel in the plants studied was surprising. Contrary to the traditional image of a masculine workplace in the automobile industry, there was a high share of women working in production in all three plants. Over half of industrial workers in the two Russian plants were not men but women in their 30s and 40s, trying to find a balance between work and taking care of their children.

The share of women in production at Westauto in 2007 amounted to about 20 per cent; as the production expanded in 2008, this number grew to 40 per cent. Most of them worked in the paint shop and final assembly. The share of women working in production in Russia was higher than at other locations of Westauto, despite the strict labour regulation regarding lifting weight for women in Russia:

> In production we have about 20 per cent female, which is relatively high for a production environment. Most of the women, maybe it's obvious, tend to work outside the body shop. There are quite strict legal limits in Russia with respect to lifting capability and weight restrictions.... I think we have practically no women in body construction for that reason, because the operators have to lift welding guns.
>
> (Interview WAH1)

In the beginning of 2008, the plant kept hiring workers but the recruitment of 'female professions' in production was stopped, as an internal advertisement at

Table 5.3 Average monthly wages at the plants studied in Russia (2007–8)

	Westauto	*Rusauto*	*Rusmet*
Average monthly wages, roubles	21,500	15,500	11,000
Average monthly wages, euros[1]	478	345	245

Source: Interviews by author

Note: 1. From here and forth: Numbers in roubles were converted to euro according to the exchange rate of 2008

What about the workers? 111

the plant stated. The official explanation by Westauto said that the plant could not employ more women without violating the Russian labour law, even though there were a lot of women willing to work in production.

The share of women in production was even higher at the Russian plants (see Figure 5.4). According to the Personnel Director at Rusauto, 90 per cent of production workers in the assembly at Carl were women aged 35–40 years; the share of men and women in the welding shop was equal. At Rusmet, 54 per cent of all employees were female; about 70 per cent of them were in their 40s.

The high percentage of women employed in traditionally male-dominated workplaces can be explained by low wages in these jobs for men. The wages paid by the plants and reliability of their payment were, however, attractive for women. A further explanation has to do with fixed working hours, which women appreciated. A third factor was the high rate of alcoholism and drug addiction among men. Women in Russia traditionally take care of the children and, due to the high rate of alcoholism among men, they also undertake the role of provider for the family. This made women ready to endure the hard working conditions at Rusmet:

> We have a high fluctuation among men. The male contingent here will soon get into the Red Book [The Red Book of rare and protected animals]. They become drunkards, drug addicts. There is the same situation at other [industrial] enterprises... We started to recruit female turners, as men just were not able to stand such work: the turners work [at the machines] with their arms in the emulsion up to the elbows, and men just could not bear that... We even tried to teach women machine setting and maintenance jobs, as we need them very much. We recruited a group but, somehow, it did not go well. Women just need something different. They need to get their work done, make a certain number of pieces, and be paid for them.
>
> (Interview RMH1)

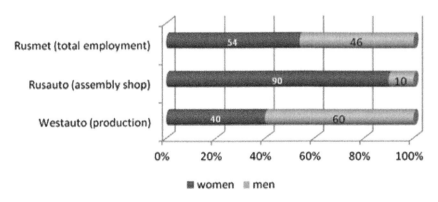

Figure 5.4 Gender distribution in employment at the plants studied in Russia.
Source: Interviews at the companies

112 *What about the workers?*

At Rusmet, the share of women in production started to grow as an 'emerging' tendency in the post-socialist years, but was, later, purposely cultivated by the management. A high share of women influenced the payment system at Rusmet. A large number of women had children and took frequent sick leave because of them. Rusmet adjusted the remuneration system in order to motivate them to avoid taking a sick leave:

> At first we paid a bonus for the harmful working conditions to the women, but we later had to cancel it because of the dissatisfaction of the men, who earned less for the same work. There is one more problem with the women: when their children are ill, they stay home. We decided not to reduce anything to them because of that, as it is not humane, but we pay a quarterly bonus for working without absences.
>
> (Interview RMH1)

This example gives an idea of how difficult it was for management to create the right incentives for female workers, but, at the same time, the ease with which management was able to change the remuneration system.

The overview of the production processes and employment at the three plants studied shows that both material and social production settings at Rusauto and Rusmet still bore the legacy of the Soviet era. Their production equipment had a patchwork character. Their staffs had inflated numbers of non-value-adding personnel. Their production workers were older than at Westauto and were more likely to have been socialised into socialist relations in production.

All three plants employed a high share of women in production jobs. Even new machinery and higher wages at Westauto could not make industrial work attractive for Russian men. Employing women at the Russian factories became a part of management strategy for dealing with the labour shortage and deviant workplace behaviour of Russian male workers.

5.2 Reforming quality assurance in production

The present section will analyse whether the principles characteristic of total quality management (TQM) were actually implemented at the level of production lines. It will discuss product quality checks, finding the root causes of problems in production, and the improvement of production processes at the plants studied (cf. Cole 1999). The section will question if change in the organisation of quality assurance affected the content of work on the shop-floor compared to the socialist path of industrial work (cf. Sections 2.5 and 3.7).

The role of managers and Western partners for the introduction of international quality management concepts

The question of internal versus external determinants of overcoming path dependence is central in path dependence theory (see Section 1.3). The following section will discuss how the initial impulse for change came about at the three plants studied and analyse the role of internal managers and external partners in the change process. It will show that collaboration with external partners was a necessary condition for change in all three cases studied.

At Westauto, expatriate managers headed all departments at the plant during the first year of its operation in Russia and played a central part in the transfer of the company's production system and QM system to the new plant. The headquarters hoped to reduce the number of expatriate managers within the first year of the plant's operation. The positions of human resource manager, manufacturing and plant engineering manager and material planning and logistics manager were among the first to be handed over to Russians. According to the German production manager, Russian managers were capable of embracing change very fast if its purpose was openly communicated to them:

> When a production system is introduced, one must take into account the cultural conditions. There are striking contrasts in England, Germany and Russia... By culture, I mean the culture where one grows up and how one perceives change. The English always have excuses, why something does not work out. The German is sluggish but runs along with you. With Russians it is so that when one explains everything openly, it runs like a locomotive. I have not experienced such fast changes until now.
>
> (Interview WAP)

Russian staff at Westauto received considerable training in new QM concepts (discussed in Section 5.4). Nevertheless, handing over of managerial positions to local Russian managers proved to be difficult. Several years after production started most management positions at Westauto in Russia were still held by expatriate managers. Only two of the departments – Westauto Production System (WPS) and the QM department – were headed by Russians at the time of the interviews. Thus, the enduring presence of expatriate managers was necessary in order to assure the sustainable functioning of the Russian location.

In both of the Russian plants, the introduction of new QM concepts was driven by newly appointed managers, who had first-hand experience of Western automotive enterprises. Besides, the plants established partnerships with Western companies to support change.

In 2006 Rusauto acquired the vehicle platform Car2 from a Western OEM. This marked the beginning of a radical change at the plant. The purchase was followed by establishment of a collaboration with a large Western multinational company that was supposed to assist Rusauto in launching the manufacturing of Car2 in Russia, including the modernisation of production system and QM. The company's strategy was to hire managers with work experience at leading Western automotive companies. As the CEO of Rusauto Holding stated in a newspaper interview, the company needed "a critical mass of change agents" for a breakthrough. Rusauto preferred to hire people from the leading international OEMs rather than developing their own staff, in order to save time. One of the new hires was a young director

114   *What about the workers?*

of the Rusauto plant; he recruited several managers from a Russian–Western automotive JV in 2007. The new managers included the quality director, personnel director, head of quality of the supplied parts department and head of the department of quality assurance in production. The new managers attempted to carry out a rapid modernisation of the Car1 production line and to use it as a trial ground for new management tools that were to be applied at the Car2 production line a year later. However, the 'old' production managers kept their positions.

The change at Rusmet was initiated by the new director appointed in 2005. He had an ambition to export the products to the West and had to overcome the other managers' scepticism regarding the feasibility of manufacturing goods complying with Western quality standards:

> Before our director told us that it was possible, we had never got the slightest idea that we could work with Germans. What do they manufacture and what do we [product quality differs a lot]? But he started to travel a lot, has been many times abroad, in Germany, and he 'fired us up'. I also did not believe that it was realisable for us.
>
> (Interview RMH1)

The new plant director both acquired first-hand knowledge of Western production locations and established contacts with prospective customers. He appointed a new quality director in 2005, a young engineer, who had already worked at Rusmet for seven years and was then trained in QM for one month off the job. In 2006, the plant started to work with management consultants on developing its QM system. First, Russian consultants were invited, but Rusmet was not satisfied with this collaboration. After that, the director hired a German management consulting company, which assisted Rusmet in its change efforts until the plant succeeded in certifying for compliance with ISO/TS 16949 and started to export. When the change was completed another plant director was appointed, a person who had built his career within the factory at Rusmet. This director put on hold or even reversed some of the new policies introduced by his predecessor.

Summing up, the introduction of new QM standards at the two Russian plants was not begun by directors rooted in these organisations but, instead, by newly appointed Russian managers with some first-hand knowledge of Western production systems. In the case of Westauto, the enduring presence of expatriate managers proved necessary. In all three cases, the management drew upon the support of foreign partners in the implementation of new QM standards in Russia.

Quality management standards introduced at the plants

The processes and outcomes of changes in path dependent processes depend on exactly what novel QM concepts organisations introduced, and also on how much space for interpretation and discretion the actors had (cf. Thelen 2009:484). The following section will describe QM standards introduced at the three plants and discuss how much room for interpretation of these standards the management had. While the three plants converged on the broad set of concepts introduced, they differed in how much room for interpretation there was.

Change at all three plants centred on production organisation and QM concepts that were firmly established in the international automotive industry. They included Toyota Production System, ISO 9000 standard and ISO/TS 16949, as well as standardised QM tools such as 5S and failure mode and effects analysis (FMEA), among others. All three plants viewed the Toyota Production System as a reference model and were certified for compliance with ISO 9000. However, these concepts were adjusted to concrete organisational settings.

Westauto transferred two core sets of standardised regulations from its head-quarters to its Russian plant: the WPS and Westauto Quality Operation System (WQOS). WPS was based upon the Toyota Production System:

> WPS is copied from the Toyota Production System. Really, completely copied. Everyone has read the books about the Toyota Production System and now they are implementing such systems. It is really the same everywhere... We at Westauto have developed the system together with people from Toyota.
>
> (Interview WAP)

WQOS was defined in an internal document as "the overall system and over-arching umbrella, under which all Westauto manufacturing processes and tools reside". WQOS used 19 key parameters for production, which included internal audits, Six Sigma and reduction of variation, as well as consumer product quality audit (audit 'by the eyes of the customer'), among others. These parameters are applied not only at the Russian plant internally, but also to evaluate Westauto's suppliers in Russia and their incoming parts.

The parameters of WQOS were broad enough to allow for adjustment of indi-cators of quality assurance functions to individual production locations. The Russian location had a much lower degree of automation of production and qual-ity control operations than other Westauto plants in Europe, different software supporting quality assurance, smaller space for production shops and longer production tact time (four minutes in 2007):

> We don't have such work intensity as at the European plants but we have a lot of hard manual work. The body shop is the hardest: a worker should lift a 100kg welding gun. [The employee does not actually 'lift' the welding gun as the Training Leader says; he probably rather manipulates a welding gun that is fastened to the welding machine.]
>
> (Interview WAH2)

The plants had discretion with regard to some issues only related to work organ-isation, such as allocation of quality checks and number of people responsible for them. Despite the adjustments, the differences in QM systems at the Russian location and other European locations of Westauto were minor, according to the Westauto managers.

116 *What about the workers?*

In addition to introduction of WPS and WQOS at the plant, the Westauto location in Russia was also certified for compliance with ISO 9001 in 2002 and, up until the time of the interviews, it was subject to regular audits by the certification company. This indicates that Westauto needed additional external audits besides the internal systems. Thus, multiple sets of indicators were in place to ensure that the Russian plant followed the same standards as other locations and which therefore limited the space for interpretation of these regulations in Russia.

The transfer of new QM concepts to Rusauto took place in two phases. Change started about 2003 and was, at first, aimed primarily at cutting down production costs. Around 2007, the focus shifted to the preparation for manufacturing of Car2.

In 2003 Rusauto hired a Western consulting company to help with implementation of the Toyota Production System. The consultants helped with standardisation and rationalisation of work operations, improvement of material logistics and provision of information regarding production defects to workers. Rusauto implemented the Japanese standards 'kanban', 'poka-yoke' and 'gemba'.[1] In 2005, the 'Department for Production Systems' was founded with the aim of developing a company-wide production system at Rusauto.

The implementation of the Rusauto Production System was still under way at the end of 2007, when the second phase of the change process at Rusauto started: Rusauto acquired the Car2 platform. This time, the emphasis was put on learning directly from other Western automotive companies. Establishing collaboration with a Western automotive multinational and hiring managers from a Western–Russian JV were part of this strategy:

> I think that no consulting firm, except the ones that specialise on a certain automaker, can give the necessary [expertise] to an automobile plant... Vehicle assemblers are self-sufficient in their [production and management] systems. Consulting companies are employed for suppliers' development.... Automobile corporations copy everything from each other and they all try to use Toyota's practices.
>
> (Interview RAQ1)

Due to these diverse learning processes, the Rusauto Production System distinguished itself from the WPS by being a term used for a large set of diverse tools and practices with different origins. These included some Japanese concepts, as well as concepts stemming from Rusauto's Western partner, from the former owner of the vehicle platform Car2 and from the Western–Russian JV, where the new managers hired by Rusauto had worked:

> We have the Department for Production Systems that implements a wide spectrum of instruments. A section of the quality department [at Rusauto plant] are members of this group. The Directorate analyses the percentage of vehicles that passed first-time-through (FTT) and the existing bottle-necks.

What about the workers? 117

The cross-functional teams that went through special training teach different systems, e.g. our Western partner's production system, 5S, HR. It is a group that has existed for a long time and we now transfer its activities into the practical field. The department is subordinate to the CEO of Rusauto. This group visits different plants; they have a manual for best practices and they monitor what there is [at present]. They work in the fields of quality, production, economy and finance.

(Interview RAQ1)

In addition to the Rusauto Production System, the plant was certified for compliance with ISO 9000, which it used "as a guideline" (Interview RAQ1). As was the case with Westauto, Rusauto also needed additional external guidance by a certification body.

Both Westauto and Rusauto developed their own production systems based on Toyota as a role model. However, while Westauto had significant experience with transferring its production system across borders, this work was, in many respects, ground-breaking for Rusauto, which was developing regulations for one location only. The Rusauto Production System had, it seems, a more patchwork-like character. Another difference is that Westauto applied a standardised quality assurance system integrated with its production system at the Russian plant. The quality assurance system was less standardised at Rusauto. Analysis of the application of new QM concepts at Rusauto also showed that some interpretation and modification of the Japanese concepts took place. The actual content of some of the practices at Rusauto differed from the conventional meanings established in the Western literature.

Unlike the two OEMs studied, Rusmet did not aim to develop an internal production system, although they did want management consultants' assistance in the implementation of the principles of lean production. Rusmet's major efforts were aimed at preparation for ISO/TS 16949 certification. This automotive QM standard sets tighter requirements to quality assurance processes than ISO 9000 (see Section 4.3 for details).

Preparation for certification started with the plant's audit by three prospective Western European customers. The interaction with prospective customers during these audits was an eye-opening event for the Russian managers, who did not even know the terms that the OEMs' representatives operated with, to say nothing about complying with them:

Company X gave us the first impression about FMEA in 2006. Company Y conducted its first introductory/preliminary audit, which we failed, in 2007. They asked us questions that we just did not understand.... The German OEM's representatives told us after their first visit to our plant that we have the potential, but the results of the audit were not satisfactory. They have conditions for collaboration [with suppliers], 'special terms', and the first of them is certification for compliance with TS or VDA 6.3.

(Interview RMQ)

118   *What about the workers?*

Rusmet failed their first audits, but sought consultants' help in the introduction of the standard ISO/TS 16949 and related standardised tools like FMEA, PPAP and statistical process control. The German OEM offered significant assistance to Rusmet to carry out the change by using its original supplier development programme '5M' to guide the change process at Rusmet (see p. 98 for details). The programme went beyond QM and required rethinking and formalisation of the core elements of production organisation at the plant.

The description of QM concepts introduced at the three plants exhibits a lot of similarity with regard to the standards and tools that they implemented. However, managers' discretion in the implementation of new concepts at Westauto and Rusmet seems to be more limited than at Rusauto. In the case of Westauto, the company headquarters controlled unification between production systems and QM systems across its locations. In the case of Rusmet, there was external control by ISO/TS 16949 certification bodies and prospective customers. Whereas Westauto and Rusmet had Western partners controlling their compliance and hence reducing the scope for interpretation of the standards, Rusauto drew on collaboration and exchange with Western partners but was not controlled by them. Therefore, Rusauto had the most space for interpretation and adjustment of the new concepts among the three plants studied.

Division of quality assurance functions between the production and quality departments

The reduction of indirect quality control was one of the aims of the introduction of Japanese concepts of QM and production organisation in the Western automotive industry (see Section 4.1). The socialist automotive industry, on the contrary, was based upon the strict separation of direct production from all indirect functions. Consequently, inflated indirect services were characteristic of socialist production, where indirect workers outnumbered direct workers on the line (cf. Section 2.3). The following section will explore whether the introduction of international QM standards at the three plants studied strengthened the role of production in quality assurance.

Managers' estimates of the importance of different forms of control in the plants' QM systems were similar at Westauto and Rusmet, while Rusauto differed from these two plants (see Table 5.4). QM at Westauto relied by up to 50 per cent and at Rusmet by up to 60 per cent on the responsibility of workers integrated into production processes. The importance of indirect quality control and experts' contribution in design of processes were similarly important at Westauto and Rusmet (20 per cent and 15 per cent, respectively); the role of technical equipment and systems was the least important (10 per cent) at both Westauto and Rusmet.

The Production Manager at Westauto attempted to develop the feeling of 'process ownership' on the shop-floor:

> I need to have the automation to rely on the technical systems. 'Experts' are also not significant, as we get developed processes. Engineers here only

What about the workers? 119

Table 5.4 Importance of forms of control in QM systems at the studied plants (%)

Forms of control	Westauto	Rusauto		Rusmet
		Car1	*Car2 (as should be)*	
Responsibility of workers integrated into production processes (workers' competence and participation)	50	no answer	no answer	60
Indirect quality control (quality control through indirect workers)	20	no answer	no answer	15
Experts' contribution (engineering competence on design of quality assurance processes in production, e.g. poka-yoke)	20	5–10	99	15
Technical equipment and systems (quality controlling equipment)	10			10

Source: Interviews by author

> develop the standard. So, there is development and support of standards. 'Indirect control' – I will never improve the quality by controlling it. I'm trying to develop a process ownership feeling [on the shop-floor].
>
> (Interview WAP)

This opinion was similar to the position of the managers at Rusmet. Both the Production Director and the Quality Director at Rusmet emphasised the importance of direct workers' responsibility for quality. The Production Director stated that workers' competence and motivation were decisive for the quality of the end product:

> Quality depends up to 60 per cent on those who manufacture. If they are competent, then everything goes well. If they don't want it, then give them any tools and there still will be no quality.
>
> (Interview RMP)

According to the Quality Director at Rusmet, about 50–70 per cent of the indirect quality inspectors had been removed since the beginning of the change process. Quality inspectors from the quality department were only responsible for the final product checks and carried out sample process audits in production. The Quality Director stated that the role of technical equipment and systems in quality assurance did not increase after the change, as Rusmet could not afford to upgrade the equipment entirely.

The Quality Director of Rusauto was reluctant to give estimates on all four forms of control. He only emphasised that the main direction of change planned for the Car2 production line, compared to the Car1 production line, would be a lesser reliance on workers and indirect inspectors. Instead, the management intended to

120 *What about the workers?*

drastically increase the significance of experts' contribution to the design of quality assurance processes and the reliance on technical equipment and systems:

> If we estimate how it is now [at Car1 production], poka-yoke and automation of quality assurance together account for 5–10 per cent of all quality control operations. At the final stage of the new project [Car2] it should be 99 per cent. If we include the experts who develop these systems, it should all come up to 100 per cent.... Ideally, the quality department should consist of engineers and white-collar staff and managers, plus product audit. It should always be a quality unit that does not depend on the directors of enterprises, that gives advice to people and gives a real picture of what is going on.
>
> (Interview RAQ1)

Rusauto hoped that a much higher automation of the Car2 production line, compared to the old Car1 line, would allow avoidance of the problems it had faced with the integration of responsibility for quality into workers' tasks at the Car1 line.

Other indicators of the degree of integration of indirect control into direct workers' tasks that were used in the study are the size of QM departments in relation to the total employment at the plants and the ratio of production workers to quality inspectors in the assembly shops (see Table 5.5).

Quality assurance tasks were integrated into the functions of direct workers to the greatest extent at Westauto, where the share of quality auditors to direct workers amounted to about 1:57. This ratio does not include the internal quality inspectors assigned to production, who carried out product quality checks at the quality control stations. Their ratio to production workers was standard for all locations of Westauto, including Russia, and amounted to 8 per cent. Agency employees were not taken into account, as their number includes not only direct workers, but also employees in material manufacturing planning and logistics.

The two Russian plants differed significantly. The share of quality department employees in the total employment at Rusauto was almost 15 times higher than at Rusmet, and the share of quality auditors to direct workers was about eight

Table 5.5 Share of quality department employees in the total in employment at the studied firms

Location	Enterprise	Percentage of quality department employees in the total employment at the plant	Ratio of quality auditors (inspectors) to direct workers in the assembly
Russia	Westauto	1.5	1:57
	Rusauto	7.3	1:3
	Rusmet	0.5	1:25
Germany	Germbrake (pilot case study)	2.6	1:103

Source: Interviews by author

times higher. Some of this difference could be due to the different character of the production processes at Rusauto and Rusmet and the fact that the quality department at Rusauto already employed some people for the Car2 production line. However, the main explanation is that such enormous numbers of quality assurance employees at Rusauto were a conscious strategy of the new managers aimed at strengthening the power of the QM department in production.

This strategy at Rusauto was intended to stop the concealing of defects in production and included two steps. A formal subordination of the 'old' production supervisors and shop managers to the Head of the Department of Quality Assurance in Production was introduced. Therefore, the number of employees in the QM department also included shift and shop managers. The other step was raising the number of indirect quality inspectors in the Car1 production line, so that their ratio to direct workers became about 1:3. This number had been decreased a few years earlier as a cost-reduction measure. According to the Head of the Department of Quality Assurance in Production, that reduction had undermined the position and status of the quality inspectors, who had been treated like 'representatives of a lower race' (*'predstaviteli nizshego sorta'*) by the production employees. The new managers thus restored the initial ratio of quality inspectors to production workers and raised the status and pay of the quality inspectors (see more on remuneration in Section 5.5). According to the Quality Director, they intended to first raise the number of indirect inspectors and then decrease it again, when "the necessary level of conscientiousness [of the direct workers] is achieved" (Interivew RAQ1). The FTT indicator, which shows the share of flawless vehicles passing quality control at the end of assembly, was to guide decisions about the number of quality inspectors in production.

The overview of the division of quality assurance tasks between the production and QM departments at the three plants shows that the degree of integration of quality-related functions into direct workers' tasks at Westauto and Rusmet was much higher than what had been typical for the old path of industrial work. Introduction of international QM standards at Rusauto, on the contrary, led to an expansion of indirect quality control staff, which was seen as a way to overcome the resistance to changes in production and to make workers and line managers report defects. In this way, the managers at Rusauto went back to the level of indirect control typical for the socialist period.

Workers' role in product quality inspection

As all indirect functions were separated from direct production in the socialist path of industrial work, workers' formal tasks did not include product quality checks. Contrary to this, expectation that workers control quality of products they manufacture was a part of the 'conscientious worker' ethos that was supported by ideological campaigns under the planned economy (see Section 2.2). In the Western automotive industry, reduction of density of indirect control by assignment of product quality checks to production was the first step in the reorganisation of quality assurance associated with lean manufacturing (cf. Section 4.2).

122   *What about the workers?*

The following section will analyse how product quality checks were organised at the three plants in Russia, and to what extent they were integrated into direct workers' tasks.

Product quality checks at the three plants included, to a varying extent, product inspection during the production process, at the end of a process (at the so-called 'quality control stations or gates') and when the assembly was completed.

Almost all product quality checks at Westauto were carried out by production workers assigned to the quality control stations or FTT. The quality of automobiles at the Russian plant of Westauto was checked during the production processes and at the end of the assembly. There were three quality control stations in the assembly shop, and one quality control station at the end of the other shops, where 100 per cent of vehicles were checked. All defects were specified in the car's travel card. At the end of the assembly, a 100 per cent visual check of vehicles was carried out and an FTT indicator was calculated. After the FTT, one car per shift was thoroughly checked in accordance with consumer product quality audit requirements. The latter was the only check performed by the QM department.

At Rusauto all product quality checks were carried out by 'quality controllers' assigned to the QM department and there was even a check carried out by the headquarters of the corporation. Quality checks included product inspections during the production process, at quality control stations, at the end of the assembly (FTT) and a new consumer product quality audit based on a Western partner's methodology. The consumer product quality audit was applied in the Car1 production plant and was to be used later at Car2 as well. Quality auditors trained and certified in Germany evaluated three randomly selected vehicles during two shifts and carried out a road test. In addition to the product quality checks performed by the Rusauto plant, the headquarters of the Rusauto Corporation carried out 'corporate' vehicle audits, thus overseeing the audits performed internally at the plant.

> Corporate checks are conducted once a quarter and then the results are compared to the plant's results. If they do not coincide, then everyone will catch it!
>
> (Interview RAQ1)

It is noteworthy that product quality checks at Rusauto had been largely assigned to production around 2003, but the new managers, who came in 2007, had reassigned these checks back to the quality department and strengthened indirect control. This step was taken because of a high level of defect concealing by workers at Rusauto and false quality reporting by production staff. Rusauto reported an FTT of about 98–99 per cent before the management change (FTT was about 50 per cent at the Westauto plant), but this indicator fell to only 60 per cent after product quality checks were reassigned to the QM department:

> When our [management] team came to Rusauto about a year ago, the number of quality controllers was increased. Before we came there it had been

reported that we were the best, and false results were published at about 98–99 per cent of FTT, which are hard to achieve even in the West. A lot of checks were under the jurisdiction of the production, and we changed this situation.

(Interview RAP)

The prevention of concealing of defects on the shop-floor became a major struggle for the new managers. Quality controllers faced strong resistance from the shop-floor at the quality control stations, as they tried to take cars with defects out of the production process:

> I am like a barrier: there are certain requirements and I either open the gate or close the gate. It is also important for me to develop these requirements. I must carry this out, i.e. to discover the deviations from the standards. I must stop this defect and just close the gate. It is a difficult moment – to close the gate. There are still fewer [quality] controllers [than production employees] and there exists a big pressure from production.

(Interview RAP)

Therefore, defects were mostly discovered and reported not by workers but by quality controllers. This required high density of indirect control, not only at quality control stations, but also during the production process. After about a year's effort of change by the new managers, reporting of defects by workers was still very rare. Nevertheless, the Quality Director hoped to soon eliminate product quality checks between the control stations.

Non-reporting of defects was also a problem at Rusmet, where about 20 per cent of workers could conceal them. However, this did not prevent the management from assigning product quality checks to the workers on the line. Workers performed statistical process control, which was implemented with the support of consultants:

> Before it was like that: [workers] checked 100 per cent [of parts] on an instrument and then a controller came and checked 10 per cent from the batch. Now a sample is defined and every fifth or tenth part is checked. We spend less time on checking.

(Interview RMP)

After workers performed quality control, they signed as having carried out the checks. In the case of a process disturbance or a defect, workers consulted a list of frequent defects, where their possible causes were specified. Both the Quality Director and the Production Director pointed to equipment as a most likely cause of defects. If the defects had already been described, workers changed the equipment settings to eliminate them. If workers could not remove the causes of defects, they stopped the production process and informed the seniors. When workers discovered a defect from their own or the previous operation, they had

124　*What about the workers?*

to sort that part out and send it to the 'isolator of not-in-order output'. A technologist, together with quality inspectors, examined the not-in-order parts and repaired them, where possible. At the end of production, quality inspectors carried out the final product quality check.

The management at Rusmet encountered resistance from workers, as they tried to integrate new quality tasks into their functions:

> We encountered opposition from the workers. They resisted when they had to write down something, i.e. to indicate that the check had been carried out and to sign. This is surely additional work. It was difficult for us as we had a lot of 50-year old employees.
>
> (Interview RMQ)

The Quality Director explained the workers' resistance by the difficulty of switching to a new way of work for older employees. Another explanation could be that new indirect quality control tasks decreased workers' wages, which depended on their productivity (remuneration is discussed in Section 5.5).

The description of product quality checks at the three plants shows that the density of indirect control in production at Westauto and Rusmet was much lower than in the socialist path of industrial work. Product quality checks were, to a high extent, integrated into the functions of production workers at both of these plants, even though Rusmet still faced a problem with defect concealing in production. Contrary to these two plants, Rusauto was increasing indirect product inspection at the time of the interviews, and could not prevent workers from concealing defects. Its major efforts were aimed at stopping the false reporting by production staff that had tended to obscure problems.

The workers' role in problem-solving

Problem-solving is a central element in new QM standards. Investigating the root causes of problems, involving workers in these activities and introducing corrective measures targeting these causes and modifying the process standards were central to the reorganisation of quality assurance at Western automotive companies in the 1980s–90s (see Sections 4.1–4.3). The gap between the formal standards and actual work and production routines in the Soviet industry inhibited learning from mistakes. Punitive measures on the shop-floor in the case of defects increased the likelihood of defect concealing by workers. Problem-solving was a not a part of workers' formal tasks, but workers tried to modify the processes anyway in order to assure the output amount. Even enterprise managers concealed the truth about their performance (Harrison 2009). The following section will analyse how the introduction of new QM standards changed problem-solving activities at the plants studied and workers' roles in these activities.

Westauto differed significantly from the two Russian plants, with a higher formalisation of problem-solving. Problem-solving at Westauto included daily and weekly circles described in detailed standards. The daily circle focused on

What about the workers? 125

defects discovered at the consumer product quality audit; the weekly circle focused on defects discovered in production.

The participants of daily meetings, where the results of the consumer product quality audit were discussed, included the heads of the shops, production supervisors and the Variability Reduction Team. If necessary, a brigade leader was invited. During the same shift, the information about additional checks and corrective measures went to the brigades' boards and to the cars' travel-cards. If the causes of defects could not be found immediately, special teams of highly qualified workers, headed by engineers, carried out thorough investigations. The whole cycle (investigation of causes, corrective measures and feedback to workers) took place within one day. Feedback on defects was delivered to the whole brigade, but responsibility for defects at Westauto was individualised, as all defects were traceable to a single worker:

> The team analyses who caused the error; 100 per cent of the errors are traceable. If you have 100 per cent anonymity, then you have no sense of responsibility. Only without anonymity, if the responsibility is attributed to individual people, can you make the employee responsible.
>
> (Interview WAP)

The brigades had goals regarding the number of defects found at the consumer product quality audit ('calls') and regarding other minor defects and process disturbances ('red marks') (see more on goal setting for brigades' performance quality in Section 5.3).

Every worker was informed of her weekly rates of defects discovered in production. All workers took part in the reduction of the numbers of defects in production through brigade discussions, with goals set with regard to maximum defect rates (described in more detail in Section 5.3). Defects discovered most frequently within the last five to six months were summarised in a special report, with an overview of the systemic measures aimed at defect reduction that had been implemented. Every shop also had goals regarding the maximum number of such defects; goal fulfilment was linked to the plant's incentive system.

Thus, workers received individual feedback regarding both types of defects at Westauto, which meant there were clear borders between individual and brigade responsibility. Workers were also involved in solving problems, although this involvement was limited to highly qualified workers in the case of defects discovered at customer product quality audits.

At Rusauto, problem-solving included the same two circles as at Westauto (defects from consumer product quality audits and defects detected in production), but it was carried out by management only. Defects discovered at consumer product quality audits were discussed twice a day at top-management meetings called 'gemba'. These meetings were primarily aimed at reporting objective information and appointing people to solve the problems:

> Twice a day we have gembas, with participation of the top management [of the plant], where the current situation is elucidated. Gembas are meant not

126 *What about the workers?*

> for the solution [of the problems], but *for stating the facts* and managers' focusing on the current problems. They take decisions on who can be involved in [solving] these matters.
>
> (Interview RAP, italics added)

The participants of 'gemba' were primarily managers. Strong involvement of the plant management in reporting the quality problems and appointing the responsible managers was used to exercise additional control over production and prevent the concealing of defects. The manager of the shop where the problem originated was in charge of the solution of the problem in the shop.

For defects detected in production, the *andon* (alarm cord) system was introduced at Rusauto. The original Japanese idea of *andon* is that a worker can pull this alarm cord and stop the conveyer in case of problems. At Rusauto, if a worker pulled the *andon* cord, this did not stop the conveyer. If the alarm was activated, two quality department employees, a brigade leader and a production supervisor attempted to 'remove' the problem while the conveyer belt was moving. If this was not possible, the conveyer was stopped and the shift manager and the production manager were informed. If they could not solve the problem, the General Director of the plant was informed. When the cause of the process disturbance was discovered, the brigade leaders and production supervisors were responsible for implementation of corrective measures and they informed the workers in all shifts. In reality, however, workers rarely pulled the *andon* cord, since they preferred not to report defects. Worker- and equipment-caused defects at Rusauto were tightly intertwined, which contributed to workers' unwillingness to expose themselves to possible sanctions.

A Western Quality Manager consulting Rusauto, pointed out another difficulty in problem-solving at the plant: there was very little collaboration between the production sections in the case of quality problems. He explained this as being the result of a high degree of separation and the individualisation of responsibility at the level of production supervisors:

> The responsibility is very much personalised. This is really so: there is one person who is in charge of a process area. This person does not care what happened before [his process area]. In Central Europe, if something is wrong before one's process area, one would call, ask, be restless, because one undertakes one's work conscientiously!
>
> (Interview RAQ2)

The narrow interest of production supervisors in their own parts of the process undermined the likelihood of finding the 'root causes' of problems.

The description of problem-solving activities at Rusauto shows a gap between the requirements of the new QM concepts and the actual behaviour of workers and production supervisors. Rusauto attempted to change problem-solving and involve brigade leaders in it while still struggling with unwillingness to report defects on the shop-floor.

What about the workers? 127

Rusmet also had two circles of problem-solving: one initiated by 'external' defects – that is, customer reclamations – and one focused on 'internal' defects discovered in production. Apart from this, workers registered the causes of the process disturbance that led to idle time in their 'personal time control cards'.

Investigation of causes of defects that reached the customer followed the international standardised tool Global 8D.[2] First, a specialist from the quality department clarified the details with the customer and then a problem-solving group was set up in the unit where the defect was manufactured. An interim containment action was taken within 48 hours after the reclamation, while the team worked on long-term corrective measures. Feedback to the workers was delivered by their immediate seniors. In the case of important defects, workers were gathered to receive the information after work or during the lunch break. This meant that this time was not paid as working time.

In the case of internal defects, reaction rules and time were less formalised:

> If a defect is clear, then the technological service takes it up. It is rather difficult to bring together people to solve a problem. Usually, a technologist, a product designer and a quality specialist are called.
>
> (Interview RMQ)

The causes of defects were discussed with workers two to four times a month on 'Days of Quality', and the accumulated data were discussed on the shop level once a month. It should be noted that, due to the remuneration rules at Rusmet, these discussions were not paid as working time, which was likely to undermine workers' engagement with them.

An additional practice that contributed to registering the causes of defects at Rusmet was 'personal time control cards'. All working time was divided into five-minute time slots and a worker had to specify if she worked or was idle. In the case of idle time, causes should be registered (e.g. equipment breakdown). The accumulated information on causes of process disturbance was manually entered into the computer, but it was not analysed at the time of the interviews. Analysis of this information had been planned at the next stage of the change process at Rusmet. However, the Plant Director who had initiated the change process at Rusmet had been substituted by the headquarters shortly before the interviews. The new director put on hold or reversed many of the initiatives of the previous director, including the use of time control cards.

The overview of problem-solving at Rusmet shows very different degrees of standardisation in the case of defects that reached the customers and in the case of internal defects. There was an indication that idle time was a problem at this plant, but its causes were not investigated. This information was only used to determine workers' pay (discussed in Section 5.5). Workers did not participate in problem-solving and were only informed about problems by management. Notably, Rusmet still used two practices stemming from the socialist approach to quality control and work organisation. 'Days of Quality' were first mentioned in the Saratov System of Defectless Work in the 1950s (cf. Section 2.3) and making

128　*What about the workers?*

workers register their time use was one of the ideas of early Soviet Taylorism (cf. Section 2.1). 'Days of Quality' under the planned economy were, to a high extent, ideologically motivated and their effectiveness at Rusmet seems doubtful, since workers were not paid for participation in them.

The analysis of problem-solving activities shows that the two Russian plants deviated from the traditional gap between the formal rules and actual work routines in case of reclamations or defects discovered at customer audits. This shows that customer satisfaction became a much more important factor in the Russian industry than it used to be under the planned economy. However, the degree of standardisation of problem-solving initiated by internal defects at the two Russian plants was much lower than at Westauto. Worker involvement in problem-solving at the two Russian plants was much lower than at Westauto as well. Participation in problem-solving only became a part of the formal tasks of brigade leaders at Rusauto.

Managers' attitudes to worker-caused defects

Fear of reporting mistakes due to the sanctions that would follow was a central characteristic of the socialist path of industrial work. Elimination of this fear was one of the imperatives of the TQM movement and an empirically proven precondition for finding the root cause of problems in production (MacDuffie 1997). The following section will analyse managers' attitudes to worker-caused defects and will try to find out if the plants departed from the 'blame mentality', which contributed to the concealment of defects by workers.

In order to answer these questions, managers at the three plants were asked to estimate the share of defects due to four basic causes: workers, production equipment, suppliers and product design or to specify other causes and to provide their explanation for the worker-caused defects (see Table 5.6).

There were significant differences with regard to estimated causes of defects between Westauto and the Russian plants. These differences had to do primarily with the high share of equipment- and supplier-caused defects at the Russian plants. Notably, the estimated share of worker-caused defects at the Russian plants was lower than at Westauto.

According to the German Production Manager at Westauto, workers' performance was by far the major cause of defects at the plant (90 per cent); flaws due to suppliers and production equipment accounted only for 10 per cent of defects. However, the Production Manager at the plant did not view human mistakes as anything alarming:

> Even a great manager makes 70 per cent correct decisions and 30 per cent erroneous... It is normal for people to manufacture defects.
>
> (Interview WAP)

He did not consider workers' negligence an explanation of the high share of worker-caused defects at Westauto, and stated instead that they were due to the

Table 5.6 Causes of defects at the three plants, as estimated by the managers

Causes of defects	Westauto	Rusauto		Head of quality of supplied parts department	Rusmet	
	Production manager	Quality director			Quality director	Production director
		All defects	Warranty time			
Workers	90%	3–5%	–	40% workers and equipment together	30% – workers 30% – equipment set-up	40%
Production equipment	5%	–	–		30%	40%
Suppliers	5%	–	30% – internal suppliers 60% – external suppliers	30–40%	0.5% or less	10%
Product design	–	–	10%	20–30%	1–2 ppm	10%
Other		99% – managers				

Source: Interviews by author

130   *What about the workers?*

low degree of automation of production and quality assurance processes. Furthermore, the management at Westauto intentionally attempted to introduce a no-blame mentality on the shop-floor (discussed in Section 5.5 on remuneration and sanctions).

At the two Russian plants, production equipment, suppliers and product design were mentioned as significant causes of defects, along with workers. According to the Quality Director and Production Director at Rusmet, workers accounted for 60 and 40 per cent of defects (respectively) and production equipment accounted for 30–40 per cent. The Quality Director specified that about half of the worker-caused defects were due to difficulties in the setting up of equipment. Moreover, he indicated that 15 per cent of the equipment-caused defects were actually due to the 'equipment of active control' – that is, the equipment that assures quality during the process by measuring and automatically adjusting machine parameters to achieve required product characteristics. Suppliers and product design accounted for a much lower share of defects than workers and production equipment. Thus, despite the partial equipment modernisation that had been carried out at Rusmet, production machinery remained a significant cause of defects. Difficulties in equipment set-up and instability meant that these two causes of defects (workers and equipment) at Rusmet were tightly intertwined.

The request for information in the form of these rough estimates was met with a lot of resistance from the managers at Rusauto. They were unwilling to put details in writing and gave their statements only orally and rather vaguely. For example, the Personnel Manager emphasised the paramount role of the low quality of supplied parts for Rusauto:

> If we, for example, had introduced the system of not letting a defect go to the next stage [of the production process], the conveyer at Car1 would be stopped and not turned on any more because of the components. They are produced in a particular production culture. It is not possible to replace the suppliers as there are no alternatives. There is no choice and no chance to substitute a supplier.
>
> (Interview RAH)

Thus, Rusauto was not able to stop the supply of low-quality parts and had to cope with it in production. The high share of low-quality components from suppliers made it necessary for quality controllers to accept minor defects that could not be detected at the consumer product quality audit – 'by the eyes of the customer':

> Our priority in communication with suppliers is criticisms [detected] in the customer product quality audit and not in the assembly process on the main conveyer.
>
> (Interview RAS2)

Negotiations about the acceptable minor defects, which were likely to appear, added to the tensions between the production and quality controllers.

What about the workers? 131

According to the Quality Director at Rusauto, almost all defects in production were caused by 'managers' and their incompetence (up to 99 per cent), and only a few – by workers (3–5 per cent). Notably, these 3–5 per cent were deliberate mistakes due to workers' dissatisfaction with pay:

> Ninety-nine per cent of causes are managers. If they are not competent, this causes problems. Three to five per cent are deliberate mistakes when a person is not satisfied with the wages and causes damage. Ultimately, everything boils down to the chief executive or general director. If there is an imbalance somewhere it will come up.
>
> (Interview RAQ1)

The Head of Quality of the supplied parts department, however, had a different opinion about the causes of defects at Rusauto. According to him, workers and old unreliable production equipment accounted for 40 per cent of defects. He found it difficult to differentiate between these two causes due to their interdependence. Suppliers accounted for 30–40 per cent of defects, and product design for the remaining 20–30 per cent. Hence, worker- and equipment-caused defects at Rusauto were intertwined, as well as at Rusmet.

The analysis of worker-caused defects shows instability of production equipment and interconnection of worker-caused and equipment-caused defects at the two Russian plants studied. This does not seem to be the case at Westauto, where the equipment was newer. This interconnection made the search for causes of defects an area of likely tensions between workers and management, but was not addressed openly in these plants' problem-solving procedures, discussed in the previous section. These tensions were intensified by the fact that attribution of responsibility or guilt to a worker implied a wage reduction for her (explored further in Section 5.5 on remuneration systems). Hence, this interconnection was likely to impede the deviation from the blame mentality at the two Russian plants.

Workers' role in improvement activities

Improvement activities were poorly planned and formalised under the planned economy. Workers were motivated to participate in them by worker mobilisation campaigns that used ideology, recognition and material incentives to encourage workers to share their ideas on higher productivity and quality. The requirement to formalise process improvement and document evidence is one of the requirements in the automotive QM standard ISO/TS 16949 (cf. Section 4.3). The following section will analyse how the introduction of international QM standards changed the improvement activities and the role of workers in them at the plants studied.

Improvement activities at the three plants significantly differed. The two Russian plants were characterised by a lower formalisation of these activates, lesser worker involvement and strong impact of the socialist legacy on their practices.

132   *What about the workers?*

Continuous improvement at Westauto included two forms: the all-company system of defect reduction and individual improvement suggestions (kaizen). These two forms of improvement were applied to all levels and units at the plant and were guided by annual targets. The goals for defect reduction for Westauto Russia were set by headquarters and 'cascaded' down to the level of a brigade at the plant (see more in Section 5.3). Every employee had to reach the target of submitting one kaizen a year, which Westauto achieved without difficulties.

The system of individual improvement suggestions at Westauto was integrated with the wage system and training system for hourly employees. To progress within a wage grade, a worker had to attend certain courses and then make improvement suggestions within three months after training. This helped to make sure that the worker mastered the course material:

> There is a practical part after every training. That is, the worker has to bring real improvements within three months after the theoretical course, i.e. real improvements, real suggestions on the organisation of the working place, either from the point of view of safety or from the point of view of ergonomics or from the point of view of waste reduction.
>
> (Interview WAH2)

Workers' contribution was expected to advance from single improvement ideas to larger projects, although the cost-reduction effect of the suggestions was not high according to the Production Manager. Workers were expected not only to develop an improvement idea, but also to contribute to its implementation (the kaizen system at the Russian plant differed from other locations of Westauto):

> If a worker wants to make a suggestion, there is a standard form on which he receives a brigade leader's signature and then the signature of the head of the shop, because maybe this suggestion will improve his own work, but will worsen it on the following section [at the next stage of the production process]. Then he registers it himself in the personnel department, as this is a condition for the grade rise.
>
> (Interview WAQ10

> Only accomplished improvements are taken into account. The operator has to initiate and to lead this process, to push it through.
>
> (Interview WAQ2)

Thus, there were no monetary rewards for suggestions at the Russian plant, but they were a precondition for moving to a higher wage grade (see Section 5.5). This way to motivate workers to submit suggestions had limitations. According to the Training Manager, workers were not willing to submit their suggestions when they achieved the maximum possible wage grade already:

> The reward is really an issue.... [Workers think:] 'I have an excellent kaizen but I will not give it to you, as I will anyway not get anything for that...

therefore I will better keep my kaizen under my hat and will not show it to anybody.'

(Interview WAH2)

At the time of the interviews, the management at Westauto started to develop a new system of rewards for suggestions that would take into account the financial benefits for the plant resulting from improvements.

Thus, improvement activities at Westauto were formalised; workers' participation in these activities was integrated with the remuneration system. Yet, workers did not submit the improvement suggestions to actually improve their working area, but had a purely instrumental attitude to kaizen.

At Rusauto improvement of production processes became one of the tasks of the Directorate for Production Systems, a multi-functional group of experts from various plants within the holding. Workers' involvement in improvement, however, still followed the socialist principles.

Improvements at Rusauto were linked to implementation and further development of the Rusauto Production System:

> The Rusauto Production System has been implemented for about five years, with the help of consultants. They take Toyota as the basis and there are steady improvements. They implement kanban, poka-yoke. If we compare how working places are organised now and used to be organised before, there are striking differences.

(Interview RAH)

The Directorate attempted to determine the 'best practices' and then to diffuse them throughout the corporation.

The system of improvement suggestions for workers, however, had not been affected by the introduction of the new QM standards. Workers submitted their improvement suggestions to their line managers and were paid 100 roubles for a suggestion (about 2.2 euros). The production supervisors also took the suggestions into account when assigning a Coefficient of Labour Participation (KTU) to the workers. However, there were no formal criteria for this coefficient (discussed in more detail in Section 5.5). Production sections competed over the number of submitted suggestions, an idea that stemmed from the socialist labour competition movement (cf. Section 2.2). Management considered the system ineffective but did not plan to change it:

> Workers can come with [improvement] suggestions, but this does not work the way it should... The wish to submit improvement ideas is quite low now.
> (Interview RAH)

The description of improvement activities at Rusauto shows that improvement activities received more attention from the management than in the past and became a domain of expert knowledge. Workers' role in improvement activities was not affected by the introduction of new QM concepts at Rusauto.

134 *What about the workers?*

There were three improvement programmes at Rusmet: an annual cost reduction ('optimisation') by experts, 'rationalisation suggestions' by employees and a 'labour competition' system. Improvement activities involving workers followed socialist principles, which were somewhat reinterpreted by the management and linked to the new QM standards.

The cost-reduction goal at Rusmet was set by the management annually and was then cascaded down to the level of the shops' chief engineers. First, the fields for cost reduction with the highest possible saving potential at the plant were defined. Then the planned cost reduction was divided between the shops. After that, special teams headed by the chief specialists in the shops were set up. Unlike in the case of the defect reduction programme at Westauto, there were no goals for brigades.

Workers could submit their improvement ideas to the coordinators for rationalisation suggestions, which existed in every shop. These were 'active workers', who combined this task with their jobs. Submitted suggestions were then discussed by a special commission headed by the Technical Director of the plant. There were no targets with respect to either the number of suggestions or their cost-reduction potential at Rusmet. According to the Quality Director, workers received 500 roubles for a rationalisation suggestion (about 11 euros). In cases where the economic effect of a suggestion could be calculated, 7 per cent of the effect was to be paid to the author. In reality, however, the management did not feel bound by these regulations, and the employees then did not get the complete reward:

> If the effect can be calculated, then the payment depends on the sum characterising the positive effect. The highest effect that we've ever had was 3 million roubles [about 67,000 euros]. We just discussed it recently. According to our regulations, we have to pay to the author (it is a specialist and not a worker) less than 10 per cent – about 7 per cent. It comes out that we have to pay to him 200,000 roubles [about 4,400 euros]!... And so, we were thinking what to do about it. We cannot not pay and discredit ourselves. Then we decided like this. This is not a suggestion that someone made alone and calculated himself. He also asked people in the laboratory to help him, to try this idea. Therefore, we decided that we will estimate the degree of his participation in this suggestion as 30 per cent [and pay him only 30 per cent of the reward].
>
> (Interview RMQ)

Thus, the management reduced the reward to 30 per cent of what it should be according to the rules and did not pay the remaining 70 per cent to other co-participants in the development of the suggestion either. This example points to the arbitrary character of rules for rewards that were easily violated by management. It is noteworthy that union representatives at Westauto assisted workers in the case of perceived injustice from the management in such matters. Likewise, in Germany works councils could interfere in cases of management–

What about the workers? 135

worker conflicts with regard to rewards for improvement suggestions (interviews GBH1 and GBT). This was not the case with Rusmet.

The third element in the system of improvement at Rusmet was 'labour competition', which had been in place since the Soviet period. Labour competition at Rusmet was a very elaborate practice, which had the motto 'For effectiveness, quality and saving'. It took place within 11 groups or categories, which embraced all hierarchical levels and division sizes at Rusmet: from shops to individual 'workers and specialists' (internal document, Rusmet):

List of categories
    I–II – production shops
    III – indirect (auxiliary) shops
    IV – technical departments (including quality assurance department)
    V – management departments
    VI – brigades
    VII – individual workers and specialists (there are six subcategories here, e.g. direct workers, production supervisors, young employees aged up to 30)
    VIII – authors of improvement suggestions (*ratsionalizatory*)
    IX – mentors (*nastavniki*)
    X – members of project groups
    XI – transient prize for the best quality of work process in the production shops (to be received by the shop manager)

All these groups were evaluated four times a year. A separate set of two to eight evaluation criteria was developed for each of the groups; different evaluators were appointed for different evaluation criteria.

Most of the evaluation criteria measured employees' compliance with the internal regulations. The list of criteria for every category of competitors included fulfilment of the output norms, absence of discipline violations and complaints from other units within the plant. There were additional performance quality-related criteria in evaluation of direct production shops and individual workers and specialists: submission of output free from defects and absence of customer complaints.

Criteria for the evaluation of brigades were the most elaborate. Two of them (criteria 4 and 5) directly referred to the new QM standards that were implemented at Rusmet in 2006 (adapted excerpt from an internal document, Rusmet):

1. Work productivity (fulfilment of the plan)
2. Daily fulfilment of the output plan
3. Submission of output with no defects
4. Mastering the 8D competencies and their application (absence of internal and external complaints, development and carrying out of effective corrective and preventive measures)

136 *What about the workers?*

5. Implementation of the quality tools required by the ISO/TS 16949 (absence of criticism from the internal auditors)
6. Order and cleanliness in the workplace ('culture of production')
7. Labour discipline (absence of criticism)
8. Work safety (absence of injuries)

The winners of the competition received a lot of recognition and were awarded 'symbolic' monetary prizes. The head of the unit and the head of the unit's union committee in all group competition categories (i.e. shops, departments or brigades) received individual rewards of 300–500 roubles (about 7–11 euros), while ordinary members of the units received petty amounts of 15–30 roubles per person (less than 1 euro). Seventy of the best individual workers and specialists from the whole plant received 500 roubles. The Head of Work Organisation and Pay Department stated that there was no enthusiasm about participating in the competition:

> People like it, when they know that their brigade is the best, when their pictures are hung out on the 'board of honours'. Though there is no heroism like before… We hand out certificates and the rewards take place in a festive atmosphere, but all that is purely symbolic.
>
> (Interview RMH1)

Thus, labour competition was a formalised practice based upon objective and measurable criteria. The content of the labour competition was slightly changed since the Soviet era, particularly for brigades, whose evaluation criteria included concepts that had not existed before the QM change. However, no thorough revision of labour competition took place and it served as an employee recognition programme, rather than as an improvement framework.

One of the factors behind this superficial bricolage of the old concept of labour competition is the absence of a substitute for the socialist ideology that used to fuel the old system. The managers at Rusmet lamented the lack of conscientiousness in employees' attitudes to work on several occasions. This was seen as the reason for the failure of the quality circles that the plant had attempted to introduce:

> We tried to organise quality circles, but at the moment it does not work – there is a lack of conscientiousness.
>
> (Interview RMP)

The notion of conscientiousness combines responsibility, diligence and awareness; it is close to internalised control, which the TQM movement aimed at. This attitude to work had been one of the goals of the Soviet ideology, aiming at workers' compliance with the requirements of the Soviet economy without the need for external compulsion, as workers were 'working for themselves' and were not being 'exploited' by the capitalists (cf. Sections 2.1–2.2). In the context of

Rusmet, a capitalist enterprise, which appropriated the manufactured surplus value, a new foundation for conscientiousness had to be created in order to facilitate internalisation of control by workers.

The discussion of improvement activities at Rusmet shows that the purpose of the plant-level programme centred on cost reduction and not variability reduction, as at Westauto, or alignment of workplace organisation with the company's production system, as at Rusauto. Brigades were not involved in this programme, as was the case with Rusauto. However, the systems of workers' improvement suggestions and labour competition at Rusmet were more elaborate than at Rusauto, even though they still drew on socialist rhetoric and ideas: 'optimisation', 'rationalisation' and 'labour competition'.

Thus, improvement activities at Westauto deviated from the socialist principles most of the three plants studied. The system of workers' improvement suggestions did not receive any management attention and rethinking at Rusauto, but was reinterpreted and linked to the new QM standards at Rusmet. Nevertheless, workers' motivation for participation in these activities was low at both Russian plants and had an instrumental character at Westauto.

Summary: change of workers' role in quality assurance

The new QM standards affected the way quality was assured in production at all three plants. They had the strongest effect in the case of Westauto, where all three of the quality assurance functions studied were structured by the new standards and deviated from the socialist practices. These functions were integrated with the WPS and the company's headquarters set key indicators for these functions. In contrast to Westauto, the socialist legacy was weakened but still present at the two Russian plants. The functions that immediately affected the customers (product quality checks and problem-solving for defects that were likely to reach the customer) changed much more than the QA functions related to internal routines (problem-solving for internal defects and improvement activities).

The content of work on the shop-floor changed following the introduction of the new standards at only two of the three plants studied – Westauto and Rusmet. At Westauto, responsibility for quality was individualised and formalised: workers' formal tasks included participation in problem-solving in brigades and development and implementation of improvement suggestions. At Rusmet, product quality checks based on statistical process control were formally integrated into all workers' functions. This differs from the socialist path of industrial work, in which only the best workers were granted a personal stamp qualifying them for inspection of their output quality (cf. Section 2.3). At Rusauto, the content of work on the shop-floor remained largely the same. The novel system of the *andon* appears not to have been used often by workers, who were reluctant to report defects. The problem with concealing of defects by workers surfaced at Rusmet as well, although to a lesser extent.

Two factors likely to explain why Westauto did not face the problem of defect concealment on the shop-floor, unlike the Russian plants, can be proposed. First, it

138 *What about the workers?*

was managers' open and no-blame attitude to mistakes at Westauto. Second, it was the possibility of tracing the defects to their cause at Westauto. At Rusauto, the management had to navigate in 'turbid waters', where the quality of supplied parts was low and could not be improved due to the suppliers' monopolist position. Both at Rusauto and at Rusmet, worker- and equipment-caused defects were difficult to distinguish. The implications of this interconnectedness for the path of industrial work will be further explored in Section 5.5 on remuneration policies.

Summing up, the content of work on the shop-floor was affected the most at Westauto, less at Rusmet and the least of the three at Rusauto. These outcomes point towards the importance of international partners for the introduction of the new QM standards, since external control was the strongest in the case of Westauto, weaker in case of Rusmet, audited by the Western customers, and the weakest for Rusauto.

5.3 Work organisation and assignment of quality assurance tasks

Brigade work played a central role in the socialist path of industrial work. Brigades were exposed to contradictory pressures. On the one hand, they bore collective responsibility for meeting output targets, but, on the other hand, they could not compensate for the shortfalls of the socialist enterprise, such as the irregularity of supplies. They were supposed to be responsible for the quality of output, but the quality of products they manufactured was subject to rigorous inspection by quality controllers. They could take some decisions about the work process, but their formal authority did not include any indirect tasks, such as participation in the development of process descriptions. These contradictions in responsibility on the shop-floor were referred to as 'negative control' by Clarke (Clarke 1993). The following section will discuss how the introduction of international QM standards changed brigade work and whether it led to the integration of quality-related tasks into the brigades' formal responsibilities.

Organisation of group work on the shop-floor

The analysis shows that while group work at Westauto differed from the approach to brigade work typical for the planned economy, the two Russian plants under study did not introduce new principles of group work coherent with the QM standards.

Westauto applied the same principles of group work in Russia as at its other locations. All team (or brigade) members were allocated paid working time and space for group discussions – not just a few members elected onto the brigade council, which was the case under the planned economy. Teams on the shop-floor were between six and ten people, depending on the process, who were responsible for the production process within their area. Brigades had a leader who knew all the working places. Although the leader was appointed by the management, it was typically someone respected by the other brigade members. Brigade leaders did not, in principle, work on the line, but substituted absent employees in case of illness. They carried out indirect tasks within the brigade's work area and were responsible for communicating problems with quality in the brigade's process area to the production supervisor. Brigade leaders received an additional premium.

Brigades had a zone for group discussions, which included quality problems along with other issues; the time allotted for discussions was 30 minutes a week in 2007 (it was reduced to 20 minutes in 2009). The brigades of two shifts also met at the end of the shift, when they had 30 minutes' overlap for discussion. Part of the discussion time was used for information from the management:

> The sheet of the plant's information with news and events is read out to the workers; they discuss quality problems, modernisation and other problems that they have.
>
> (Interview WAQ1)

Brigades could also discuss distribution of operations, attendance of training courses and 'some improvements to facilitate work and the safety' and material orders. According to the Trade Union Coordinator for Work Safety though, it was the brigade leader who distributed operations and ordered material for work.

Brigade leaders also submitted suggestions on how to improve process descriptions to production specialists. This represents a major difference from the socialist path of industrial work, where only actual work practices were changed. According to the Trade Union Coordinator, workers did not participate in the development of process descriptions. Even though management stated that they did, line managers were unwilling to interact with workers:

> Those are mere words that [work] instructions are developed together with the workers. But, in fact, they are sent down. They [production specialists and technologists] cannot cross the threshold of communication between the manager and the subordinate.
>
> (Interview WAT)

This suggests that even Russian employees who used to work on the production lines themselves demonstrated unwillingness to involve workers after they were appointed to more senior positions. Workers, however, viewed the imperfect work process descriptions rather pragmatically. According to the Trade Union Coordinator, they followed them as long it was possible to do so with only minor deviations and then submitted corrections. This indicates that work process descriptions actually guided work processes and that workers did update them, even though they faced some resistance from the Russian managers.

At Rusauto, the principles of brigade work were not changed during the introduction of international QM standards. Production lines at Rusauto were divided into 'sections' of 20–30 workers, led by a production supervisor. There were several brigades of five to six workers in each section. Workers rotated within a

140   *What about the workers?*

brigade with the purpose of learning multiple operations and increasing the flexibility of operation assignment. As was the case at Westauto, brigade leaders, in principle, did not work on the line, but substituted an absent employee in case of illness or personnel shortage. Brigade leaders received an additional premium.

The German Quality Manager from the Western partner company noted that brigade work at Rusauto differed significantly from group work in Europe. It was marked by a strong individualisation of tasks, low support between peers and social disapproval of interference into the work of colleagues. Workers did not perceive work goals as common or shared, contrary to the Soviet collectivist rhetoric about brigade work:

> In Russia there is no 'group work' in the European sense of the word. There is the 'collective' or it may also be called 'brigade', 'group', or 'team', in which everyone has his own tasks. But in a team it is so that everyone supports the other, help each other, etc. The Russians have pride in exactly what they do. Therefore, they do not want to interfere in what the other does and do not doubt if the other makes [his work] properly. The boundaries between different jobs in Europe are becoming blurred and in Russia it is quite different at the moment.
>
> (Interview RAQ2)

This observation indicates that both peer support and pressure to perform work well in brigades was very low at Rusauto. Brigades at Rusauto represented rather a group of workers performing separate tasks, than a unit for mutual support in carrying out the work. Such behaviour was likely to be reinforced by a remuneration system at Rusauto that relied on sanctions (explored further in Section 5.5 on remuneration). Workers were likely to be unwilling to interfere or criticisise their colleagues' work, as this could affect their fellow workers' bonuses. The low significance of brigades as social units at Rusauto is confirmed by the fact that KTU was distributed within a production section and not within a brigade (see more on the history of KTU in Section 2.3).

Overall, brigade work played a rather marginal role at Rusauto. Workers were organised in brigades but cohesion in brigades was low. Workers carried out individual tasks and were paid individual wages.

Brigade work at Rusmet still followed the principles stemming from the Soviet era as well. The very definition of a brigade in the company's internal regulation was loaded with Soviet collectivist rhetoric:

> The production brigade is a primary cell of the labour collective of the unit. A brigade unites workers for the joint and most effective carrying out of production task on the basis of mutual comradely help, joint interest and responsibility for work results.
>
> (Internal regulations on brigade work, Rusmet, 2007)

Brigades were rather large, consisting of 20–30 people from both shifts working on one process or on a part of a process. Notably, members of large brigades

What about the workers? 141

could also include a production supervisor and/or other engineering and technical employees. When needed, brigades were divided into smaller groups, *zven'ya*, on the basis of the functions carried out by workers; *zven'ya* united workers from the same shift. There was no paid working time for brigade or *zveno* discussions, but management expected that brigades discuss work matters during the shift change.

Every brigade and *zveno* had leaders (*brigadir* and *zven'evoi*). Workers elected brigade leaders and *zveno* leaders themselves, but the appointments were to be made by the management. Brigade leaders could be elected both from workers and RSS. *Zveno* leaders were subordinate to brigade leaders, and the latter to production supervisors. Brigade leaders belonged to the lowest management level and had disciplinary functions.

> Brigade leaders substitute the production supervisor and monitor work distribution and that workers are busy [don't stop working]. The brigade leader also has disciplinary functions when the production supervisor is absent.
>
> (Interview RMH1)

Brigade work principles were integrated with the remuneration system at the plant. Brigade leaders participated in ascribing KTU and the bonuses to the workers (KTU at Rusmet is discussed in Section 5.5). Brigade leaders received an additional premium of 300–600 roubles (7–13 euros), depending on the size of the brigade; zveno leaders received half of a brigade leader's premium. The premium was only paid if the brigade fulfilled its production plan.

Another characteristic of brigade work inherited from the socialist past was the brigade council (*sovet brigady*), elected by brigades. They consisted of several skilled and respected workers (no less than three members), who met at least once a month. A production supervisor and a union representative participated in these meetings. Brigade councils carried out multiple functions. They were supposed to prepare improvement suggestions within the brigade's working area, to assist workers in fulfilling production norms, to raise workers' qualification level, to assist trainees in the brigades, and to suggest candidates for the internal personnel development programme. Apart from these responsibilities, the brigade council played an important role in assuring production and labour discipline. It prepared suggestions to management with regard to sanctions for discipline violations.

According to the Production Director, the Soviet approach to brigade work was deliberately kept at Rusmet and management did not plan to change it. The management believed that the Soviet approach to brigade work had strong potential to raise workers' conscientiousness. Brigade work at Rusmet was integrated with labour competition and remuneration, which also still rested upon Soviet principles:

> We have had the brigade form of remuneration, [labour] competition and a link between performance quality and [labour] competition. We took the decision to keep this, and we will also apply these methods in the future.... One can often hear now that everything that there was in the past is bad. I think there were also some good methods, particularly the ones that have to

142   *What about the workers?*

do with ideological work aimed at raising [workers'] conscientiousness. Working with workers, clarifying [something to them], convincing [them].

(Interview RMP)

The official description of brigade work at Rusmet emphasised the collective responsibility for the production process within the brigade's working area. In addition, it was stated that, along with individual responsibility and brigade leaders' responsibility, brigades bore collective responsibility for fulfilling the production plan on time and for assuring a high quality of products and work.

Summing up, the brigade work at Rusmet could be considered an example of 'negative control' on the shop-floor, characteristic of the punitive path of industrial work (cf. Chapter 2). High expectations regarding brigades' responsibility were not backed up by brigades having real authority. The brigade was not a unit that consisted of workers only: it could also include engineers and managers. Neither was it a unit that acted in the interest of workers: the brigade leader and the brigade council's major purpose was assisting in meeting the production targets and disciplining workers. Brigades at Rusmet were not given any time and space for autonomous decisions within the working area: only brigade councils held discussions and even here a production supervisor was present.

Westauto was the only one of the plants studied where teamwork was aligned with the international QM standards introduced. Brigade work at Rusauto was characterised by inertia of the socialist principles of brigade work that were not reconsidered by the management. Rusmet followed the traditional organisation of teamwork deliberately.

Integration of quality assurance responsibilities into brigades' tasks

Introduction of Japanese QM concepts in the Western automotive industry led to the involvement of groups on the shop-floor in kaizen activities, and resulted in other forms of group contributions to the company's performance targets. The following section will discuss which quality assurance responsibilities were integrated into brigade tasks in the three plants under study.

At Westauto, most of the tasks related to quality assurance within the working area were carried out by brigade leaders. Whole brigades were involved in problem-solving and were integrated into top-down goal setting for defect reduction, along with all other hierarchical levels at the plant. Brigade leaders also kept statistical records about defects in accordance with WPS, took care of the graphs for the brigade board (some of them were filled out once a day, others once a week or a month) and performed paperwork for registration of kaizen activities.

A defect or a process disturbance in a brigade was called a 'red mark'. Brigade leaders took the first decision on whether the defect could be fixed while the line was moving or if the car in question should be taken off the line. Production workers at Westauto did not try to conceal defects and reported them to the brigade leader:

When a worker has noticed a defect, he always reports it to the brigade leader. It is the brigade leader's job [to handle the defect]. The brigade leader

What about the workers? 143

takes a decision: either the defect is removed on the line (this is done by the brigade leader or by the worker if he has time) or this is done not on the line but in the repair zone.

(Interview WAT)

Problems that brigades encountered at work were classified as one of five categories: safety, quality, people, environment and delivery. Then it was decided whether the problem could be solved within a brigade. If this was not the case, a production supervisor was involved. This would typically be serious problems, such as equipment breakdown.

Problems that could be solved within a brigade were discussed at the brigade meetings. According to the Trade Union Coordinator, there was a real team spirit during such discussions:

If a problem can be solved within a brigade, then the brigade looks for a solution and writes it down. Then we work like a team indeed!

(Interview WAT)

Brigade leaders participated in breaking down the goals for defect reduction to the level of their brigades, after the plant-level goals were set by the headquarters and department-level goals were defined. The goals included the five above-mentioned defect categories (safety, quality, people, environment and delivery) and were formulated in accordance with the type of work the brigade was performing. The Production Manager emphasised that, although the brigade goals were not negotiable, they were achievable. Goal achievement was reviewed every three months.

The involvement of workers in quality assurance at Westauto met with some resistance, or at least misunderstanding from the local white-collar and engineering personnel:

The only way to assure quality is that one is responsible for the quality of one's own work. However, the main challenge is not how to involve [workers into quality assurance], but to want to involve them.

(Interview WAQ1)

The Human Resource Manager at Westauto observed that his tendency to ask for feedback from employees was not approved by the local specialists. The local Russian managers preferred 'a hard' treatment of employees to employee encouragement:

Russians can respect strong leadership in a way that might be offensive to Western Europeans. For example, your employees could say you need to be firmer as an example, you need to have more managerial assertiveness with employees. Whereas if we were from Britain or Germany we treat people a

144 *What about the workers?*

lot more softly and try and encourage them to do things, which is not necessarily the case here.... The good Russian managers tell me that I have to be harder [pressing with the thumb on the desk]. They tell me I have to be at least three times harder than I am.... I'm learning to recognise these things, so in making major decisions in implementing something, a new programme or whatever, I need to be careful to ask the locals: "Am I doing this the right way?" "Is this being presented in the right way?"

(Interview WAH1)

Thus, two work cultures were present at Westauto – the 'softer' Western culture, involving employees in quality assurance, and the authoritarian local culture of not engaging in a dialogue with subordinates. While the work procedures were formulated very much in the spirit of the participative culture, the Western managers faced some difficulties in winning backing from the specialists; this also surfaced with regard to workers' participation in updating work process descriptions discussed earlier.

At Rusauto, only brigade leaders participated in decisions about defects and repairs in the production line; their primary responsibility was to react to an *andon* signal along with the head of the production section and two employees from the quality department. They decided together whether the problem could be eliminated or the conveyer belt had to be stopped. Brigade leaders also collected information about the defects and they were instructed to update this information once an hour (compared to once a day at Westauto). The Head of the Department of Quality Assurance in Production observed, though, that production supervisors did not always look at this information once an hour, and this rule was a 'formality'. Hence, the regulations regarding quality were not stictly followed.

Brigades had no role in the exchange of information about quality-related problems between the shifts. According to the Head of the Department of Quality Assurance in Production, this was done at the level of line management. As discussed earlier, the major aim of the new managers at Rusauto was not to engage workers in quality assurance but to stop the concealing of defects on the shop-floor. The Personnel Director stated that the workers' resistance to the reporting of defects was due to the old production managers, who had not been and could not be substituted at the Car1 production line:

As we gain experience [with new QM concepts], we will involve direct workers into quality control operations, but there is a different ideology at Car1 now. Production and quality control are on different sides of the barricades. The former want to submit [the car to the quality inspectors] at any price and the latter are responsible for its quality. The main problem is management at all levels: from the Shop Manager to the Production Director – they all cannot be substituted at once.

(Interview RAH)

What about the workers? 145

Thus, Rusauto was very far from integrating quality assurance responsibilities into brigade tasks at the end of 2007. Production employees exercised pressure on the quality inspectors, trying to pass on the non-compliant vehicle. This behaviour was characteristic not only for workers, but also for production managers, who had not been substituted when the new managers were appointed at Rusauto. One explanation could be that the production managers lacked knowledge of new QM concepts. They continued to work as they used to under the planned economy, as they did not have the experience that the recently appointed managers had gained at the Russian–Western JV. Another explanation though might have to do with the remuneration system at the plant: the wage fund of the shop was directly linked to its output (see Section 5.5 for details). Resistance to reporting defects could therefore be the result not only of the inertia of the old work habits, but also of a rational strategy to increase pay.

Organisation of group work at Rusmet was still dominated by Soviet rhetoric, but contained some new elements. Brigade leaders carried out several concrete tasks related to quality assurance: repairs of defects and prevention of process disturbances and equipment breakdowns. However, brigade regulations contained a long list of other brigade leaders' tasks, which were hardly changed since the socialist era. These tasks addressed process improvement in a vague and formalistic way, without any reference to the new QM standards. For example, in 2007 the internal regulation on brigade work at Rusmet prescribed, among others:

- actively participating in introduction of the new progressive forms and advanced methods of work organisation, combination of qualifications, and multiple machine operation, to strive for raising work productivity and the decrease of product costs;
- developing and supporting brigade workers' initiative… in decreasing the labour-intensiveness of the products;
- organising the [labour] competition in the brigade together with the union representative, strengthening the labour and production discipline, facilitating the growth of qualifications and of the economic competencies of the brigade's members in every possible way; development of mentoring, invention and rationalisation.

Even though this description contained improvement tasks carried out by brigade leaders and brigade councils, they were not mentioned by management as a form of continuous improvement. This is a further indicator of the ritualistic character of these tasks.

Whole brigades competed for the best quality of work performance in the plant's 'labour competition' (described in Section 5.2 above). Contrary to the regulations on brigade work, criteria for evaluation of brigades in the labour competition were rethought and integrated with the new QM standards. However, workers' engagement in labour competition was not very high according to the management.

146   *What about the workers?*

The Quality Director observed that changing the personnel's attitude towards quality control had been the most challenging aspect of the introduction of new QM standards. Nevertheless, the management perceived that it had carried out a tremendous change in both employees' and specialists' attitudes to quality. The very concept of responsibility for quality vis-à-vis the customer had been new both for workers and engineering personnel at the start of the change process:

> The issue of the role of workers is more difficult than the others. It is more difficult to work with it. It is more difficult to find a person who is writing non-objective things. It is easier to find a systemic mistake. The 2.5 years that we spent on preparation for the certification are due to the personnel. I don't mean only workers, but also engineers. Before, we did not have the understanding of responsibility for quality.
>
> (Interview RMQ)

As was the case with Rusauto, Rusmet had to overcome false reporting during the introduction of new QM standards. However, in contrast to Rusauto, it used a strategy of intensive personnel training and also practised mentorship on the shop-floor to train the newcomers (discussed in the following section).

The form and degree of integration of quality-related tasks into the brigades' functions at the three plants differed. Westauto involved brigades in quality assurance on the basis of the principles that it applied at its other locations. Work organisation at the two local plants under study was still based on the principles of brigade work characteristic for the socialist path of industrial work. However, while Rusmet adjusted some of the old concepts to new QM standards following the logic of bricolage, brigade work at Rusauto did not get attention from a management whose main struggle was stopping defect concealment.

Summary: change in brigade work

The analysis of work organisation at the three plants shows that the introduction of new QM standards influenced brigade work only in two of the cases: Westauto and Rusmet. They had no significant impact in the case of Rusauto. Brigades at Westauto did not have the negative responsibility in production, characteristic of the socialist path of industrial work. Quality assurance tasks were an integrated part of brigades' formal functions. In the case of Rusmet, the socialist principles still dominated work organisation but some of these old ideas were reconsidered by the management and integrated with the new quality standards. Brigade leaders' functions were substantially changed, but brigades' tasks were only weakly affected. In the case of Rusauto, only brigade leaders received new responsibilities related to quality.

All three plants faced resistance from the local line management and employees in the course of change. While all three plants reported about resistance from the local specialists and line managers, Westauto was the only plant that did not mention employee resistance to the new tasks related to quality. It also seems to

What about the workers? 147

have succeeded in weakening resistance from local specialist and managers better than the two domestic plants. This can be explained, in part, by its entry mode to Russia as a greenfield plant, which freed it from some of the socialist legacy. At the same time, the union representatives at Westauto contributed to releasing the tensions on the shop-floor, a factor that was not present at the two local plants. Finally, the new approach to group work for Russia at Westauto was supported by its training and remuneration policies, discussed below. These policies at the two domestic plants still bore a significant legacy of the socialist time, which continued to reinforce the old path of industrial work.

5.4 Employee development and quality assurance competencies

A narrow technical approach to workers' qualifications and the exclusion of indirect competencies had been characteristic of the socialist path of industrial work since the early 1920s. This approach was taken as a basis for the *Soviet Wage Rate and Qualification Handbook for Workers* (*ETKS*), which had been obligatory under the planned economy and was still applied in the public system of vocational training and at many Russian companies after the market reforms. This approach to workers' qualification was both complementary to the principles of the organisation of production and work in the Complex Systems of production management and led to development of learning effects reinforcing the old path of industrial work.

In the West, the need to involve employees in quality assurance in accordance with the new QM concepts changed the competence requirements for direct workers. Employees on the shop-floor needed quality-related competencies and a better knowledge of production processes (cf. Sections 4.1–4.2). The following section will analyse if the introduction of international QM standards in the three plants under study resulted in a change in the companies' approaches to employee development and in a change of requirements for workers' competencies.

Qualification requirements and organisation of employee development

The entry-level qualification requirements at the three plants differed due to differences in production processes (see Section 5.1 above). Therefore, the present section will describe these requirements first and then analyse if the organisation of employee development was changed due to the introduction of new QM standards.

Production operators recruited by Westauto typically had a technical vocation school certificate (70 per cent) or engineering college certificates (26 per cent). Among operators, 4 per cent had completed higher education. Westauto did not pay attention to the specialisation the candidates had. According to the Trade Union Coordinator, less than 5 per cent of the workers had worked in a conveyer production plant before working at Westauto.

148   *What about the workers?*

The management at Wesauto emphasised that production processes in Russia did not require a highly qualified workforce. For example, welders in the body shop, who were among the most qualified, had to have a qualification corresponding to the third qualification rate out of six described in the *ETKS*. Due to a low degree of automation in production, the plant was primarily interested in the reliability of the workers:

> We train people but most of the processes and operations are very basic. Maybe we would train graduates less than people with a limited education, but all the processes are very basic. For instance, the process says: take a part, use one screw here and one screw there.
>
> (Interview WAS1)

> Here I need people with a lower qualification than in Europe. One needs highly qualified workers there to keep automation running. Here it is not about qualification, but about reliability [of workers].
>
> (Interview WAP)

However, even such relatively low entry qualification requirements were difficult to maintain due to a shortage of qualified workers in the local labour market.

It was difficult for Westauto not only to recruit people, but also to keep employees, as there was a very high attrition rate at the plant. This turned training into 'a conveyer belt' next to the production conveyer belt. Westauto carried out about 63.5 hours training per employee a year, which allowed it to train the newly hired employees and to compensate for the high employee turnover:

> Last year we had 25 per cent attrition on the hourly [employees], and about 20 per cent attrition in the office staff. That has improved this year, but we have to cope with an extremely high level of turnover. Imagine, this means that the whole personnel changes on average every four years. It's a big turnover... So, attrition is a problem for us and recruitment is a problem for us, because *we have to keep running to stand still*, but nevertheless we are doing well at the moment.
>
> (Interview WAH1, italics added)

> Before the employers used to choose employees for themselves, now it is the candidate who chooses an employer.... *Personnel training is a conveyer next to the [production] conveyer...* Qualification volume for the last year amounted to 145.978 hours, and these are only internal programmes.
>
> (Interview WAH2, italics added)

The Training Manager stated, though, that a significant part of training was so-called 'licence trainings', which permitted workers to perform certain kinds of work – that is, training on dangerous materials or work safety.

Employee development programmes at Westauto did not follow the *ETKS*, but were based on a qualification matrix developed by Westauto. In order to support

What about the workers? 149

on-the-job training, an internal system of mentoring had been introduced at the plant. Some brigade leaders appointed as mentors by the management were responsible for training and support of less experienced workers. Mentors were freed from direct work unless there was a shortage of workers. They could also be sent to other locations of Westauto for additional training.

Thus, Westauto did not rely much upon the public system of vocational training and carried out intensive employee training in house. This way, it did not have to align its list of required qualifications with the *ETKS* still in use in vocational schools and colleges.

Worker qualification requirements at Rusauto were not high either. According to the Personnel Director, the entry qualification requirements for workers at the Car1 line at Rusauto included completed secondary school or high school (nine or 11 years of schooling) or vocational school. Some of the production workers held technical college certificates and academic education diplomas.

Rusauto still followed the list of qualifications described in the *ETKS* and had collaboration agreements with vocational schools and technical colleges in the region. Trainees of these schools had an internship opportunity (*praktika*) at the plant and could then be employed by Rusauto. These schools shared the weaknesses common for Russian vocational training: obsolete equipment (even compared to the old machines at Rusauto) and outdated training content that did not include any information on the new approaches to QM and production organisation. Apart from this, these schools could train workers up to the third or fourth qualification rate only, which was not enough for real production settings. The average qualification rate at the plant was fifth to sixth. New employees could raise their qualification level at the Rusauto Training Center. The Center also trained people for the much needed qualifications of equipment maintainers and electro-mechanics. Many workers at Rusauto obtained an additional qualification in the Training Center, which increased the flexibility of job assignment for the plant. Workers were interested in having two qualifications, as they received a premium for substituting a colleague with a different qualification than what was stated in their employment contracts.

Qualification requirements for the Car2 production line were higher than for the Car1 line. Due to a much higher degree of automation at Car2, the plant needed a lot of equipment maintenance employees and software specialists and far fewer direct workers. There was a shortage of the required candidates in the labour market, but Rusauto attempted to attract new employees anyway to avoid retraining the people from the Car1 line. The new managers feared that the transfer of employees and line management from Car1 would cause the transfer of the old 'system of relations' in production, contributing to pushing a vehicle with defects further along the production process:

Partially, the people from Car1 [production line] will move to Car2 [production line], but we are afraid to transfer the system of relations that developed at Car1 along with transferring the employees. There shouldn't be too many of them.

(Interview RAH)

150 *What about the workers?*

In order to eliminate the old system of relations, all line management – from production supervisors to the shop managers – were to be newly recruited at the Car2 line. Both the Personnel Director and the Quality Director emphasised that the soft competencies of the candidates would play a crucial role in recruitment decisions. Openness, ability to learn and interest in working in the automotive industry were required from all candidates – from shop managers to workers.

The Personnel Director stated that Rusauto was considering stopping the use of the *ETKS* and instead developing a more simple classification of qualification levels for the Car2 production line. They discussed the option of having only three levels within a qualification for workers. In the meantime, the old Car1 line was characterised by the inherited labour force, outdated competence descriptions and old attitudes to work.

The educational background of employees at Rusmet was similar to that at the two other plants. The majority finished either secondary school or vocational training school (about 85 per cent). About 12 per cent had a technical college degree and 2 per cent had an academic education. Rusmet collaborated with a local vocational school and gave its students an internship opportunity at the plant during study time. The plant attempted to entice the trainees from the vocational school by remunerating the best of them. Depending on the trainees' skills and productivity, they could be paid per piece or paid a monthly premium. Trainees who came to the plant were assigned to a mentor (*nastavnik*), a highly qualified worker experienced in working with trainees.

The introduction of international QM standards at Rusmet had a profound impact on the organisation of employee development at the plant. In 2006, Rusmet developed a complete list of the skills and competencies at the plant, including new quality-related competencies, as a part of the preparation for QM audits by the foreign customers. The matrix was used to assess the needed and available competencies. The Head of Work Organisation and Pay Department stated that the matrix was also used to develop a completely new formalised approach to employee remuneration at the plant. Every direct and indirect worker's skills and competencies, and the actual operations and tasks she performed, were assessed. Subsequently every worker was ascribed a so-called 'appraisal rate' (*otsenochnyi uroven'*). This rate was used as a basis for calculation of monthly wages (see more in Section 5.5). The appraisal rates were updated every quarter. However, this new skill matrix was applied only at the plant internally, as vocational schools kept using the *ETKS*.

Another novelty with regard to employee development at Rusmet was that all training at the plant was structured according to the '5M' programme implemented by the German OEM, aimed at purchasing from Rusmet (see more on '5M' programme in Section 4.6). A new position was introduced during the change process, the 'Chief Auditor', who was responsible for auditing the QM system at the plant and also for managing all training activities there. The new programme was deployed gradually. First, the best workers, who were to work at the production line assigned to the German OEM, were selected and trained. After that, all other employees at Rusmet obtained additional training in

What about the workers? 151

quality-related competencies and skills. According to the plant's Training Coordinator, 370 people attended formal training in 2007. This number included those who attended at least one of the 'special' courses that were organised on request from the shops. Each of the courses lasted from ten to 40 hours.

Introduction of new QM standards also raised the importance of mentorship at Rusmet. Mentorship (*nastavnichestvo*) was applied at Rusmet to train newly employed workers and for further training:

> If a middle-aged or older person comes to us, he is sent to a mentor. If someone comes with the third [qualification] rate and we need the fourth, he is also sent to a mentor. When someone comes without any rate [without a vocational qualification], then he is assigned to a mentor for almost half a year.... Sometimes, people want to master one more qualification. Then they do it in their free time.
>
> (Interview RMH2)

As a result of the introduction of new QM concepts, management changed the system of remuneration for mentorship. In the past, only a small one-off premium was paid to the mentors. At the end of 2008, mentors started to get a much higher premium linked to their qualification level. They also started to receive a premium that depended on the trainees' grades at the final exam, which made mentorship very attractive, according to the Chief Auditor and Training Leader.

Introduction of new QM standards at Rusmet resulted in the development of a plant-specific formal system of competencies that was not based upon *ETKS*. Employee development activities became more formalised and a more intensive use of in-house training and learning began.

While all three plants operated under the same system of vocational training, two of the plants studied, Westauto and Rusmet, developed their own employee qualification systems, while Rusauto still relied on *ETKS* at the end of 2007. Intensive in-house employee development programmes were organised at both Westauto and Rusmet, and mentorship was used as a key mechanism for competence development on the shop-floor.

Quality assurance competencies on the shop-floor

Exclusion of indirect competencies had been characteristic of the socialist path of industrial work and was reinforced by the use of *ETKS*. Therefore, the following section will investigate if the introduction of new QM standards resulted in integration of quality-related competencies into direct workers' competence profiles.

At Westauto, quality assurance skills were an integral part of a worker's training, starting from their first day at the plant. The induction programme for new workers contained a large quality-related content. The programme included information on ISO 9000, work safety, environmental safety and the WPS. The workers first obtained some formal knowledge on quality assurance; then they were

152   *What about the workers?*

taught to look for the causes of problems ('fish-bone' diagram); after that, they learnt to implement these competencies in a game:

> Induction is conducted by internal trainers who are specialists in the departments. It lasts for three days. On the first day half an hour is devoted to quality issues; on the second day half a day is spent on the fish-bone method. On the third day there is a business game 'Henry's House'. It is organised as an imitation of the conveyer belt, and there is also the FTT [quality inspection].
>
> (Interview WAH2)

Quality-related training was also integrated into further training programmes at the plant as a part of technical skills training. Most of the technical training was highly relevant for quality assurance – for example, problem-resolution methodology, Six Sigma training, gauge evaluation, manufacturing engineering and synchronous material flow. About 10 per cent of the training time was dedicated to general skills training (e.g. leadership and communication skills). Thus, Westauto provided employees with the skills needed for working in accordance with WPS and WQOS without relying on the skills that workers had obtained during their vocational training or previous work experiences. It should be noted, though, that most of the training took place at the weekends and was not paid as working time.

Most of the content of the training programmes (for both technical and general skills) was transferred to Russia from Westauto's headquarters and then adjusted locally. Whereas the technical programmes were conducted almost unchanged in Russia (only with translations and minor terminological adjustments), the general skills programmes were adjusted more strongly to the local work culture. One of the adjustments was aimed at teaching the local line management to accept feedback and objections from workers. Another adjustment aimed at teaching production supervisors not to use threats in communicating with workers:

> We conduct such programmes as leadership through Russian providers... We adapt them to the cultural problems, such as 'I'm the boss and you're a fool'[3] – that is, to our system of communication and the system of blackmailing. For example, [the production supervisor says] "Do this and if you refuse, I will go to the Human Resource Manager" – this is taken into account in the leadership programme for [production] supervisors.
>
> (Interview WAH2)

Thus, Westauto attempted to change the local managers' negative attitudes to bottom-up communication with subordinates through training programmes.

Westauto carried out some training in house and some with external partners in the city. The practical technical training was conducted in house; the general skills programmes (e.g. leadership) were entrusted to local organisations. Formal courses on standardised QM and production organisation concepts (e.g. kaizen, waste elimination, total productive maintenance (TPM)) were conducted off the

What about the workers? 153

job at the local technical university. The first quality auditors at Westauto had been trained in ISO 900 at an international certification organisation in Russia, since there had been no specialists for the QM department in the local market when Westauto opened the Russian plant.

In sum, quality assurance competencies played a central role in Westauto's training programmes. This represented a novelty compared to the persistent path of industrial work in Russia. Westauto provided employees with competencies they needed for working according to the WPS and WQOS without any collaboration with the local vocational schools, which still adhered to the *ETKS*.

Rusauto did not plan to carry out any quality-related training for the shop-floor workers at the end of 2007. In the future, the Personnel Director hoped to begin employing workers who had studied in the new vocational training programmes recently started by Rusauto Holding. These programmes were developed for schools and colleges collaborating with Rusauto, with the aim of bringing the skills of vocational school graduates to a level corresponding to the requirements of the industry. On-the-job training time was to be reduced to a month, students were supposed to learn two to three qualifications and lean production was to be a part of the study programme. This initiative was, however, too recent to cover the current needs of the Rusauto plant for workers for both Car1 and Car2 production lines.

Instead of retraining workers for the Car2 production line, Rusauto planned to reduce their role in quality assurance and to invest in engineering competence in design of quality assurance processes and automated means of quality inspection. The quality department had to be expanded by the start of Car2 production, but finding specialists was difficult. At the end of 2007, requirements for the candidates included technical education and English-language skills; no knowledge of QM was expected. The Quality Director admitted that they were ready to recruit people without prior work experience in the automotive industry and train them internally. The training might also include study visits to the Western partners' locations abroad.

Introduction of new QM concepts at Rusauto did not result in integration of quality-related competencies into the competence profiles of shop-floor workers. Both Car1 production line and the prospective Car2 line were characterised by exclusion of indirect competences from direct workers' competence profiles.

At Rusmet, introduction of international QM standards resulted in the integration of quality-related competencies in workers' training programmes. In addition, a group of prospective line managers was established, who were trained in the new QM philosophy and techniques by German management consultants.

Rusmet organised in-house training in quality-related competencies for the shop-floor. Training in quality-related competencies became a part of the induction and about one third of the formal courses at the plant were devoted to QM – for example, working with reclamations. Induction was organised as a two-week off-the-job training programme. Training for new employees could last from four to six months, depending on their job and qualification. All employees at the plant were trained in new topics: knowledge of the enterprise's policy regarding QM,

154 *What about the workers?*

statistical process control and knowledge of the critical characteristics in the technical drawings in connection with FMEA. A prospective German customer assisted Rusmet in learning to apply FMEA (a standardised approach to prevention of defects that is carried out before the start of the series phase of manufacturing), along with other QM standards.

Although all workers in the plant were trained in quality-related competencies, the management introduced a special 'pass' that personnel needed to be allowed to work at the German production line. The export production line had priority in terms of manning in case of personnel shortages and differed from the other production facilities, with a slower pace of work.

> People, who work for the German OEM are assigned to this equipment. We keep special training protocols for these people.... However, it is difficult for us to keep this assignment because of personnel fluctuation.
>
> The order from the German customer has priority for us. When necessary, we transfer people there from other work. People appreciate that, even though they would be able to earn more if they work on an order for, say, a Russian agriculture machine manufacturer. There they can just 'hammer out' [manufacture fast and not necessarily accurately] more within the same time.
>
> (Interview RMH2)

More accurate and slower pace of work at the export line meant lower wages for workers due to the piece-rate remuneration at Rusmet (see Section 5.5). Therefore, the need for the special pass might have to do with the need to select the workers who would not strive to increase their pay by compromising with quality of work performance.

In addition to training shop-floor workers, Rusmet had a programme of 'continuous learning' for prospective line managers. This programme was conceived as a way to solve the problem of the absence of qualified line managers that Rusmet was facing. Technical employees at Rusmet lacked the competencies needed for working according to the new QM principles in order to be promoted. Additionally, there was a generation gap between the 'older' and 'younger' managers:

> We have a problem with managers now. If our managers are young, then they don't quite have the understanding. If they are old, then they have difficulty switching to something new.
>
> (Interview RMH1)

The Director of Rusmet, who initiated and led the QM change, started up this programme for line management together with the German consultants. About 20–5 'talented and young' people aged 25–40 were selected in production. They were trained for three months by the German management consultants and were then trained further by the quality assurance department.

What about the workers? 155

The group existed for a whole year, but was abandoned after a new plant director had been appointed by the holding headquarters. The new director did not support the programme:

> This group was conceived as people who would later spread the received knowledge within the plant. It was the so-called 'turbo-group'... The goal of our former director was continuous learning.... Now this has died and there is no further advancement. Some of the employees from the turbo-group have even already left the plant.
>
> (Interview RMH2)

The lack of interest in the 'turbo-group' from the new director might be explained by the fact that he was appointed when Rusmet had already introduced international QM standards and qualified for exporting to the West. He might have perceived the start of exporting as the achievement of the ultimate goal rather than reaching a tentative state that had to be continuously sustained and developed further. Apart from the discontinuation of the 'turbo-group', the new director suspended the link between wage and qualification level of the employees (see Section 5.5).

The introduction of new QM concepts at Rusmet resulted in a departure from the exclusion of indirect competencies from direct workers' qualification, characteristic of the old path of industrial work. With assistance from a German customer and a German consulting company, Rusmet was able to establish in-house training in quality-related competencies for both workers and prospective line managers.

Summary: change in employee development

Two out of the three studied enterprises, Westauto and Rusmet, deviated from the narrow technical approach to direct workers' qualification, which had been characteristic of the planned economy and was still reinforced by the *ETKS* after the market reforms. At these plants, the introduction of international QM standards created a need for new quality assurance competencies on the shop-floor.

Westauto and Rusmet developed new training programmes without collaborating with the public vocational training institutions. Westauto adapted its internal training programmes applied at other locations and collaborated with local QM certification organisations and a university. Rusmet drew on its collaboration with German partners, when it developed new employee training programmes. Both Westauto and Rusmet revived the socialist practice of mentorship on the shop-floor. Mentorship enabled dissemination of knowledge on quality assurance and other aspects of production and work within the company. New organisation of employee development at these plants weakened the coordination effects with the public system of vocational training, still applying the *ETKS*.

Learning effects reinforcing the old path of industrial work were weakened at Westauto and Rusmet as well. However, the scope of quality-related competencies

156   *What about the workers?*

in workers' training at Westauto was broader than at Rusmet, which corresponded to quality-related responsibilities integrated into production workers' functions at these two plants. Both Westauto and Rusmet developed line managers' quality-related competencies along with those of workers.

Development of plant-specific competence lists at Westauto and Rusmet became the basis for the personnel development programmes and remuneration systems at these two plants (discussed in the following section). High formalisation of personnel development activities and the clarity of the impact of employees' qualifications and competencies on their wages restricted the arbitrariness of management decisions regarding remuneration and so weakened the punitive character of industrial work at these two plants.

No change in employee training programmes was made at the Car1 line at Rusauto. Instead of developing the competencies of their own employees for the Car2 line, Rusauto planned to attract new workers. Rusauto hoped to eliminate unwanted behaviour on the shop-floor by hiring new staff, despite the shortage of qualified staff at all levels, which all three plants were facing. At the time of the study, learning effects reinforcing the old path of industrial work remained in place and hampered the new managers' efforts to change employees' behaviour in production.

The analysis also shows that the personal traits and the soft skills of local employees, and line managers in particular, played a significant role in the introduction of new QM standards, along with quality-related competencies. All three plants were eager to find employees who possessed such qualities as 'openness' and 'ability to learn'. However, only Westauto viewed authoritarian communication in Russia as a barrier to its production and QM systems. Therefore, development of egalitarian communication skills was a part of line managers' training at Westauto. In this way, Westauto attempted to combat the persistent deeply rooted work attitudes and communication skills that its Russian personnel had developed prior to their employment at Westauto. These efforts were, however, challenged by the high attrition at the plant, which meant short employment periods.

5.5 Remuneration, bonuses and sanctions for performance quality on the shop-floor

The Soviet approach to remuneration bound the elements of the socialist path of industrial work together. Calculation of the constant share of pay in the industry was based upon workers' qualifications described in the *ETKS*. The variable share of pay consisted of diverse bonuses. Some of them targeted the 'quantitative side of work' and were designed to assist the management in meeting output targets; others aimed at achieving an acceptable level of product quality by rewarding the 'quality of work performance'. Calculation of bonuses was not transparent and clear for employees; management had high discretion in decisions on wages. Remuneration systems were also linked to work organisation on the shop-floor: many of the bonuses were paid for brigade performance and the borders between individual and brigade responsibility were blurred. Thus the

What about the workers? 157

socialist approach to remuneration was integrated with other elements of the socialist path of industrial work. The complementarity of these elements impeded the change of individual elements, such as quality control, even after the market reforms.

Management continued to use withdrawal of bonuses to discipline workers after the market reforms. Its discretion with regard to calculation of bonuses increased due to poor reinforcement of the labour laws in the post-socialist era. This sharpened the punitive character of remuneration systems after the start of the transition (see Section 3.7).

Fear of admitting mistakes on the shop-floor hampered employees' contribution to quality assurance, which is central in the new QM ideas (see Section 4.1). Therefore, the following section will analyse whether the plants designed new remuneration systems that supported integration of quality assurance tasks – product quality checks, solving problems and improving production processes – into functions of the shop-floor workers. The section will first present a general overview of the remuneration systems at the plants and then discuss bonuses and sanctions related to quality of work performance.

Remuneration systems and bonuses for quality of work performance

Approaches to remuneration at two Russian plants still bore characteristics inherited from the past: the variable share of pay played a central role in disciplining workers and the borders between individual and brigade contributions to work results were blurred. Westauto did not use monetary incentives to discipline workers. Instead, the management at this plant linked pay to in-house competence development and career progression.

The expatriate managers at Westauto observed the paramount importance of pay for Russian employees; all non-monetary incentives played an inferior role:

> Obviously pay is very important, but in some of our other locations maybe there are some supplementary benefits that always also get a lot of attention, but here it tends to be mainly pay. You know, 'Yes we are interested in some supplementary benefits,' but 'What's the pay?'
>
> (Interview WAH1)

Yet, the remuneration system at this plant did not contain a variable share of pay. The wage system for hourly paid employees comprised a few career steps with clearly defined progression criteria. There were only two grades (A and B), with four wage levels in each of them. All unskilled jobs (e.g. cleaning, unpacking) had been outsourced. The wage grades regulated career progression for semi-skilled or skilled workers only.

A-grade was for semi-skilled production operators and B-grade was for skilled mechanics, electricians or technical maintenance workers. A worker had to gain work experience on the job, obtain the skills for doing more than one job and complete some mandatory training in order to progress within a grade. A worker

158 *What about the workers?*

could move from A1 to A2 after half a year, from A2 to A3 after a year and from A3 to A4 after 1.5 to two years. Beginning with the switch from A2 to A3, kaizen activities were included in progression requirements. In order to move from A2 to A3, a worker had to submit three improvement suggestions; in order to move from A3 to A4, a worker had to complete a project within the working area and to show ability to train other people. The Training Manager notes, however, that workers could quickly reach the maximum wage level within A-grade (within 1.5 years). But progressing to the B-grade was problematic, as there were few vacancies at this grade. Thus, workers were not motivated to improve their performance after 1.5 years of employment at Westauto.

Westauto had no monetary incentives for quality of work performance. Quality of individual work performance was not even evaluated. Yet, the quality of brigade performance was measured by the number of 'red marks' that a brigade received (see Section 5.3 on work organisation above). The brigades that received the fewest 'red marks' were given small symbolic rewards:

> Until now we have not found a universal reward method. We practised the 'board of honours' in the shop, gave out vouchers for Ikea for 500 roubles [about 11 euros]. We tried to order a pie for a brigade in our canteen, as a brigade form [of incentive], which the brigade could then eat when convenient... There is no strict link 'fulfilled – received'.
>
> (Interview WAQ1)

The union attempted to convince the management to introduce monetary incentives for quality improvements. They had two suggestions: to link the size of rewards to the amount of savings resulting from improvement suggestions (this practice was common at the German automotive firms, where pilot interviews were conducted) or to pay a premium to the brigades that show the best performance (as in the traditional approach to pay). The management declined both options, even though they admitted that the motivating effect of the symbolic rewards was low.

Thus, the remuneration system at Westauto was based on a career progression scheme, which motivated new production operators to acquire new competencies, improve quality of their work performance and train others during the first 1.5 years of employment. The management refused using monetary incentives at its Russian location, despite requests from the union.

The management at Rusauto did not change the remuneration system for production workers; their pay still contained a high variable share. They did, however, change the rules for pay to quality inspectors in order to combat informal deals between quality inspectors and workers about passing the defects along the line.

The workers' remuneration consisted of three parts: a time-based wage, an individual bonus and a shop bonus. Time-based wage was calculated on the basis of workers' qualification and wage rates – Rusauto still used the *ETKS* at the end of 2007. But if workers had qualifications that were difficult to find in the labour

What about the workers? 159

market, the management made special individual remuneration agreements with them.

Production supervisors disposed of funds that they used for individual bonuses to workers within their production sections. They appraised every worker's performance monthly, using the KTU, which helped distribute the money within the production section:

> There are no criteria for the performance of individual workers; there are only criteria for a production section. Within a production section, the production supervisors appraise their people through the so-called KTU. The KTU is ascribed monthly and this bonus is paid from the production supervisor's fund. There are no formal criteria. Production supervisors appraise the workers subjectively.
>
> (Interview RAH)

The absence of formal criteria in assigning KTU allowed for a high degree of arbitrariness in production supervisors' decisions.

The shop bonus was very important to the workers, since it amounted to about 30 per cent of the basic wage. The size of the shop wage fund depended on the monthly output of the shop. Workers were paid the highest shop bonus if the shop reached the output targets and they had not manufactured defects. If quality inspectors discovered defects, workers' bonuses were reduced. The Quality Director stated that production workers would strike informal deals with quality inspectors about not reporting the defects and keeping the bonuses. According to him, the existing remuneration system reinforced this practice:

> Workers at our plant get the highest bonus for the quantity of outcome and for the number of defects. I think it is wrong. Taking into account the poverty, 1,000 roubles [about 22 euros] can be a question of a family's survival. Our people are simple – there will be deals, kickbacks in a production line, when production workers give part of their earnings to the controllers to keep the bonuses.
>
> (Interview RAQ1)

Workers at Rusauto not only did not want to report defects, but also were ready to bribe the quality inspectors in order to keep their bonuses. At the same time, some workers deliberately caused damage in production. The Quality Director explained this by workers' dissatisfaction with the size of wages and estimated that 3–5 per cent of defects were caused deliberately.

The new managers were aware of the drawbacks of workers' remuneration system, but its future direction remained ambiguous. The Personnel Director advocated greater transparency and clarity of remuneration system for workers and simplification of qualification and wage rates. He believed that the workers should see how their performance influenced their earnings. The Quality Director supported simplification of bonus payments as well and wanted to substitute

160   *What about the workers?*

monthly shop bonuses with an annual bonus. He thought, however, that employees' performance should have no direct impact on the size of their bonuses:

> We are considering an option where bonuses are paid once a year – for example, 5 per cent a year.... The idea is that the person does not know when he is remunerated and there is no sense of creating a special [informal bargaining] system.
>
> (Interview RAQ1)

The Quality Director believed that the only way to stop informal bargaining between workers and quality inspectors was to remove the link between the variable share of pay and the quality of work performance.

In the meantime, the new managers tried to strengthen the ability of quality inspectors to resist production by formally subordinating production to the quality department and changing the inspectors' remuneration. Until that change, quality inspectors had earned less than production workers. They had typically been approaching retirement age, had not been respected by the production staff and had even feared them. The earnings of quality inspectors had depended positively on the quality of the vehicles – that is, the more defects they found, the lower their bonus was:

> We fundamentally changed the motivation system. When we came, it was so that the more defects the quality controllers found, the lower their bonus was. We removed all special reasons that could influence the work of the quality department. We made it independent from everybody.
>
> (Interview RAQ1)

> The inspectors are the same people now as before, but they have more responsibility. They are given a voice now. We 'revitalise' the person, and teach him not to be afraid of the production staff. *They* are responsible for the quality of this vehicle and *not production*.
>
> (Interview RAP, italics added)

By changing the remuneration to quality inspectors, the new managers at Rusauto struggled to better detach responsibility for quality from production functions and not to integrate it.

At the time of the interviews, the socialist legacy was very strong in the remuneration system at Rusauto. Generally low pay, high discretion of line managers in determination of its variable share and workers' fear of withdrawal of bonuses gave the remuneration system at Rusauto a punitive character. The pay system at Rusauto differed from the traditional way of remunerating workers under a planned economy by lower significance of brigade bonuses. These were substituted by bonuses to production sections.

Rusmet developed a new remuneration system while it was preparing for the audit by its prospective German customer. The new system was based upon

What about the workers? 161

formal personnel appraisal and the new competence matrix discussed above. Three main elements of the new system included the employee's *appraisal score* (AS), productivity and quality of work performance. The new remuneration rules were tested in the production line for the German OEM first and then applied throughout the plant in 2006. The trade union at the plant supported the new remuneration system, as workers' bonuses were not reduced arbitrarily, and the system was more just than before. The new system was, however, changed again by the new plant director appointed by the holding headquarters in 2008. He took this decision without prior discussion with the Head of Work Organisation and Pay Department and despite resistance in production. The second change represented a U-turn to collectivist remuneration, with a strong focus on the amount of output and much less attention to quality.

The first change in the remuneration system

Rusmet carried out systematic appraisal of all employees and workplaces as a part of the introduction of the new QM standards. All workers received an AS, which was based on all competencies (including quality-related ones) and actual tasks performed. This system represented an alternative to the qualification and wage rates described in the *ETKS*. The ASs varied from 1 to 6; the basic wage for these scores varied between 2,550 and 8,000 roubles. They were used as a base for calculation of two bonuses (for 'productivity' and for 'quality of work performance'). This way, workers were motivated to raise their qualification level and attain new competencies.

A productivity bonus was designed to stimulate workers' output; no limits to the output were set. Quite to the contrary, workers were stimulated to produce up to double their norms and even higher. If a worker fulfilled her output plan (100 per cent of the norm), she received 25 per cent of the AS; the higher the output, the higher the bonus she received. Thus production outputs varied a lot as more productive workers compensated the poor performance of their less productive colleagues.

The bonus for quality of work performance was aimed at assuring the workers' compliance with the new quality regulations. Rusmet used the following criteria to calculate it:

1. Defects discovered by the quality inspectors.
2. Fulfilment of the requirements of the QM system.
3. Carrying out statistical quality checks.
4. Filling out 'productivity' documents.
5. Labour discipline (coming late, drinking etc.).
6. 'Production culture' (order and cleanliness in the workplace, which was checked by a special commission once a week).

If an employee did not receive warnings in any of the criteria, her bonus for quality of work performance amounted to 50 per cent of the AS. One warning reduced

162 *What about the workers?*

the bonus to 35 per cent and two to 20 per cent. With three or more warnings the worker did not receive any bonus for quality of work performance. The Head of Work Organisation and Pay Department noted that the size of the bonus had a strong motivating potential, but workers could get the whole bonus without much effort. Therefore, she believed that the management should have designed more challenging criteria.

Although the remuneration system was time-based, workers were paid only for the time they actually worked. They were not paid for idle time, irrespective of its causes. In order to register the causes, the management introduced the 'personal time control cards' discussed above, which was supported by the union. Workers registered their working time on the. Workers' bonuses were only reduced if they were responsible for the interruptions in production.

The company U-turn on the remuneration system

The new director eliminated the individual ASs from the remuneration system and returned to piece-rate wages. According to the Head of Work Organisation and Pay Department, he hoped that this would assist Rusmet in reducing the idle times and meeting the output targets. As under the planned economy, piece-rate wages were calculated for the whole brigade and were then distributed among the brigade members on the basis of the KTU:

> KTU will be the basis of the new system... KTU will be linked to fulfilling the output norm [by the brigade]. For example, if the output norm is the production of 600 parts, then it will be one KTU for a brigade. It will then be divided between the brigade's members, depending on the individual contribution.
>
> (Interview RMH1)

The new director also reduced the weight of the bonus for quality of work performance from 50 per cent to 20 per cent of the basic rate. Thus, the role of quality of work performance weakened and employees' competence levels did not influence earning any longer. The Head of Work Organisation and Pay Department believed that the new remuneration system would not help reduce idle times, as they were caused by the weakness of internal material planning and logistics. She noted that the new pay rules were a quick fix to the problem and not a working solution:

> We have large losses of working time. People keep sitting as they cannot work. At the same time, we say that there is a shortage of people. When a shop manager says, let us send people home and shorten the working day, then the shop manager is fired, as one must not tell the truth. It was different under our former director [of the plant].
>
> (Interview RMH1)

The second change in the remuneration system was followed by other signs of a return to arbitrary management behaviour at Rusment.

What about the workers? 163

Production employees resisted the collectivist remuneration system and resorted to strikes. They were dissatisfied with the levelling of the earnings in the new system. Levelling seemed inevitable to both the Head of Work Organisation and Pay Department and the production supervisors:

> Production supervisors come and complain to me that this will be a kolkhoz [collective farm] again... We've always had the 'bees', who come and work without raising their heads. And there are 'flies', who come, sit down, put their heads on their arms and, if they are not urged to work, then they won't do hardly anything. Our [previous] system gave these bees a chance to earn and weeded the flies out. And if we depart from the current system, it will be a levelling again. It will just make no sense to work for the bees. Some of them have a husband, others – not. Before, they could even stay until eight, as they knew that they would earn for that. If all that is divided equally, they won't do it. Who will work then? KTU worked in the Soviet time, when we had the conscientiousness. We could then divide everything equally, but now it won't work. There will be a war on KTU again.
>
> (Interview RMH1)

Workers' attitudes to work were very diverse – from extreme diligence to complete negligence. The new pay system was not able to raise productivity by rewarding the effort, as production processes and material planning were very uneven. The Head of Work Organisation and Pay Department noted that employees tended to justify the underperforming colleagues and assign equal KTUs:

> It is difficult for us to work with KTU. We are kind-hearted: we take pity in everybody and smooth out [the conflicts]. We say, it is not his fault, as there was no metal [material for working].
>
> (Interview RMH1)

The first change in remuneration at Rusmet aimed to support the introduction of new QM standards based on transparent rules rewarding individual output and quality of work performance. The new Plant Director at Rusmet, appointed when the QM standards had been in place, returned to brigade-based piece rates – a Soviet remedy to uneven production processes. He took this authoritarian decision despite the opposition of middle management and production supervisors, and the trade unions' protests against the new rules did not prevent the new director from introducing them. The ease of this change at this Russian enterprise shows how important individual actors are for the sustainability of new policies.

The analysis of remuneration systems at the three plants shows that Westauto departed from the socialist approach to pay the most. This plant developed a simple, formalised and transparent system that did not contain monetary bonuses linked to either workers' output or quality of work performance. Rusmet first developed a formalised remuneration system linked to individual performance,

164 *What about the workers?*

and integrated with the requirements of the new QM standards. Then, however, Rusmet abandoned the new system and returned to the Soviet approach to pay. This case shows how reversible and shaky the achieved change at Russian industrial enterprises was. Rusauto followed the old remuneration approach: it used *ETKS* to calculate wages and had a high variable share of pay on the shop-floor. Rusauto only changed the pay rules to quality inspectors. Their status at the plant was improved to allow them to better resist the pressure from production. Workers at both Rusauto and Rusmet continued to conceal defects in fear of losing bonuses.

Sanctions for quality of work performance

Sanctions were an important means of control on shop-floor in the socialist path of industrial work. The TQM movement emphasised, on the contrary, that elimination of fear was an indispensable precondition for finding the root causes of problems on the shop-floor. The very notion of 'sanctions' is absent from the contemporary debate on incentive systems in Western industry. The following section will discuss which sanctions were applied in the three plants studied and how these sanctions depended on the quality of work performance on the shop-floor.

There were three levels of sanctions at Westauto: verbal warning, the first written warning and second written warning, followed by a dismissal. Quality Manager 1 notes, however, that dismissals were very rare. The management tried to keep the employees due to the high attrition rate at the plant. Therefore, employees who received the second warning were moved to a less responsible job:

> If it happens for the second time, we lower the responsibility level of the station [where the employee is working]. If he is working at the control station – this work is cushy and is considered a good working place – then he can be transferred to the assembly operation. I cannot remember any dismissals. It is always possible to find a less interesting and difficult job, where the employee can be transferred, up to a cleaner. There is no limit to perfection as the saying goes.
>
> (Interview WAQ1)

The fact that the management avoided dismissing employees resembled the 'punish-but-retain' logic applied under a planned economy (discussed in Sections 2.2 and 2.5). Westauto's approach was, however, very different, since the employee was not allowed to carry out the same job.

Both the Production Manager and the Human Resource Manager at Westauto emphasised the importance of developing a 'no-blame' attitude towards mistakes:

> We don't want to use any disciplinary measures. We want to motivate and have no fear. Under normal quality measures, there is no need to use

What about the workers? 165

disciplinary means. There is no punishment, as it causes anxiety. When workers are afraid, they do not communicate any longer… In order to optimise the process together with employees, you need open communication.

(Interview WAP)

The management distinguished between unintended and deliberate misconduct and only applied sanctions in the case of intended misconduct or violation of process requirements:

Sanctions are applied in cases of malicious damage – for example, [a recent case with] bumper painting. The employee has not followed the process [description] in order to save 50 per cent of the cycle time.

(Interview WAP)

The Trade Union Coordinator confirmed that sanctions at Westauto were only applied in cases of deliberate discipline violation.

While the expatriate management tried to avoid punitive measures, in order not to cause fear on the shop-floor, this attitude was not common among the local line managers. The Production Manager stated that this approach was new for his Russian colleagues and developing it was the main challenge in his work at Westauto in Russia. Local line management and specialists resisted the expatriates' attempt to have open communication with workers.

Three factors seem to explain the abating occurence of threats at Westauto, compared to the local industrial plants. There was no variable share of pay, hence the discretion of the line management was restricted. Westauto also developed the local employees' ability to communicate without threats in soft skills training (discussed in Section 5.4). Finally, the independent and active union played an important role in the prevention of the abuse of power by line management:

It used to be different earlier. There were cases of power abuse by the management. For example, in 2003 a manager refused to sign for a worker's grade [switch], only because the manager didn't know him [the worker] in person. Now there are no such tensions. When a manager wants to talk to a worker, a union representative is invited. They [the managers] even prefer such an invite.

(Interview WAT)

The absence of threats in communication on the shop-floor was, thus, a result of continued efforts, not only by the expatriate managers, but also by the union.

The management at Rusauto had only two formal sanctions: a reprimand from a production supervisor signed by the shop manager and a severe reprimand, which was supposed to be followed by dismissal. Workers were frequently dismissed for drinking. For example, ten people in the welding shop were fired for drinking within the month prior to the interviews at the plant.

The managers noted, however, that only the most blatent discipline violators were fired. In other cases, the management tried to avoid dismissals, as it was

166 *What about the workers?*

difficult to find substitutes for the employees fired. Most frequently, the management withdrew bonuses in the case of misconduct:

> For example, at the Russian–Western OEM where I worked before, the only sanction would be to fire an employee; here we take away the bonus. One of the managers at an American supplier in Russia, for example, says 'If, after a warning, we have to make another warning then why is he working here?' So, their policy is persuasion and training first, and then if something is wrong – firing straight away. We could also fire a lot of people, but where will we get new ones?
>
> (Interview RAQ1)

The management at Rusauto did not see any alternative to punishing-but-retaining the misbehaving workers in their jobs.

There were no elaborate formal criteria for either the shop bonus or individual bonus at Rusauto, as discussed above. Therefore, the management had significant discretion over administering the bonuses. At the same time, worker-caused defects were tightly intertwined to equipment-caused mistakes at Rusauto (see Section 5.2), which gave the withdrawal of the bonus an arbitrary character. Such use of sanctions demotivated workers from reporting defects in production and thus perpetuated the old logic of quality control.

Rusmet followed the sequence of sanctions that included a first reprimand, second reprimand and then dismissal. Management at Rusmet also faced a shortage of workforce and was reluctant to fire employees. Employees were not fired on quality-related issues; only drinking could lead to a dismissal:

> The point is that we have now encountered the lack of workforce in the labour market. The wages at our plant are higher than the average in the city, but we can still feel the shortage of personnel. The reasons sufficient for a dismissal are drinking, unexplained absence... but now, even after an unexplained absence, people are not necessarily dismissed.
>
> (Interview RMQ)

Rusmet had to put up with severe violations of work discipline, and attempted to discipline workers by monetary sanctions. The primary sanction applied at Rusmet was withdrawing a part of a worker's bonus. The bonus was decreased in the case of a violation of quality assurance regulations or when a worker passed on a defective part. If a worker did not fill out the statistical control card, for example, 1,500 roubles were withdrawn from her bonus.[4] When a defective product was passed on, the worker responsible for it had the cost of the part deducted from his bonus.[5] Rusmet did not distinguish between unintended and deliberate misconduct when reducing the bonuses:

> Sanctions are applied in case of damage caused by the employees' fault [sic]. For example, he set up the machine wrongly or missed a defect or committed

What about the workers? 167

something else *unintentionally*.... We punish materially – we withdraw a part of the bonus. This is defined by a production supervisor, the head of the shop or by the technologist. The worker pays up to 100 per cent of the damage, which makes about 30–40 per cent of his earnings.

(Interview RMQ, italics added)

Sanctions for unintended damage were likely to cause tensions among workers and a resistance to reporting defects for two reasons. First, worker-caused defects at Rusmet were tightly intertwined with equipment-caused defects, as equipment was unreliable (see Section 5.2). Second, workers' earnings depended primarily on the number of parts produced and workers were not paid for idle times, even if these were not due to workers' conduct.

The Production Director noted that, ideally, no sanctions should be needed, but about 20 per cent of the workers at the plant would deliberately pass on the defective part to the next operation in order to receive the pay for it:

It ought to be that workers don't need a whip. This should be already in their blood, like with the Japanese. Now we have cases when, after manufacturing a defect, they attempt to pass it on [along the process]. The ratio [of workers who do it and not] is approximately 80 to 20; 80 per cent are conscientious workers who send the defect to the 'isolator' and 20 per cent are the ones who allow the defect to pass on to the next operation. But this is a defect that they discover after the work has already been invested and then they want to get paid for it. There are no cases when someone finds a defect and passes it on.

(Interview RMP)

Thus, the monetary sanctions demotivated workers from reporting defects. The management, however, did not address this mechanism, as they believed that employees behaved this way due to the lack of conscientiousness in their attitudes to work.

The application of sanctions at Rusmet bears a lot of similarities to the case of Rusauto. In both cases, withdrawal of bonuses allowed management to 'punish-but-retain' the employees under the condition of a labour shortage. At the same time, fear of losing bonuses and piece-rate pay pushed workers not to report defects. From the three plants studied, only Westauto did not use the variable share of pay as punishment on the shop-floor.

Summary: change in the remuneration systems

The analysis shows that all three enterprises studied changed their remuneration systems following the introduction of the new QM standards. Only Westauto, however, designed a remuneration system that supported integration of quality-related tasks into direct workers' functions. Remuneration systems at both Rusauto and Rusmet continued to reinforce the old path of industrial work. Even

168 *What about the workers?*

though Rusmet had first significantly deviated from the punitive principles of pay, with the introduction of the new QM standards, it returned to them again when the change of QM was completed.

While Westauto radically deviated from the socialist approach to pay, the two Russian plants modified the traditional principles. Westauto and Rusmet developed new competence matrixes for their employees and thus weakened the complementarity with the narrow worker qualification profiles described in the *ETKS*. The subsequent return to piece-rate pay at Rusmet, however, made workers' qualification level insignificant for their pay. The remuneration system at Rusauto was still based upon the *ETKS*.

Other principles of the socialist approach to pay were high reliance on withdrawable bonuses to discipline workers, significant management discretion in determining them and blurred borders between individual and collective responsibility. Westauto did not use the variable share of pay to either reward or to punish employees. Both Rusmet and Rusauto still saw no alternative to the withdrawable bonuses in order to punish-but-retain their employees, as was the case under the planned economy. The management at the two Russian plants withdrew bonuses in cases of both intentional and unintentional mistakes, in spite of the fact that production machinery was unreliable and worker- and machine-caused mistakes were hard to distinguish. The rules for calculation of the variable share of pay allowed for management discretion and blurred individual and collective responsibility. The amount of pay at these plants allowed for management discretion and blurred individual and collective responsibility.

As a result, workers at both Russian plants were afraid of revealing mistakes. All in all, the punitive character of such remuneration systems sharpened compared to the socialist era. As social welfare shrank after the market reforms, the amount of pay became more important for family survival in Russia.

5.6 Conclusion: impact of international quality management standards on the path of industrial work in Russia

The introduction of international QM standards affected production work in all three plants studied. Yet, the patterns of change in the four elements of industrial work differed. The following section will first summarise the change in each of the four elements analysed and will then discuss the role of foreign partners and internal learning processes in this change.

The first element of industrial work analysed in the chapter was organisation of quality assurance. The aim was to find out whether the change in quality assurance led to integration of new quality-related tasks into the functions of shop-floor workers. All three plants implemented some of the international management standards regulating the way they assured quality. These standards included ISO 9000, lean production and statistical process control (SPC), among others. At Westauto these concepts were integrated under the umbrellas of the WPS and WQOS. Both Rusauto and Rusmet stated that they introduced the principles of lean production at the plants, but their approaches to organisation of production

What about the workers? 169

and QM had a more patchwork-like character. Employees at Westauto were involved in systemic work related to production system. At the two Russian plants problem-solving and improvement activities were generally carried out by management and technical experts.

The introduction of new QM standards at the two Russian plants followed different patterns for the quality assurance functions that directly affected the customer and the ones that did not. In the case of product quality checks and problem-solving for defects that might or actually did reach the customers, old routines were substituted with new ones. Problem-solving for internal defects and improvement activities that did not directly affect the customers changed following the patterns of layering and bricolage. New international concepts coexisted with old principles that were, in some cases, adjusted to the new QM systems, as is the case with labour competition at Rusmet. While international QM standards prescribed clear formalised responsibilities and action plans, traditional quality assurance routines were characterised by looser sequences of reaction and blurred responsibilities.

The introduction of international QM concepts resulted in change in work content on the shop-floor in two of the cases: Westauto and Rusmet. In the case of Westauto, production workers were responsible for product quality checks, participated in reduction of defects, problem-solving and improvement activities. In the case of Rusmet, workers' new tasks were limited to product quality checks: they carried out statistical quality control, filled out the statistical control cards and sorted parts with defects. At Rusauto, the management did not attempt to introduce new quality-related tasks into workers' responsibilities. Instead, they tried to strengthen indirect control over production. Thus, integration of new quality assurance responsibilities weakened the socialist principle of separation of direct production from indirect functions only at two of the studied plants.

The Russian plants had to accomplish two tasks at the same time: formalisation of production and work processes and employee involvement in quality assurance and improvements within their working areas. They had to develop clear and realisable standards for production processes and quality assurance and to drastically reduce the gap between formal rules and actual production and work practices. They also had to reduce the amount of indirect quality inspections and involve workers in quality assurance. At Westauto transferring the standardised production system (WPS) from the headquarters to the Russian plant was an important factor for solving both tasks, as WPS contained standardised requirements concerning the integration of quality assurance tasks into production workers' functions. Rusmet managed to formalise quality assurance functions that affected the customers most and to integrate product quality checks into workers' functions. It then struggled simply to maintain the tentative state achieved and did not plan to delegate other quality-related functions to the shop-floor. Rusauto attempted to solve the tasks of formalisation and involvement in a sequence. It postponed the idea to involve workers in quality assurance for an indefinite time and concentrated on setting standards and rules in production. The task of elimination of false reporting and prevention of defect concealment per se was already a major challenge for Rusauto.

170   *What about the workers?*

The change in work organisation, employee development and remuneration at the three plants followed different patterns. The modes of change included substitution of old principles with new ones, layering and superficial and deep bricolage of the old rules. Brigade work was not changed much at the two Russian plants. Rusauto did not reconsider brigade work during the change process and still followed socialist principles. Brigade leaders were tasked with reacting to *andon* signals, but otherwise the rules were not changed. Another minor change was that the collective bonus was divided within a production section and not within a brigade. Nevertheless, the complementary effects between the elements of production work that used to reinforce the old path remained in place. At Rusmet, the socialist principles of brigade work were deliberately kept by the management, with only superficial reorganisation. Brigade leaders' responsibilities for product quality inspection were modified and new criteria for labour competition were developed. The principle of 'negative control' that characterised brigade work under the planned economy still applied in part to work organisation at Rusmet. Brigades bore the major responsibility for output and its quality. Yet, brigades' productivity was undermined by the instability of production machinery and material flow in the plant. Brigades, however, were not authorised to take decisions regarding production processes. The borders between individual and collective responsibility were blurred by the reintroduction of collective piece-rate remuneration at Rusmet, after international QM standards had been implemented. Westauto developed new rules for brigade work, which made brigades' indirect responsibilities clearer and more limited than at Rusmet. At the same time, brigades at Westauto were given space and paid working time to make a contribution to quality assurance. Therefore, brigade work at Westauto represented a mechanism stabilising the new approach to QM at this plant.

The introduction of international QM standards resulted in the development of completely new descriptions of workers' competence profiles at two of the studied plants – Westauto and Rusmet. These two plants followed the logic of substitution: they did not rely on the *ETKS*, but instead integrated new competencies required by the international QM concepts into their in-house employee development systems. Competence profiles of direct workers included competencies and skills that were formulated on the basis of actual production and work processes, and included those relating to quality assurance. In the case of Westauto, these new competencies covered the broad range of QM concepts introduced at the plant – from ISO 9000 to the fish-bone diagram. In the case of Rusmet, all workers were trained in only three new competencies: the company's QM policies, SPC and FMEA. However, the fact that Rusmet developed a new matrix of all competencies, which became the basis for the new wage rates, represented a mechanism stabilising the new QM standards in production. Rusauto still adhered to the *ETKS*, which reinforced the old path of industrial work.

Remuneration plays a key role in the punitive character of industrial work in Russia; therefore changing it was particularly important for interrupting the logic of the old path. This punitive approach was formed by three principles: the use of a high variable share of pay as a means to discipline workers, the great degree of

What about the workers? 171

managers' discretion in calculation of the variable share and blurred borders between individual and collective contributions to work results.

All of these principles still applied to the remuneration system at Rusauto, and application of these rules perpetuated the old path of industrial work and poor acceptance of responsibility by workers for quality in production. Westauto radically deviated from these principles of remuneration characteristic of the local industrial enterprises. Variable share of pay did not play any role in Westauto's remuneration system: wages were paid to individuals and not brigades, and there was a focus on the personalisation of responsibility for mistakes. Rusmet first substituted some of the old remuneration principles with new ones; the most significant change was related to individual focus and formalisation of pay. Although the plant still used a variable share of pay, managerial discretion in its calculation was significantly reduced. This step, however, was followed by a return to collective piece-rate pay. The pattern of change in remuneration at Rusmet indicates the shakiness of the change achieved, as the self-reinforcing dynamics behind the old path were weakened but not eliminated, and mechanisms stabilising the new QM concepts were not strong enough. Application of sanctions without distinguishing between intentional and unintentional mistakes, tight interconnection between worker- and machinery-caused defects and the weakness of employee interest representation at the two Russian plants further sharpened the punitive character of work.

The analysis of the patterns of change in the four elements of production work studied shows that Westauto deviated from the old principles in all four of them. At Rusmet the content of work on the shop-floor and the approach to employees' development were changed. Remuneration system at Rusmet was affected as well, but the old principles were reintroduced with the appointment of a new plant director. At Rusauto insignificant or no change was found in the four dimensions analysed.

In order to draw a conclusion about whether the punitive path of industrial work was broken at the plants, three factors should be combined: the novelty in the four dimensions, the self-reinforcement dynamics behind the old path and the mechanisms sustaining the new QM concepts. The overview of the change patterns shows that the old path of industrial work was only broken in the case of Westauto. Yet, the old work attitudes and behaviour on the part of local line managers were still present there. Some complementarity between the new principles evolved, but, overall, the mechanisms stabilising the new path were rather weak. This undermined the sustainability of the achieved state and indicates that Westauto did not switch to a new path of industrial work. At Rusmet the punitive path of industrial work was only weakened since most of its reinforcement mechanisms were still in place. In the case of Rusauto, the old path of industrial work persisted.

The analysis of change processes at the shop-floor level points to both a crucial role of internal learning processes and to the indispensable role that Western partners played in all three cases. Westauto's headquarters transferred the Westauto Production System and quality operation system to the Russian location and set performance targets for these two systems at the plant. The enduring presence of expatriate managers was vital not only for stabilising these systems, but also for sustaining the new

172 *What about the workers?*

communication style between the local line management and employees. Bottom-up communication and exclusion of threats and blame for mistakes posed a continued challenge for Westauto. In the case of Rusauto, Western partners assisted in both introducing new QM concepts at the Car1 line and preparing for the manufacturing of Car2. External partners played a crucial role in changing the quality assurance at the plant, even though this did not significantly affect workers' role in it. In the case of Rusmet, Western customers and consultants were directly involved in introducing new QM concepts and developing new personnel policies. The production line for the German customer became the trial ground for the novel concepts that were then applied in the whole plant. The cases of Rusmet and Rusauto also indicate the importance of the enduring presence of local top and middle managers with experience of organisation of production and QM outside the locked-in path of work in Russian industry. The new managers at Rusauto who were able to critically question the existing quality assurance routines worked at a JV previously. At Rusmet, a top manager with personal experience in the organisation of production in Germany, who carried out the change, was substituted with a director who had built his career within the factory at Rusmet. This resulted in the weakening or elimination of many of the mechanisms stabilising the new QM standards at Rusmet and even in the reintroduction of the old principles characteristic of the punitive path of industrial work.

Notes

1 'Kanban' – a tool in lean production, which helps to level production, depending on the actual demand of the customers; 'poka-yoke' – mistake-proofing mechanisms in lean production, which help a machine operator to avoid mistakes; 'gemba' – a Japanese term for 'shop-floor', used to signify the importance of the shop-floor, where value-adding activities take place, for solving problems and getting ideas for improvements.
2 Eight Disciplines Problem Solving - problem-solving cycle including eight steps – from defining the problem to implementation of permanent corrective actions and the recognition of the problem-solving team.
3 The Training Leader refers to the Russian proverb: "I'm the boss – you are a fool; you're the boss – I am a fool."
4 The average wage at Rusmet in 2007–8 was 11,000 roubles.
5 Rusmet manufactured relatively small metal parts.

6 Conclusion

This book undertook a journey to the shop-floor of industrial enterprises in Russia to analyse the encounter between international management standards and the persistent Soviet era practices on the shop-floor. The prevailing argument in the literature states that efforts to change the industrial workplace failed to reach the production line level, and high management discretion and use of punitive methods on the shop-floor persisted, despite the reforms. Quality control and work organisation remained particularly repellent to change. The empirical study in this book focused on the introduction of international quality management (QM) standards in the Russian automotive industry, which was exposed to international competition in the 2000s. Drawing on path dependence theory, the study first reconstructed the core elements that constituted the path of industrial work in Russia and identified the mechanisms that perpetuated the path, despite the multiple waves of reforms in the economy of recent decades. With this background, it analysed the agency aimed at introducing the international QM standards at the industry and company levels, and the change outcomes.

The results of the study allow for cautious optimism. They show that the introduction of international QM standards can lead to breaking away from the Soviet legacy in the Russian industrial workplace. Such change requires a combination of pressure and support from international partners or headquarters and sustained learning processes at the company level. The change is a gradual and lengthy process, since it entails weakening of self-reinforcement mechanisms perpetuating the old path of industrial work and establishing mechanisms stabilising the new management principles.

The conclusions will pull together the three lines of analysis in the book, following the logic of breaking path dependence. They will first describe the path dependence in the Russian industrial workplace; then discuss the supporters and challengers of the international QM standards at the industry and company levels; the final part will discuss the implications of change for the Russian industrial workplace and outline the prospects.

6.1 Decomposing path dependence in the Russian industrial workplace

The historical analysis in the book showed that a specific pattern of elements constituting the Soviet path of industrial work had become locked in by the 1980s. The adoption

174 *Conclusion*

of NOT, a Soviet interpretation of Taylorism, in the 1920s brought about a strict division of tasks between the production and quality control departments and a narrow technicist approach to worker qualification, excluding any indirect competencies, also the ones relevant for quality assurance. These two elements were later integrated with a high degree of informal steering in production. The development and diffusion of the standardised Complex Systems of Management of Output Quality institutionalised two more elements of the Soviet path of industrial work – specific approaches to group or *brigade* work and remuneration. Brigades bore collective responsibility for both the amount of the output and its quality, while having very limited formal authority. Brigade pay contained a significant variable share. Although this share was linked to output level and 'quality of work performance', management had high discretion in determination of the variable share and withdrawal of bonuses to discipline workers. Such a pay system, combined with high responsibility and low formal authority of brigades in the production process and a high degree of informal steering in production, resulted in an overall punitive character of production work in Russia under the planned economy.

Enterprises' struggles for high product quality played an important role in shaping the character of work under the planned economy, along with struggles to fulfil plans and raise productivity. The Soviet standardised systems of organisation of production, work and remuneration contributed to *complementary effects* between the elements constituting the path of industrial work. These effects impeded the change of single principles governing the shop-floor, while the other elements remained in place. One more mechanism perpetuating the path was *learning effects* that evolved due to the narrow qualification profiles, which were formalised in the *Soviet Wage Rate and Qualification Handbook for Workers* (*ETKS*). Narrow qualification profiles hindered extending the scope of formal authority on the shop-floor. Finally, the Soviet path of industrial work was a product of joint efforts of the state, major industrial companies, research institutes and the public system of vocational training. This led to the formation of *coordination effects* on the established path of production work, which made it difficult for individual companies to deviate from the pattern followed by most other actors.

These three self-reinforcement mechanisms explain the persistence of the punitive path of industrial work despite the market reforms. The reforms did not challenge the Soviet path but they removed the moderating elements of the socialist production regime, such as employment guarantee. Labour legislation was liberalised and violation of labour rights became commonplace. The path of industrial work in the post-socialist period, therefore, combined the worst of both the planned economy and a liberal market economy.

6.2 Supporters and challengers of the international quality management standards

The two central ideas underlying the new QM standards – involvement of shop-floor workers in operational decisions and flexible standardisation – completely contradicted the punitive path of industrial work. Introduction of the international

Conclusion 175

QM standards was not possible just by substitution of the old approach to quality control. It challenged the whole path of industrial work and required weakening of the reinforcement dynamics behind the old practices governing the shop-floor. The scale and duration of the change seemed prohibitively demanding to most local enterprises. Therefore, they did not start to change their quality policies even after the radical shift of the industrial policy in the Russian automotive industry, which opened it to international competition. Instead, industry-level agency, aimed at diffusion of the new QM standards, played a key role in this process. Foreign companies that established production in Russia became main actors supporting the diffusion of the new QM standards in the industry. They both introduced the new standards at their own local plants and supported the introduction of these standards at domestic suppliers' plants. The role of domestic car manufacturers gradually shifted from being a challenger to a hesitant supporter of the new standards.

Internationalisation of the Russian automotive industry represented an opening of this industry to new actors and organisational 'fields' where alternative solutions to organisation of production and quality control were in place (cf. Crouch and Farrell 2004). This could be a way for domestic companies to gain awareness of the need to change the persistent path, along with knowledge on alternative solutions. Yet, there was little overlap in membership and scarce interaction between the domestic and the foreign segments of the industry. The domestic associations of car makers and suppliers viewed lobbying protectionist industrial policies for the domestic segment as their primary aim as late as 2007. The domestic automakers' first actions aimed at introducing international QM standards at their supplier plants also took place within the domestic segment. The Association of Russian Automakers (OAR) established its own version of the international automotive QM certification. No mechanisms for verifying compliance with the standards were established locally. These certificates were not recognised internationally. The closeness of the domestic automotive segment led to only a slow weakening of the coordination effects reinforcing the old approach to quality control.

Western OEMs that established manufacturing in Russia had knowledge and experience of the international QM standards from their headquarters and other locations. They both introduced the new standards at their own plants in Russia and supported their implementation at their prospective local suppliers' plants. Since they were present in multiple national contexts, they also possessed experience in transferring standardised production systems and QM systems across borders. Their collaboration with suppliers, based on supplier development programmes, was applicable in different national contexts. They aimed at modernisation of suppliers' quality assurance systems, along with other key elements of the production system and human resource policies, such as employee development system. The OEMs' agency combined support and control of suppliers' change efforts. Yet, the number of Russian firms supplying foreign OEMs in Russia or abroad remained very small. Their products had to fit with the OEMs' localisation strategies. More importantly, the management at local enterprises often showed resistance to change.

176   *Conclusion*

At the company level, actors' inclusion into networks outside the domestic industry segment and personal experience with international QM concepts played an important role as well. Expatriate managers or local Russian managers with work experience in joint ventures were more likely to establish mechanisms stabilising the new standards and to weaken the mechanisms perpetuating the old path of industrial work. Their presence was a condition both for the start of the change process and for the sustainability of the results achieved. Typical challengers of the new QM standards were local managers in production whose work experience was limited to the domestic industry segment. They lacked the knowledge of new management concepts and, what is even more important, they had deeply ingrained beliefs that quality is something that they can negotiate with quality inspectors and that workers behave best when afraid of punishment.

6.3   Change in the Russian industrial workplace

The book presented nuanced causal accounts of the introduction of international QM standards at three companies: Westauto, a multinational automobile manufacturer; Rusmet, a Russian supplier to a Western OEM; and Rusauto, a Russian automobile manufacturer. The change outcomes in these three companies differed.

In order to judge whether the punitive path of industrial work was broken, and a new path evolved, two conditions are important. At least some new elements deviating from the persistent logic should be introduced, and self-reinforcement mechanisms perpetuating the old path should be eliminated or significantly weakened. A new path evolves when the behaviour in question is guided by new organisational logic rather than the path dependent one and mechanisms supporting a new solution are created.

Westauto managed to break away from the punitive path of industrial work characteristic of the Russian industry. It succeeded in transferring its production and QM systems to Russia. These systems had a strong impact on the content of work on the shop-floor: both individual workers and brigades received quality-related tasks. Work organisation was guided by new principles as well: brigades were paid for working time to participate in problem-solving. Fulfilment of these tasks was not conditioned by bonuses but was linked to career progression. The remuneration system developed at Westauto did not follow the punitive logic of the old path. The system of personnel development supported the new path of work as well. Intensive employee training was organised, including off-the-job training at local organisations. Formal training of local line managers in soft skills and their gradual socialisation at the plant helped overcome their resistance to the new non-punitive and no-blame culture at Westauto. A combination of training and socialisation allowed weakening of the learning effects reinforcing the old path. Participation of the new independent union at Westauto in management–employee talks represented an additional barrier to the punitive behaviour of the local managers. Nevertheless, Westauto did not switch to a new path that would consistently value employees' discretionary effort to improve production and work processes. The lack of sufficiently strong mechanisms stabilising the new path and persistence of punitive attitudes among the Russian managers made the sustainability of the achieved state a continued challenge for the plant management.

Conclusion 177

Rusmet only weakened the persistent path on the shop-floor. This case showed both the changeability of the character of work on the shop-floor and the reversibility of the change achieved at a Russian enterprise. The implementation of international QM standards led to change in work content on the shop-floor, establishment of a new personnel development system and considerable change in remuneration principles. These weakened the reinforcement mechanisms underlying the punitive path of production work. Some of the achieved change was reversed, however, when the plant director was substituted after having completed the change process. The new director, who had built his career within the factory walls, reintroduced the socialist remuneration principles and abandoned some of the personnel development programmes. This contradicted to the new approach to quality assurance and caused tensions with the workers. While Rusmet significantly weakened the mechanisms reinforcing the punitive path of industrial work at the first stage of the change process, the new logic on the shop-floor was challenged after the substitution of the director.

Path dependence persisted at Rusauto. This plant introduced some new QM concepts, but most of the principles constituting the core of the punitive path of industrial work remained in place. Separation of indirect tasks from workers' responsibilities was not challenged. Remuneration systems relied on bonuses and were characterised by a high degree of management discretion and unclear borders between individual and collective responsibility. Employees' qualification profiles were still based upon the *ETKS*. Thus, both complementary and learning mechanisms reinforcing the punitive path remained in place. Strengthening the formal regulations in production was hard as the production equipment was unreliable, suppliers delivered low-quality parts and production attempted to push through defects in order to secure the wage fund that was linked to output. Rusauto struggled to standardise and formalise production and work processes and to reduce workers' participation in quality assurance.

Some of the differences in change outcomes at the three plants were due to starting conditions at the plants and strength of control from international industry partners. Westauto was a greenfield production site, while Rusmet and Rusauto were formerly state-owned, privatised enterprises. Westauto did not have to overcome complementary effects between the elements constituting the old path, but was able to prevent them by designing new work and personnel policies at its Russian location. Decisions regarding Westauto's production and QM systems were taken by the European headquarters. Rusmet, a supplier to Western customers abroad, was exposed to both support and rigorous control of its change progress by these companies. Rusauto's collaboration with Western automotive companies had a more consultative character.

The elements constituting the persistent path of industrial work at the Russian plants did not change simultaneously. Change went faster in dimensions that influenced the customer most. The international partners of the enterprises paid most attention to organisation of quality assurance and workers' role in it and to workers' competence development systems. Organisation of brigade work and remuneration systems at the two domestic enterprises studied seem to have been at the periphery of the attention of international industry partners during the change process.

178 *Conclusion*

The case studies of Westauto and Rusmet showed that the international management standards affected the Russian industrial workplace in two ways. They led to a higher formalisation of work and production processes and to greater employee involvement in decisions within their operation areas. The enterprises reduced the divergence between written and actual processes and personnel policies, including employee development and remuneration. By doing this, they diminished managers' discretion and arbitrariness of their decisions. The enterprises also provided shop-floor workers with indirect competencies that allowed for a broader range of responsibilities. Yet, the scope of workers' decisions remained limited, particularly at Rusmet.

Pursuing both the aims of strengthening the degree of formalisation compared to the traditional path and increasing employee involvement had higher chances for success than pursuing only one of them. Both cases where change did take place, Westauto and Rusmet, aimed at both. Rusauto, on the contrary, tried to reduce employee participation in production processes and postponed increasing employee involvement to the indefinite future. This plant faced continued struggles between production and quality departments; workers kept concealing defects even several years after the start of the change process.

6.4 Prospects

The book offered a rather positive perspective on the international management standards. These standards have the potential to create a more transparent, predictable and less punitive work environment in industrial enterprises in Russia. This work environment is, however, more restrictive and more standardised than at traditional local enterprises. The new environment takes away the porosity of a working day and demands higher work intensity. It also relies on a high density of control, even though the forms of control change from direct overseeing to more individualised forms of responsibility built into production processes. Yet, the study indicated that such approaches to work were more likely to be perceived as fair by the workers than the rules governing the traditional industrial workplace. A key reason for this was the new management standards' imperative to look for systemic flaws in organisation of production processes instead of taking a shortcut and blaming workers. Since high-quality products can only originate from stable production processes, management focus on systemic measures also benefits the companies' competitiveness.

While learning to find and resolve systemic shortages in organisation of production and work required significant exertion and time, the return to the punitive path of industrial work appears to be happening rather effortlessly. This return is facilitated by persisting weakness of labour law enforcement and employee interest representation and the current economic downturn in Russia, which led to growing unemployment and labour lay-offs at industrial enterprises. In this context, collaboration with international industrial enterprises, where sanctions are not a central element in governing the industrial workplace, can play an important role in tipping the balance away from the punitive legacy.

Appendix

Table A.1 Overview of the sources of data complementing the interviews

Types of sources	
Company documents	Internal documents
	Annual reports
Observation	Guided tours of automotive plants
	Attendance of seminars for representatives of the automotive industry
	Attendance of automotive fairs
Internet-based sources	http://gazeta.ru/auto
	http://auto.lenta.ru
	http://www.autosphere.ru
	http://www.rbcdaily.ru
	http://www.zr.ru
Industry data and reports	Statistical data from Verband der Automobilindustrie
	Reports from the Germany Trade and Invest – the economic development agency of Germany *Branche kompakt*, issues "Russland / Kfz-Industrie und Kfz-Teile"
	Magazine *Automobilproduktion*, special issues and newsletters on Eastern Europe
	Reports by Ernst & Young

Source: Author

Table A.2 Supplementary expert interviews

Organisation	Interview location	Date
Standardisation of quality management		
European Foundation for Quality Management	Brussels	10.04.2006
Deutsches Institut für Normung (German Institute of Standardisation)	Berlin	27.04.2006
TÜV Akademie (Academy of the Technical Inspection Association)	Berlin	23.10.2006
Management consulting companies		
Valeocon	Berlin	16.03.2006
Haensch Qualitätsentwicklung	Berlin	05.10.2006
TQM 2000	Leipzig	15.12.2006
QM Consulting	Berlin	08.03.2007
Steinbeis	St Petersburg	17.04.2007
We Plan	Cologne	24.09.2007
Automotive industry		
VDA-QMC – Association of German Automotive Industry – Quality Management Center	Oberursel	26.03.2007
Rhineland-Palatinate Supplier Association	Kaiserslautern	13.02.2006
German Manufacturer of Bearings	Herzogenaurach	13.04.2007
Association of Russian Automobile Manufacturers (OAR)	Moscow	30.08.2007
Research Institute for Automobiles and Automotive Engines (NAMI)	Moscow	24.09.2008
Education, vocational training and personnel training related to quality assurance		
Bundesinstitut für Berufsbildung (Federal Institute for Vocational Education and Training)	Berlin	23.02.2006
Vocational Training Centre UniVera	Berlin	05.06.2008
St Petersburg State Electro-Technical University	St Petersburg	20.04.2007
Education Committee of St Petersburg Government	St Petersburg	16.06.2008
Klimov Aircraft Engines Works	St Petersburg	19.06.2008
St Petersburg Academy of Postdiplom Education	St Petersburg	20.06.2008
Education Committee of St Petersburg Government	St Petersburg	24.06.2008
Ecopsy Consulting	Moscow	18.11.2008

Source: Author

Table A.3 Pilot interviews at metal industry and automotive plants

Plant location	Plant	Product	Number of interviews	Date
Russia	Irkutsk Machine Building Works	Machines for heavy metal industry	1	03.02.2006
	Severstal Cherepovets	Steel for metal industry	1	03.02.2006
Germany	Germtrans	Transmissions	2	22.11.2005
	Germauto	Automobile assembly	2	09.01.2006
	Germfilt	Filters	1	14.02.2006
	Germheat	Heaters	1	14.02.2006
	Germtool	Metal parts	1	16.02.2006
	Germplastic	Plastic exterior parts	1	16.02.2006
	Germbrake	Brakes	1	17.02.2006

Source: Author

Table A.4 Pilot case studies of German-owned automotive plants

Plant	Ownership	Product	Location	Number of employees	Interviewee's position	Date
Polengine	German	Engines	Poland	*c.* 1000	Quality Manager	07.06.2006
					HR Manager	07.06.2006
					Manager of the Q-Centre	07.06.2006
Germbrake	German	Brakes	Germany	*c.* 1000	Quality Assurance Manager	29.01.2007
					Production Manager	29.01.2007
					Deputy Head of the Works Council	29.01.2007
					Head of Personnel and Administration Department	30.01.2007
					Head of Personnel Development and Guidance Department	30.01.2007

Source: Author

References

1979. *Kompleksnoe sovershenstvovanie upravleniya proizvodstvom, organizatsii i oplaty truda po opytu VAZa: Materialy seminara.* Moscow: MDNTP.

2003. *Edinyy tarifno-kvalifikatsionnyy spravochnik rabot i professiy rabochikh.* Moscow: Kniga servis.

2005–8. *Automobilproduktion Newsletter für Osteuropa.*

Ackermann, R. 2003. "Die Pfadabhängigkeitstheorie als Erklärungsansatz unternehmerischer Entwicklungsprozesse" *Managementforschung*: 13: 225–255.

Alasheev, S.Y. 1995a. "Neformal'nye otnoshenia v protsesse proizvodstva: 'vzgliad iznutri'" *Sotsiologicheskie Issledovania*: 2: 12–19.

Alasheev, S. 1995b. "Informal relations in the Soviet system of production", in *Management and Industry in Russia: Formal and Informal Relations in the Period of Transition*, edited by S. Clarke. Aldershot: Edward Elgar, pp. 28–68.

Alasheev, S. 1995c. "On a particular kind of love and the specificity of Soviet production", in *Management and Industry in Russia: Formal and Informal Relations in the Period of Transition*, edited by S. Clarke. Aldershot: Edward Elgar, pp. 69–98.

Alasheev, S. and Romanov, P. 1997. *Dinamika "rabochego mesta" na rossiyskom predpriyatii.* Paper presented at the seminar of the Russian Research Programme of Warwick University, Moscow.

Aleshin, B.S. 2006. *O realizatsii v srednesrochnoi perspektive (2005–2008 gg.) prioritetnykh zadach v sootvetstvii s «Kontseptsiei razvitiya avtomobil'noi promyshlennosti Rossii». Parlamentskie slushaniya na temu «Zakonodatel'noe obespechenie razvitiya otechestvennoi avtomobil'noi promyshlennosti»*, Moscow.

Altshuler, A., Anderson, M., Jones, D., Roos, D. and Womack, J.P. 1984. *The Future of the Automobile: The Report of MIT's International Automobile Program*, Cambridge Mass: MIT Press.

Andreeva, T.E. 2006. "Upravlenie personalom v period izmeneniy v rossiyskiy kompaniyakh: metodiki rasprostranennye i rezul'tativnye" *Rossiyskiy zhurnal menedzhmenta*. 4:25–48.

Anisimova, G. and Sobolev, E.N. 2010. "O strategii menedzhmenta v oblasti oplaty truda na rossiyskikh predpriyatiyakh" *Chelovek i trud*: 1: 32–36.

Appelbaum, E., Bailey, T. and Berg, P. 2001. "Do high performance work systems pay off?", in *The Transformation of Work*, edited by S.P. Vallas. Amsterdam: JAI, pp. 85–107.

Arthur, B.W. 1989. "Competing technologies, increasing returns, and lock-in by historical events" *Economic Journal*. 99 (394): 116–131.

References 183

Association of Automotive Engineers. 2010. *Official Internet Portal.* Retrieved from www.autoengineer.org/history.htm on 2 August 2012.

Bacon, N. and Blyton, P. 2000. "High road and low road teamworking: perceptions of management rationales and organizational and human resource outcomes" *Human Relations.* 53 (11): 1425–1458.

Barker, J.R. 1993. "Tightening the iron cage: concertive control in self-managing teams" *Administrative Science Quarterly.* 38: 408–437.

Barley, S.R. and Kunda, G. 1992. "Design and devotion: surges of rational and normative ideologies of control in managerial discourse" *Administrative Science Quarterly.* 37: 363–399.

Basov, V.V. 2001. *Upravlenie kachestvom i konkurentosposobnost'u produktsii avtomobile stroeniya: monografiya,* Nizhny Novgorod: Volgo-Vyatskaya Akademiya Gosudarstvennoi Sluzhby.

Beck, N. and Walgenbach, P. 2005. "Technical efficiency or adaptation to institutionalized expectations? The adoption of ISO 9000 Standards in the German mechanical engineering industry" *Organization Studies.* 26: 841–866.

Belobragin, V.Y. 2003. *Kachestvo: uroki proshlogo i sovremennost',* Moscow: ACMC.

Bennett, A. and Elman, C. 2006. "Complex causal relations and case study methods: the example of path dependence" *Political Analysis.* 14 (3): 250–267.

Bizyukov, P. 2005. "Sluzhby personala - upravlencheskaya periferiya", in *Praktiki upravleniya personalom na sovremennykh rossiyskikh predpriyatiyakh,* edited by V.I. Kabalina. Moscow: ISITO pp. 36–67.

Björkman, I., Fey, C.F. and Park, H.J. 2007. "Institutional Theory and MNC subsidiary HRM practices: evidence from a three-country study" *Journal of International Business Studies.* 38 (3): 430–446.

Bluhm, K. 2001. "Exploring or abandoning the German model?: Labour policies of German manufacturing firms in Central Europe" *European Journal of Industrial Relations.* 7 (2): 153–173.

Bogner, A. and Menz, W. 2002. "Expertenwissen und Forschungspraxis: die modernisierungstheoretische und die methodische Debatte um die Experten. Zur Einführung in ein unübersichtliches Problemfeld", in *Das Experteninterview. Theorie, Methode, Anwendung,* edited by A. Bogner, B. Littig and W. Menz. Wiesbaden: VS Verlag für Sozialwissenschaften, pp. 7–30.

Borisov, V.A. and Clarke, S. 2001. "Predislovie", in *Profsoyuznoe prostranstvo sovremennoy Rossii,* edited by V.A. Borisov and S. Clarke. Moscow: ISITO, pp. 7–18.

Borisov, V.A. and Kozina, I.M. 1994. "Ob izmenenii statusa rabochikh na predpriyatii" *Sotsiologicheskie Issledovania:* (11) 16–29.

Boxenbaum, E. and Battilana, J. 2005. "Importation as innovation: transposing managerial practices across fields" *Strategic Organization.* 3 (4): 355–383.

Boyer, R., Charron, E., Jürgens, l. and Tolliday, S. eds. 1998. *Between Imitation and Innovation. The Transfer and Hybridization of Productive Models in the International Automobile Industry,* Oxford: Oxford University Press.

Breev, B. 2003. "Trud v usloviakh rynochnoi transformatsii [Work under market transformation]" *Obshchestvo i Ekonomika:* 1: 93–101.

Brunsson, N. and Jacobsson, B. 2002a. "The contemporary expansion of standardization", in *A World of Standards,* edited by N. Brunsson and B. Jacobsson. Oxford: Oxford University Press, pp. 2–17.

Brunsson, N. and Jacobsson, B. eds. 2002b. *A World of Standards,* Oxford: Oxford University Press.

184 *References*

Bulmer, M. 1988. "Some reflections upon research in organizations", in *Doing Research in Organizations*, edited by A. Bryman. London: Routledge, pp. 151–161.

Bundesagentur für Außenwirtschaft. 2008. *Branche kompakt: Russland - Kfz-Industrie und Kfz-Teile*, Cologne.

Burawoy, M. 2001. "Transition without transformation: Russia's involutionary road to capitalism" *East European Politics and Societies*. 15 (2): 269–290.

Burawoy, M. and Krotov, P. 1992. "The soviet transition from socialism to capitalism: worker control and economic bargaining in the wood industry" *American Sociological Review*. 57: 16–38.

Burnyshev, K. 2001. "Innovacii i problema kachestva [Innovation and the quality issue]" *Voprosy ekonomiki*: 7: 33–47.

Burnyshev, K. and Donova, I. 2007. "Upravlenie innovatsiyami na predpriyatii: novye konteksty i starye problemy" *Sotsiologicheskie Issledovania*. 5 (5): 31–37.

Burnyshev, K. and Zubaidulina, L. 2000. *Innovatsii i upravlenie kachestvom*. Working paper. Warwick University.

Burnyshev, K., Vandyshev, M. and Priamikova, E. 2006. "Kachestvo v rossiyskoi promyshlennosti: mechanizmy obespechenia" *Ekonomicheskaya Sotsiologia*. 7 (3): 53–68.

Campbell, J.L. 1999. "Mechanisms of evolutionary change in economic governance", in *Evolutionary Economics and Path Dependence*, edited by L. Magnusson. Cheltenham: Edward Elgar, pp. 10–32.

Campbell, J.L. 2004. *Institutional Change and Globalization*, Princeton, NJ: Princeton University Press.

Campbell, R.W. 1972. "Management spillovers from Soviet space and military programs" *Soviet Studies*. 23 (4): 586–607.

Capoccia, G. and Kelemen, D.R. 2007. "The study of critical junctures: theory, narrative, and counterfactuals in historical institutionalism" *World Politics*. 59 (3): 341–369.

Charmaz, K. 2006. *Constructing Grounded Theory*. Los Angeles: Sage.

Christensen, P.T. 1999. *Russia's Workers in Transition: Labor, Management, and the State under Gorbachev and Yeltsin*, Dekalb: Northern Illinois University Press.

Clarke, C. 2005. *Automotive Production Systems and Standardisation: From Ford to the Case of Mercedes-Benz*, Heidelberg: Physica-Verlag Heidelberg.

Clarke, S. 1993. "The contradictions of 'State Socialism'", in *What About the Workers? Workers and the Transition to Capitalism in Russia*, edited by S. Clarke, P. Fairbrother, M. Burawoy and P. Krotov. London: Verso, pp. 5–29.

Clarke, S. 1995. *Management and Industry in Russia: Formal and Informal Relations in the Period of Transition*, Aldershot: Edward Elgar.

Clarke, S. 1996. *Conflict and Change in the Russian Industrial Enterprise*, Aldershot: Edward Elgar.

Clarke, S. 1998. *Structural Adjustment without Mass Unemployment? Lessons from Russia*, Cheltenham: Edward Elgar.

Clarke, S. 2007. *The Development of Capitalism in Russia*, London: Routledge.

Clarke, S. and Pringle, T. 2009. "Can party-led trade unions represent their members?" *Post-Communist Economies*. 21 (1): 85–101.

Clarke, S. and Pringle, T. 2011. *The Challenge of Transition: Trade Unions in Russia, China and Vietnam*, Basingstoke: Palgrave Macmillan.

Clarke, S., Fairbrother, P., Burawoy, M. and Krotov, P. eds. 1993. *What About the Workers? Workers and the Transition to Capitalism in Russia*, London: Verso.

References 185

Clement, U. and Lacher, M. eds. 2006. *Produktionssysteme und Kompetenzerwerb. Zu den Veränderungen moderner Arbeitsorganisation und ihren Auswirkungen auf die berufliche Bildung*, Stuttgart: Franz Steiner Verlag.

Cole, R.E. 1979. *Work, Mobility, and Participation: A Comparative Study of American and Japanese Industry*, Berkeley: University of California Press.

Cole, R.E. 1999. *Managing Quality Fads: How American Business Learned to Play the Quality Game*, New York: Oxford University Press.

Collier, D. 2011. "Understanding process tracing" *PS: Political Science and Politics*. 44 (4): 823–830.

Coyle-Shapiro, J.A.M. 1999. "Employee participation and assessment of an organizational change intervention: a three-wave study of total quality management" *The Journal of Applied Behavioral Science*. 35 (4): 439–456.

Crosby, P.B. 1979. *Quality is Free: The Art of Making Quality Certain*, New York: The New American Library.

Crouch, C. and Farrell, H. 2004. "Breaking the path of institutional development? Alternatives to the new determinism" *Rationality and Society*. 16 (1): 5–43.

David, P.A. 1985. "Clio and the economics of QWERTY". 75 (2): 332–337.

Deeg, R. 2001. *Institutional Change and the Uses and Limits of Path Dependency: The Case of German Finance. MPIfG Discussion Paper 01/6*, Köln: Max-Planck-Institut für Gesellschaftsforschung.

Deeg, R. 2005. "Change from within: German and Italian finance in the 1990s", in *Beyond Continuity: Institutional Change in Advanced Political Economies*, edited by W. Streeck and K. Thelen. Oxford: Oxford University Press, pp. 169–202.

Deming, E.W. 1982. *Quality, Productivity, and Competitive Position*, Cambridge, MA: MIT Press.

Deming, E.W. 1986. *Out of the Crisis*, Cambridge, MA: Massachusetts Institute of Technology, Center for Advanced Engineering Study.

Dickenson, R.P. and Blundell, B. 2000. "Transferring quality management experience to the Russian aerospace industry" *Total Quality Management*. 11 (3): 319–327.

Doletskyi, V.A. 1976. *O rabote kollektiva Yaroslavskogo ob'edinenia po proizvodstvu avtomobilnykh dvigatelei "Avtodizel" po povysheniu kachestva i uvelicheniu motoresursa dvigatelei*, Moscow: NIINAVTOPROM.

Donova, I. 2005. "Izmenenia v sistemakh oplaty truda", in *Praktiki upravlenia personalom na sovremennykh rossiyskikh predpriatiakh*, edited by V.I. Kabalina. Moscow: ISITO, pp. 116–136.

Edelman, O. 2003. "Biomehanicheskiy chelovek" *Otechestvennye zapiski* (3) Retrieved from www.strana-oz.ru/?numid=12&article=557 on 26 November 2008.

Edwards, R. 1979. *Contested Terrain: The Transformation of the Workplace in the 20th Century*, New York: Basic Books.

Egermayer, F. 1979. "Quality control in socialist countries", in *Quality Control Handbook*, edited by J.M. Juran, F.M. Gryna and R.S. Bingham, Jr. New York: McGraw-Hill, pp. 48A-1–48A-10.

Eisenhardt, K.M. 1989. "Building theories from case study research" *Academy of Management Review*. 14: 532–550.

Epochintsev, Y.K. 1980. *Effektivnost' novyh form i metodov organizatsii truda i sistemy oplaty v avtomobilnoy promyshlennosti*, Togliatti: Filial NIINavtoproma.

186   References

Epochintsev, Y.K., Saushkina, A.A. and Klement'eva, G.V. 1989. *Osobennosti organizatsii i normirovaniya truda v usloviyakh novogo khoziaistvennogo mekhanizma v avtomobilestroenii: Obzornaya informatsia*, Togliatti: Filial TsNIITEIavtoproma.

Epochintsev, Y.K., Saushkina, A.A., Klement'eva, G.V. and Nasenkov, E.N. 1988. *Brigadnaya forma organizatsii i normirovania truda na VAZe v novyh ekonomicheskih usloviah. Obzornaia informatsia*, Togliatti: Filial TsNIITEIavtoproma.

Epochintsev, Y.K., Saushkina, A.A. Dolgacheva, L.N. and Deinega, L.A. 1990. *Analiz ispolzovania trudovykh resursov na predpriyatiyakh avtomobilestroyenia*, Togliatti.

Ernst & Young. 2007. *The Russian Automotive Market: Industry Overview.*

Ernst & Young. 2008. *Automotive Market in Russia and the CIS: Industry Overview.*

Ernst & Young. 2013. *An Overview of the Russian and CIS Automotive Industry: March 2013.*

Federal'naya Sluzhba Statistiki. 2012. *Rossiyskii Statisticheskii Ezhegodnik 2012. Statisticheskii Sbornik.* Moscow.

Feigenbaum, A.V. 1961. *Total Quality Control Engineering and Management*, New York: McGraw-Hill.

Fey, C.F. 2008. "Overcoming a leader's greatest challenge: involving employees in firms in Russia" *Organizational Dynamics.* 37 (3): 254–265.

Fey, C.F. and Björkman, I. 1999. *The Effect of Human Resource Management Practices on MNC Subsidiary Performance in Russia. Working Paper 99-105*, Saint Petersburg: Stockholm School of Economics in Russia.

Fey, C.F., Engström P. and Björkman, I. 1998. *Learning to Harness Russia's Most Valuable Resource: A Study of Human Resource Management Practices of Foreign Firms in Russia. Working Paper 98–103*, Saint Petersburg: Stockholm School of Economics in Russia.

Fey, C.F., Nordahl, C. and Zätterström, H. 1998. *The Secret to Success: Developing and Understanding of What Makes a Foreign Firm's Organizational Culture Effective in Russia. Working Paper 98–102*, Saint Petersburg: Stockholm School of Economics in Russia.

Flick, U. 2007. *Managing Quality in Qualitative Research*, London: Sage.

Fontana, A. and Frey, J.H. 2000. "The interview: from structured questions to negotiated text", in *Handbook of Qualitative Research*, edited by N.K. Denzin and Y.S. Lincoln. Thousand Oaks: Sage, pp. 645–672.

Forker, L.B. 1991. "Quality: American, Japanese, and Soviet perspectives" *Academy of Management Executive.* 5 (4): 63–74.

Freyssenet, M., Mair, A., Shimizu, K. and Volpato, G. eds. 1998. *One Best Way? Trajectories and Industrial Models of the World's Automobile Porducers*, Oxford: Oxford University Press.

Friese, S. 2014. *Qualitative Data Analysis with ATLAS.ti*, Los Angeles: Sage.

Gastev, A.K. 1973. *Trudovye ustanovki*, Moscow: Ekonomika.

Gerber, T.P. 2006. "Getting paid: wage arrears and stratification in Russia" *American Journal of Sociology.* 111 (6): 1816–1870.

Gerber, T.P. and Hout, M. 1998. "More shock than therapy: market transition, employment, and income in Russia, 1991–1995" *The American Journal of Sociology.* 104 (1): 1–50.

Gesellschaft für Außenwirtschaft und Standortmarketing mbH. 2010. *Branche kompakt: Russland - Kfz-Industrie und Kfz-Teile (März 2010)*, Cologne.

Gimpelson, V.E. 2010. *Nuzhny li nashey promyshlennosti kvalifitsirovannye rabotniki? Istoriya poslednego desyatiletiya*, Moscow: Higher School of Economics.

References 187

Gimpelson, V. and Kapelyushnikov, R.I. eds. 2007. *Zarabotnaya plata v Rossii: evolutsia i differentsiatsia*, Moscow: Higher School of Economics.

Goertz, G. and Mahoney, J. 2011. *A Tale of Two Cultures: Contrasting Qualitative and Quantitative Paradigms*, Princeton, NJ: Princeton University Press.

Goldberg, P. 1992. "Economic reform and product quality improvement efforts in the Soviet Union" *Soviet Studies*. 44 (1): 113–122.

Golikova, V.V., Kuznetsov, B.V., Yasin, E.G., Gonchar, K.R. and Yakovlev, A.A. 2007. *Rossiyskaya promyshlennost na pereput'e. Chto meshaet nashim firmam stat' konkurentosposobnymi*, Moscow: HSE.

Gontmacher, E. 2007. "Rossiyskaya zarplata: shtrihi k portretu [Russian wages: features to the portrait]" *Otechestvennye zapiski*. (3) Retrieved from www.strana-oz.ru/?numid=37&article=1479 on 24 March 2008.

Gorlin, A.C. 1981. "Observations on Soviet administrative solutions: the quality problem in soft goods" *Soviet Studies*. 33 (2): 163–181.

Gostev, V.I. 1980. *Metody upravlenia kachestvom produktsii. Krupno-seriynoe i massovoe proizvodstvo*, Moscow: Mashinostroenie.

Griffin, R.W. 1988. "Consequences of quality circles in an industrial setting: a longitudinal assessment" *Academy of Management Journal*. 31: 338–358.

Grinberg, M.S. 1993. "Repressii 20-50-h godov i printsipy ugolovnogo prava" *Pravovedenie:* 5: 73–79.

Guest, D. 1997. "Human resource management and performance: a review and research agenda" *International Journal of Human Resource Management*. 8 (3): 263–276.

Gurkov, I.B. 2003. *Innovatsionnoe razvitie i konkurentosposobnost'. Ocherki razvitia rossiyskikh predpriyatiy*, Moscow: TEIS.

Gurkov, I.B., Zelenova, O.I., Gol'dberg, A.S. and Saidov, Z.B. 2009. "Sistema upravleniya personalom na rossiyskikh firmakh v zerkale mezhdunarodnogo sravneniya" *Mir Rossii:* 3: 132–150.

Hackman, R.J. and Wageman, R. 1995. "Total quality management: empirical, conceptual, and practical issues" *Administrative Science Quarterly*. 40: 309–342.

Hancké, B. and Casper, S. 1996. *ISO 9000 in the French and German Car Industry: How International Quality Standards Support Varieties of Capitalism*, Berlin: WZB Discussion paper FS1 96-313.

Harrison, M. 2009. "Forging success: Soviet managers and false accounting, 1943 to 1962" *Warwick Economic Research Papers, discusssion paper No. 909*.

Hedlund, S. 2000. "Path dependence in Russian policy making: constraints on Putin's economic choice" *Post-Communist Economies*. 12 (4): 389–407.

Hill, M.R. 1985. "Soviet product quality and soviet state standards" *International Journal for Quality and Reliability Management*. 2 (1): 49–64.

Hill, S. 1995. "From quality circles to total quality management", in *Making Quality Critical: New Perspectives on Organizational Change*, edited by A. Wilkinson and H. Willmott. London: Routledge, pp. 33–53.

Holstein, J.A. and Gubrium, J.F. 2002. "Active interviewing", in *Qualitative Research Methods*, edited by D. Weinberg. Malden: Blackwell, pp. 112–126.

Hopf, C. 1991. "Qualitative interviews in der Sozialforschung. Ein Überblick", in *Handbuch qualitative Sozialforschung. Grundlagen, Konzepte, Methoden und Anwendungen*, edited by U. Flick. München: Psychologie-Verl.-Union, pp. 177–182.

188 References

Institut kompleksnykh strategicheskikh issledovaniy. 2005. *Rossiyskiy rynok avtomobiley: prognoz razvitiya i rol' gosudarstvennogo regulirovaniya*, Moscow.

International Standards Organization. 2006. *The ISO Survey 2006.* Retrieved from www. iso.org/iso/survey2006.pdf on 2 March 2012.

International Standards Organization. 2008. *The ISO Survey – 2008.*

International Standards Organization. 2009. *ISO/TS 16949:2009. Quality Management Systems: Particular Requirements for the Application of ISO 9001:2008 for Automotive Production and Relevant Service Part Organizations.*

International Standards Organization. 2010. *The ISO Survey of Certifications 2010.* Retrieved from www.iso.org/iso/iso-survey2010.pdf on 11 May 2012.

Ishikawa, K. 1985. *What is Total Quality Control? The Japanese Way*, New York: Prentice-Hall.

Juran, J.M. 1979. "Motivation", in *Quality Control Handbook*, edited by J.M. Juran, F.M. Gryna and R.S. Bingham, Jr. New York: McGraw-Hill, pp. 18-1–18-52.

Juran, J.M. 1988. *Juran on Planning for Quality*, New York: Free Press.

Jürgens, U. 1995. "Lean production and co-determination: the German experience", in *Lean Work: Empowerment and Explotation in the Global Autoindustry*, edited by S. Babson. Detroit: Wayne State University Press, pp. 292–310.

Jürgens, U. 1997. "Germany: implementing lean production", in *After Lean Production: Evolving Employment Practices in the World Auto Industry*, edited by T.A. Kochan, I.D. Lansbury and J.P. MacDuffie. Ithaca: Cornell University Press, pp. 109–116.

Jürgens, U. and Krzywdzinski, M. 2009. "Work models in the Central Eastern European car industry: towards the high road?" *Industrial Relations Journal.* 40 (6): 471–490.

Jürgens, U. and Krzywdzinski, M. 2013. "Breaking off from local bounds: human resource management practices of national players in the BRIC countries" *International Journal of Automotive Technology and Management.* 13 (2): 114–133.

Jürgens, U. and Krzywdzinski, M. 2016. *New Worlds of Work: Varieties of Work in Car Factories in the BRIC Countries*, Oxford: Oxford University Press.

Jürgens, U., Malsch, T. and Dohse, K. 1989. *Moderne Zeiten in der Automobilfabrik:. Strategien der Produktionsmodernisierung im Länder- und Konzernvergleich*, London: Springer.

Jürgens, U., Malsch, T., and Dohse, K. 1993. *Breaking from Taylorism: Changing Forms of Work in the Automobile Industry*, Cambridge: Cambridge University Press.

Kabalina, V.I., ed. 2005. *Praktiki upravlenia personalom na sovremennykh rossiyskikh predpriatiakh*, Moscow: ISITO.

Kamiske, G.F. and Brauer, J. 2003. *Qualitätsmanagement von A bis Z*, Berlin: Hanser.

Kapelyushnikov, R.I. 2007. "Mekhanizmy formirovaniya zarabotnoy platy v rossiyskoy promyshlennosti", in *Zarabotnaya plata v Rossii: evolutsia i differentsiatsia*, edited by V. Gimpelson and R.I. Kapelyushnikov. Moscow: Higher School of Economics, pp. 97–140.

Kartha, C.P. 2004. "A comparison of ISO 9000:2000 quality system standards, QS9000, ISO/TS 16949 and Baldrige criteria" *The TQM Magazine.* 16 (5): 331–340.

Klimova, S. and Clement, K. 2004. "Rol' novogo Trudovogo kodeksa v reglamentatsii trudovykh otnoshenii v Rossii", in *Stanovlenie trudovykh otnoshenii v postsovetskoi Rossii*, edited by J. DeBardeleben, S. Klimova and V. Yadov. Moscow: Akademicheskii proekt, pp. 12–23.

Koch, J. 2007. "Strategie und Handlungsspielraum: Das Konzept der strategischen Pfade" *Zeitschrift Fuehrung & Organisation*: 5: 183–291.

References 189

Kononova, V.Y. 2006. "Modernizatsiya Proizvodstvennykh Sistem Na Rossiiskikh Promyshlennykh Predpriyatiyakh: Sovremennoe Sostoyanie i Perspektivy" *Rossiiskii zhurnal menedzhmenta*. 4: 119–132.

Köper, J. and Zaremba, H.J. eds. 2000. *Quality Management And Qualification Needs 2. Towards Quality Capabilities of Companies and Employees in Europe*, Heidelberg and New York: Physica-Verlag.

Kozichev, E. 2009. "Istoriya poshlin na inomarki v Rossii" *Vlast'* (4) Retrieved from www.kommarsont.ru/doc.aspx?DocsID=1111783 on 15 November 2010.

Krasnyi, Y.G. and Bartseva, S.A. 1976. *Organizatsia kontrolia i obespechenie kachestva produktsii na VAZe*, Kuybyshev: Kuybyshevskoe knizhnoe izdatel'stvo.

Kravchenko, A. and Shcherbina, V. 1998. "Sotsiologia truda i proizvodstva", in *Sotsiologia v Rossii*, edited by V. Yadov. Moscow: Institut Sotsiologii RAN.

Krzywdzinski, M. 2011. "Neuordnung der Macht. Die industriellen Beziehungen in der russischen Automobilindustrie wandeln sich." *WZB-Mitteilungen*: 131: 29–33.

Lacher, M. and Vollmer, T. 2007. "Kompetenzentwiklung für ganzheitliche und standardisierte Produktionssysteme", in *Kompetenzentwiklung in realten und virtuellen Arbeitssystemen. 53.Kongress der Gesellschaft für Arbeitswissenschaft*, edited by Gesellschaft für Arbeitswissenschaft. Dortmund: GfA-Press, pp. 109–112.

Lytkina, T.S. 2008. "Upravlencheskie strategii reorganizatsii osnovnogo proizvodstva postsovetskogo predpriyatiya: stimul i kontrol' za rabochimi", in *Sotsial'nye problemy truda v usloviyakh perekhoda k innovatsionnomu razvitiyu obshchestva. Materialy vserossiyskoi nauchno-prakticheskoi konferentsii, Saint Petersburg, April 24–26 2008.* Saint Petersburg.

MacDuffie, J.P. 1997. "The road to "root cause": shop-floor problem-solving at three auto assembly plants" *Management Science*. 43 (4): 479–502.

Mahoney, J. 2000. "Path dependence in historical sociology" *Theory and Society*. 29: 507–548.

Mahoney, J. and Thelen, K. 2010a. "A theory of gradual institutional change", in *Explaining Institutional Change: Ambiguity, Agency, and Power*, edited by J. Mahoney and K. Thelen. New York: Cambridge University Press.

Mahoney, J. and Thelen, K. 2010b. *Explaining Institutional Change: Ambiguity, Agency, and Power*, New York: Cambridge University Press.

Mandel, D. 2004. *Labour After Communism: Auto Workers and their Unions in Russia, Ukraine, and Belarus*, Montreal: Black Rose.

Martinez-Lorente, A.R., Dewhurst, F. and Dale, B.G. 1998. "Total quality management: origins and evolution of the term" *The TQM Magazine*. 10 (5): 378–386.

McCabe, D. 1999. "Total quality management: antiunion Trojan horse or management albatross?" *Work, Employment and Society*. 13 (4): 665–691.

McCarthy, D.J., Puffer, S.M. and Naumov, A.I. 2000. "Russia's retreat to statization and the implications for business" *Journal of World Business*. 35 (3): 256–274.

Meuser, M. and Nagel, U. 2002. "ExpertInneninterviews - vielfach erprobt, wenig bedacht. Ein Beitrag zur qualitativen Methodendiskussion", in *Das Experteninterview. Theorie, Methode, Anwendung,* edited by A. Bogner, B. Littig and W. Menz. Wiesbaden: VS Verlag für Sozialwissenschaften, pp. 71–93.

Michailova, S. 2002. "When common sense becomes uncommon: participation and empowerment in Russian companies with Western participation" *Journal of World Business*. 37: 180–187.

Ministry of Industry and Energy of the Russian Federation. 2004. *Vystuplenie zamestitelya ministra Minpromenergo Rossii Materova I.S. na mezhdunarodnom avtomobil'nom*

190   References

simpoziume 08.12.20004. Moscow. Retrieved from www.minprom.gov.ru. on 4 September 2006.

Monden, Y. 1983. *Toyota Production System: Practical Approach to Production Management*, Atlanta Norcross: Industrial Engineering and Management Press.

Novitskiy, A. 2005. "Perestan'te pokupat' trubu ot grammofona." *Standarty i kachestvo.* 3: 75–76.

OAO AvtoVAZ. 2008. *Godovoi Otchet Otkrytogo Aktsionernogo Obshchestva «AVTOVAZ» za 2007 god.* Togliatti.

Odegov, Y.G., Freze, V.I. and Meshkov, Y.V. 1988. *Formirovanie i ispolzovanie trudovogo potentsiala VAZa: Obzornaya informatsia*, Togliatti: Filial TsNIITEIavtoproma.

Parker, W.H. 1980. "The Soviet motor industry" *Soviet Studies.* 32 (4): 515–541.

Pierson, P. 2000. "Increasing returns, path dependence, and the study of politics" *American Political Science Review.* 94 (2): 251–267.

Pivovar, E.I. 1983. *Sovetskie rabochie i NTR: Po materialam avtomobilnoi promyshlennosti SSSR, 1966–1975*, Moscow: Mysl'.

Plotnikova, E.B. 2005. "Rabotniki Kak Sub"ekty Trudovykh Otnosheniy", in *Sotsial'no-trudovye issledovaniya*, edited by V.V. Komarovskiy, E.V. Klopov and E.S. Sadovaya. Moscow: IMEMO RAN, pp. 48–60.

Plotnikova, E.B., Germanov, I.A. and Plotnikova, E.V. 2005. "Problemy sotsial'nogo dialoga na promyshlennykh predpriyatiyakh (po itogam monitoringovogo obsledovaniya)", in *Sotsial'no-trudovye issledovaniya:* edited by V.V. Komarovskiy, E.V. Klopov and E.S. Sadovaya. Moscow: IMEMO RAN, pp. 20–28.

Polovikov, V.I., Gorbunov, Y.K., Kulikov, K.S., Kuklin, N.I., Podsobliaev, S.V., Ponomarev, V.F. and Temirov, Y.S. 1977. *Kompleksnaya systema upravleniya kachestvom produktsii. Opyt predptiyatiy avtomobilnoi promyshlennosti*, Togliatti: Filial Nauchno-issledovatel'skogo instituta informatsii avtomobilnoi promyshlennosti.

Posadskov, E. 2002. "Stimuliruyushchie sistemy: opyt i sovremennaya praktika" *Chelovek i trud:*(4) 76–80.

Raack, E. 2008. "Was lange währt, fährt endlich gut? ISO/TS 16949: 2002 - Der Standard für die Automobilindustrie" *QZ - Qualität und Zuverlässigkeit.* 53 (3): 20–22.

Robson, C. 1993. *Real World Research: A Resource for Social Scientists and Practitioner-Researchers*, Malden: Blackwell.

Roland Berger Strategy Consultants. 2005. *Developing a Competitive Russian Automotive Supplier Industry: Findings of a Study Carried Out by "Ost-Ausschuss der Deutschen Wirtschaft" and Roland Berger Strategy Consultants*, Berlin, Moscow, Munich.

Rosstat. 2012. *Index Proizvodstva po Rossiyskoy Federatsii*, Moscow. Retrieved from www. gks.ru/wps/wcm/connect/rosstat/rosstatsite/main/enterprise/industrial/# on 5 November 2012.

Russell, R. 2002. "The influence of ownership and organisational conditions on employee participation in Russian enterprises" *Economic and Industrial Democracy.* 23 (4): 555–584.

Ryvkina, R.V. and Kolennikova, O.A. 2007. "Kadrovyi krizis na promyshlennyh predpriyatiyah Rossii" *Sotsiologicheskie issledovaniya* 8: 52–57.

Sabel, C.F. 1982. *Work and Politics: The Division of Labor in Industry*, Cambridge: Cambridge University Press.

Schreyögg, G., Sydow, J. and Koch, J. 2003. "Organisatorische Pfade - von der Pfadabhängigkeit zur Pfadkreation?" *Managementforschung.* 13 (13): 257–294.

Schwartz, G. and McCann, L. 2007. "Overlapping effects: path dependence and path generation in management and organization in Russia" *Human Relations.* 60 (10): 1525–1549.

Semkina, M. 2005. "Kak Rossii stat' liderom avtoproma?" *Standarty i kachestvo* (5) Retrieved from www.stq.ru/riasite/index.phtml?tbl=tb 888&id=1053 on 11 August 2005.

Sharonov, A. 2003. "Proizvoditeli avtomobilei uluchshayut kachestvo" *RBC Daily*, June 27.

References 191

Shcheglov, A. and Sergeev, M. 2008. "Finansovyy krizis udaril po zarplatam. V avguste prosrochennyy dolg po zarplate vyros v masshtabakh strany bolee chem na 14%" *Nezavisimaya gazeta,* September 22.

Shekshnia, S. 1998. "Western multinationals' human resource practices in Russia" *European Management Journal.* 16 (4): 460–465.

Shershneva, E. and Feldhoff, J. 1999. *Kultura truda v protsesse sotsial'no-ekonomicheskih preobrazovaniy: opyt empiricheskogo issledovania na promyshlennyh predpriatiah Rossii,* Saint Petersburg: OOO Petropolis.

Shibaev, A.A. 2009. *Aktualizatsia Edinogo tarifno-kvalifikatsionnogo spravochnika rabot i professiy rabochikh (ETKS).*

Shulzhenko, E. 2009. "Modernizatsiya upravleniya kachestvom v rossiyskoi avtomobilnoi promyshlennosti: rol' avtoproizvoditeley", in *Modernizatsia Ekonomiki i Globalizatsiya. Vol. 3,* edited by E.G. Yasin. Moscow: Higher School of Economics, pp. 28–37.

Shulzhenko, E. 2012. "Human resource management and labour relations in post-socialist Russia", in *AutoUni-Schriftenreihe, vol. 29, Human Resource Management and Labour Relations in the BRICs: A Review of the Research Literature,* edited by U. Jürgens. Berlin: Logos Verlag, pp. 63–102.

Sidorskyi, I.A. 1988. *Na krutom povorote. Pervye itogi ekonomicheskogo eksperimenta v ob'edinenii "AvtoVAZ",* Kuybyshev: Kuybyshevskoe knizhnoe izdatel'stvo.

Siegelbaum, L.H. 1988. *Stakhanovism and the Politics of Productivity in the USSR, 1935–1941,* Cambridge: Cambridge University Press.

Slider, D. 1987. "The brigade system in Soviet industry: an effort to restructure the labour force" *Soviet Studies.* 39 (3): 388–405.

Sobolev, E.N. 2008. *Sotsial'no-trudovye otnosheniya v Rossii: istoriya, sovremennoe sostoyanie, perspektivy,* Moscow: Institut ekonomiki RAN.

Sochor, Z.A. 1981. "Soviet Taylorism revisited" *Soviet Studies.* 33 (2): 246–264.

Springer, R. 1999. "The end of new production concepts? Rationalization and labour policy in the German auto industry" *Economic and Industrial Democracy.* 20: 117–145.

Stake, R.E. 2000. "Case studies", in *Handbook of Qualitative Research,* edited by N.K. Denzin and Y.S. Lincoln. Thousand Oaks: Sage, pp. 435–454.

Stark, D. 2001. "Ambiguous assets for uncertain environments: heterarchy in postsocialist firms", in *The 21st Century Firm: Changing Economic Organization in International Perspective,* edited by P.J. DiMaggio, W. Powell, D. Stark and E. Westney. Princeton, NJ: Princeton University Press, pp. 69–104.

Stark, D. and Bruszt, L. 1998. *Postsocialist Pathways: Transforming Politics and Property in East Central Europe,* Cambridge: Cambridge University Press.

Stark, D. and Bruszt, L. 2001. "One way or multiple paths: for a comparative sociology of East European capitalism" *The American Journal of Sociology.* 106 (4): 1129–1137.

Strang, D. and Kim, Y. 2005. "The diffusion of scientific management, quality circles, and TQM between the United States and Japan", in *The Oxford Handbook of Work and Organisation,* edited by S. Ackroyd, R. Batt, P. Thompson and P.S. Tolbert. Oxford: Oxford University Press, pp. 177–199.

Streeck, W. and Thelen, K. eds. 2005a. *Beyond Continuity: Institutional Change in Advanced Political Economies,* Oxford: Oxford University Press.

Streeck, W. and Thelen, K. 2005b. "Introduction: institutional change in advanced political economies", in *Beyond Continuity: Institutional Change in Advanced Political Economies,* edited by W. Streeck and K. Thelen. Oxford: Oxford University Press, pp. 1–39.

192   *References*

Sydow, J., Schreyögg, G. and Koch, J. 2005. *Organizational Paths: Path Dependency and Beyond*, paper presented at 21st EGOS Colloquium, 30 June–2 July, Berlin, Germany.

Sydow, J., Schreyögg, G. and Koch, J. 2009. "Organizational path dependence: opening the black box" *Academy of Management Review*. 34 (4):689–709.

Taguchi, G. 1986. *Introduction to Quality Engineering: Designing Quality into Products and Processes*, Tokyo: Asian Productivity Organization.

Taylor, F.W. 1911. *The Principles of Scientific Management*, New York and London: Harper & Brothers.

Temnitsky, A.L. 2007. "Sobstvennost' i strategii trudovogo povedenia rabochikh v usloviakh reform" *Sotsiologicheskie Issledovania*: (2) 40–50.

Thelen, K. 1999. "Historical institutionalism in comparative politics" *Annual Review of Political Science*. 2:369–404.

Thelen, K. 2009. "First annual lecture of the BJIR: institutional change in advanced political economies" *British Journal of Industrial Relations*. 47 (3): 471–498.

Tikhonov, V.I., Klevlin, A.I. and Kocharova, K.V. 1983. *Sovershenstvovanie organizatsii obrabotki informatsii po trudu i zarabotnoi plate v usloviakh ASU. Obzornaya informatsia*, Togliatti: Filial Nauchno-issledovatel'skogo instituta informatsii avtomobilnoi promyshlennosti.

Tolliday, S., Rober, B., Charron, E. and Jürgens, U. 1998. "Introduction: the transfer and hybridization of productive models in the international automobile industry", in *Between Imitation and Innovation: The Transfer and Hybridization of Productive Models in the International Automobile Industry*, edited by R. Boyer, E. Charron, U. Jürgens and S. Tolliday. Oxford: Oxford University Press, pp. 1–19.

Tuckman, A. 1995. "Ideology, quality, and TQM", in *Making Quality Critical: New Perspectives on Organizational Change*, edited by A. Wilkinson and H. Willmott. London: Routledge, pp. 54–81.

Vedeneeva, V. 1995. "Payment systems and the restructuring of production relations in Russia", in *Management and Industry in Russia: Formal and Informal Relations in the Period of Transition*, edited by S. Clarke. Aldershot: Edward Elgar, pp. 224–239.

Verband der Automobilindustrie. 2006. *International Auto Statistics*, Frankfurt am Main.

Verband der Automobilindustrie. 2010. *Daten zur Automobilwirtschaft. April 2010*, Berlin.

Walgenbach, P. 2000. *Die normgerechte Organisation. Eine Studie über die Entstehung, Verbreitung und Nutzung der DIN EN ISO 9000er Normenreihe*, Stuttgart: Schäffer-Poeschel Verlag.

Walgenbach, P. 2001. "Historisch-institutionalistische Analyse der QM-Entwicklung", in *Qualitätsmanagement in Organisationen. DIN ISO 9000 und TQM auf dem Prüfstand*, edited by H. Wächter and G. Vedder. Wiesbaden: Gabler, pp. 3–26.

Wang, C.L. 1951. "Setting new output norms in Soviet industry" *Soviet Studies*. 2 (4): 403–412.

Ward, C. 1990. *Russia's Cotton Workers and the New Economic Policy: Shop-floor Culture and State Policy 1921–1929*, Cambridge: Cambridge University Press.

Wetzel, A. 2005. *Das Kozept der Pfadabhängigkeit und seine Anwendungsmöglichkeiten*. Discussion Paper number 52. Berlin: Osteuropa-Institut der Freien Universität Berlin.

Wilkinson, A., Allen, P. and Snape, E. 1991. "TQM and the management of labour" *Employee Relations*. 13 (1): 24–31.

Womack, J.P., Jones, D.T., and Roos, D. 1990. *The Machine that Changed the World*, New York: Rawson Associates.

References 193

Yin, R.K. 2009. *Case Study Research: Design and Methods*, Los Angeles: Sage.
Zaslavskaya, T.I. and Shabanova, M.A. 2002a. "K probleme institutsionalizatsii nepravovykh sotsial'nykh praktik v Rossii: sfera truda" *Mir Rossii*. 11 (2): 3–38.
Zaslavskaya, T.I. and Shabanova, M.A. 2002b. "Nelegalnye trudovye praktiki i socialnye transformacii v Rossii sotsiologicheskie. 6: 3–17.

Index

Ackermann 12
Alasheev, S. 49–50, 51
Aleshin, B.S. 7, 8
Altshuler, A. 77
Andreeva, T.E. 62
Appelbaum, E. 11
Association of Russian Automobile
   Manufacturers (OAR) 85–6, 87–9, 90,
   102, 175
automation: under Fordism 71; at Rusauto
   105–6, 120, 149, 153; at Rusmet 130; at
   Westauto 115, 118–20, 128–30, 148
automotive industry in Russia 10;
   AvtoVAZ 9, 10, 32–3, 87–8; domestic
   vehicle production 7, 8, 10; domestic
   vehicle sale 7, 9; female workers 50,
   110–12; Ford Motor Company 8, 26,
   66; GAZ 4, 9–10, 25–6, 50, 59, 64, 88;
   industrial associations 85–6, 87–9, 90,
   102, 175; international competition
   5–6, 8–10, 84–6, 101–2, 173; protective
   policies 6, 8, 85–6, 175; Toyota 8,
   50, 59, 63, 64; Volkswagen 8, 50, 59,
   63, 64, 66; *see also* Rusauto; Rusmet;
   Westauto
AvtoVAZ (formerly VAZ) 9, 10, 32–3, 87–8;
   requirements for suppliers 87–8, 90, 95,
   99–100; in Soviet era 32–7, 40–1, 44

Bennett 12, 17, 27
Björkman, I. 3–4, 59, 62, 63, 64
blame mentality 3, 131; no-blame
   mentality 97, 138, 164, 172, 176
blue-collar workers: agency work 107;
   average wages 110; brigade (group)
   work 54–6, 138–47; compliance on
   the shop-floor 2, 45–6, 49–50, 54, 56,
   135, 161; female workers 50, 110–12;
   in-house training and development 58–60,
148–56; involvement in operational
   decisions 1, 4, 84, 121–4, 124–8, 131–7,
   142–7, 169, 178; pay systems 60–5,
   157–68; qualification requirements
   147–8, 149, 150; role in improvement
   activities 131–7; role in problem-solving
   124–8; role in quality inspection 121–4;
   share in staff 107–108; vocational
   training 56–7, 59, 147, 153, 155–6, 174;
   see also work discipline
Bogdanov, A. 24, 26, 47n1
breaking path dependence 13–15, 173,
   174–8; *see also* self-reinforcement
   mechanisms
Brezhnev, L. 32
bricolage 14–15, 136, 169
brigade work (group work) 33–7, 39–46,
   54–6, 64, 108–9, 125–6, 138–42, 145–7,
   170–1, 174, 176–7; quality assurance
   tasks 138, 142–6; role in improvement
   activities 132–8; pay and incentives to
   156–8, 160, 162–3; self-organisation on
   the shop-floor 49, 54–6
Bruszt, L. 12, 14
Burawoy, M. 11, 48–9, 54–5, 104
Burnyshev, K. 3, 52–3

Campbell, J.L. 14
Campbell, R.W. 31, 33, 46
Capoccia, G. 12, 23
case studies in Russia *see* Rusauto;
   Rusmet; Westauto
Christensen, P.T. 28, 29, 46
Clarke, C. 80
Clarke, S. 2–3, 11, 28–9, 42, 47n10, 48–9,
   53, 65–6, 104
Cole, R.E. 1–2, 72, 73–4, 75, 80
companies studied in Russia *see* Rusauto;
   Rusmet; Westauto

Index 195

competition: in Russian automobile industry 5–6, 8–10, 84–6, 101–2, 173; in the West 73, 77, 75, 81; *see also* market economy in Russia
continuity in the Russian industrial workplace *see* path dependence
continuous improvement process: cost reduction 134, 137; *kaizen* 78, 79, 103n3, 132–3, 142, 152, 158; quality circles 73–5, 136; suggestion systems 50, 56, 133–5, 139, 141, 158; variability reduction 80, 125; *see also* blue-collar workers; lean production; workplace competitions
critical juncture 12, 23, 32, 101
Crouch, C. 13, 15, 175

discipline *see* work discipline

Edelman, O. 24–5
Elman, C. 12, 17, 27
employees *see* blue-collar workers; white-collar workers
employment relations *see* labour market in Russia; trade unions; works councils
empowerment of employees in Russia 55–6; *see also* involvement of workers in operational decisions
Ernst & Young 8, 9, 10
expatriate managers 113, 157, 165, 171, 176; *see also* leadership style

Farrell, H. 13, 15, 175
feedback mechanisms in path dependence *see* self-reinforcement mechanisms
Fey, C.F. 3–4, 55–6, 59, 62, 63, 64
Flick, U. 19
Ford Motor Company 8, 26, 66
Ford, H. 24, 71, 77
Fordism 25, 71; *see also* Taylorism; Taylorism in Russia

Gastev, Alexei 24, 25, 26
GAZ 4, 9–10, 25–6, 50, 59, 64, 88
Gerber, T.P. 14, 43, 48, 61
Germany: diffusion of lean 79–80, 134; support of change in QM in Russia 106, 114, 122
Goertz, G. 17
Gorbachev, M. 32, 35, 39, 42–7
grounded theory 17
group work in the West 79, 83; *see also* brigade work

high performance work practices 11
human resource management practices *see* blue-collar workers; personnel management; white-collar workers

ideology *see* Soviet ideology
industrial relations *see* labour market in Russia; trade unions; works councils
industrial workers *see* blue-collar workers
industrialisation 24, 26–9, 71; five-year plans 27, 32; *see also* worker mobilisation
institutional change 12–15
international quality management standards 80, 84; dissemination in Russia 6, 51, 101–3, 114–18; impact on the Russian workplace 168–72; ISO 9000 80–2, 51, 52, 53, 89–90, 115, 117, 151; ISO/TS 16949 80, 82–3, 86–9, 90–5, 117–18; TQM 52, 72, 75–7, 82; VDA 6.3 93, 117; *see also* lean production
involvement of workers in operational decisions: in Japan 72; in Russia 1, 4, 84, 121–4, 124–8, 131–7, 142–7, 169, 178; in Soviet era 30; in the West 1, 70, 75–6, 78; *see also* worker mobilisation

Japan 1, 72; lean production in 77–9, 83; quality circles in 32, 70; quality management in 37, 72–5
Jones, D.T. 1, 77, 79
Jürgens, U. 2, 71, 77, 78, 79; research on work in BRIC countries 3–4, 11, 50, 53, 56, 57, 58, 59, 62, 63, 64, 66

kaizen 78, 79, 103n3, 132–3, 142, 152, 158; *see also* continuous improvement
Kelemen, D.R. 12, 23
Kerzhentsev, P.M. 24, 26
Khrushchev, N.S. 30, 32, 39
Koch, J. 12–13, 14, 15, 27
Kononova, V.Y. 3, 52
Kravchenko, A. 25, 26, 28
Krotov, P. 11, 48, 49, 54–5, 104
Krzywdzinski, M. 3–4, 11, 50, 53, 56, 57, 58, 59, 62, 63, 64, 65, 66

labour market in Russia: labour law enforcement 61, 65, 67, 178; labour shortage 57–8; liberalisation 48
leadership style: authoritarian 1, 56, 143–4, 156, 163; fear on the shop-floor 78, 128, 157, 160, 164–5; management

196   *Index*

arbitrariness 51, 67, 84, 134, 159, 161, 166, 178; management discretion 60, 63–4, 65, 160, 165, 166, 168, 171, 178; *see also* blame mentality; resistance to change

lean production 70, 72; 5S 52, 115, 117; *andon* pull cord system 126, 137, 144; *kaizen* 78, 79, 103n3, 132–3, 142, 152, 158; production systems 11; Rusauto Production System 116–7, 168; in Russia 1, 3, 4, 51–2, 54, 68, 92, 98, 117, 153, 168; Toyota Production System 54, 70, 77, 115–17; in the West 77, 79–80; Westauto Production System (WPS) 92, 113, 115, 116, 137, 142, 151–3, 168, 169, 171; *see also* automation; Soviet systems of production organisation

Lenin, V.I. 24, 25

lock-in 12, 13, 172

Mahoney, J. 12, 15, 17

management *see* leadership style; lean production

market economy in Russia: competition 1, 5–6, 8–10, 43, 50, 59, 84–6, 101–2, 173; market reforms 48

McCann, L. 2, 11, 51, 55

National Association of Automotive Component Manufacturers (NAPAK) 85, 87

national institutional systems 79, 80, 83

Parker, W.H. 25

path dependence 11–15; in the Russian industrial workplace 1, 3, 27, 173–4, 176–7; *see also* critical juncture; self-reinforcement mechanisms

Pay and incentive systems 60–1, 65, 156–7; Coefficient of Labour Participation (KTU) 64, 133, 140, 141, 159, 162–3; grade and appraisal systems 157–8, 161–2; management discretion 60, 63–4, 65, 160, 165, 166, 168, 171, 178; non-monetary incentives 157, 158; piece-rate pay 3, 29, 30, 39–40, 71, 154, 162, 167, 171; variable share of pay (bonuses) 61–5, 68, 112, 134, 158–64; *see also* blue-collar workers; Soviet pay and incentive systems; Wage Rate and Qualification Handbook for Workers *(ETKS)*; workplace competitions

performance management *see* lean production; pay and incentive systems

personnel management: alcohol problems 49, 111; labour shortage 57–8; punish-but-retain logic 29, 61, 164, 168; recruitment 110, 147–8, 149–50; turnover (fluctuation) 58, 111, 148, 154; *see also* blue-collar workers

planned economy *see* industrialisation; Soviet industrial workplace

production systems *see* lean production

punctuated equilibrium 13

punitive measures on the shop-floor *see* blame mentality; leadership style; work discipline

quality circles 73–5, 136

quality control 5; after market reforms 1–3, 5, 49, 51–4, 67–8, 84–6, 90, 95, 101–3, 173, 175; quality inspection (indirect quality control) 118–21; quality inspectors (quality controllers) 130, 160; tensions with production over 130, 144; in Soviet era 23, 29–32, 34–7, 41–4, 138, 174; workers' role in 122–4, 146, 166, 169; *see also* continuous improvement; international quality management standards; quality management; Total Quality Management

quality management 5; competencies on the shop-floor 147, 151–6; diffusion in Russia 1–6, 15–16, 18–20, 51–4, 68, 70, 86–101, 102–3; diffusion in the West 1–2, 70, 72–7, 80–4; in production 112–21; in supply chains 4–6, 10, 52–3, 81–3, 85–103, 117–18, 175; workers' role in 137, 119–28, 131–8, 142–7, 168–9, 170, 177; *see also* quality control

quality of products: quality of Russian cars and supply parts 9–10; under planned economy 28–30; concealment of defects 26, 42, 50, 121, 122–4, 126, 137–8, 142–3, 144

recruitment 110, 147–8, 149–50

remuneration *see* pay and incentive systems

research design of the study: access to companies 17–18; case study overview 17–18, 20, 22n4; interviews 18–21; methodology and data 17–20, 179–81; research dimensions 5; research questions 15–16; triangulation 19, 20

resistance to change: from line managers and white-collar staff 55, 121, 139, 143,

146–7, 176; from suppliers 98–101; from workers 55, 123–4, 144, 146, 161, 167
rewards *see* pay and incentive systems
Roos, D. 1, 77, 79,
Rusauto 17, 18, 91, 105–6, 113, 169; brigade (group) work 139–40, 144–5; change agents 113–14, 172; pay and incentives system 158–60, 165–6; personnel composition 107–8, 109–11; quality management 116, 119–21, 122–3, 125–6, 130–1, 133; requirements to suppliers 93–5, 99, 101; Rusauto Production System 116–17, 168; Soviet legacy 170–1, 177; worker qualification and development 149–50, 153, 156
Rusmet 18, 91, 106; change agents 114, 172; collaboration with Western partners 91, 93, 95, 97–8, 172; group work (brigade work) 140–2, 145–6; lean production 168; pay and incentives system 112, 160–4, 166–8, 171; personnel composition 109, 111–12; quality management 114, 117–20, 123–4, 127–8, 130, 134–7, 169; Soviet legacy 170; worker qualification and development 150–1, 153–6, 171

Schreyögg, G. 12–13, 14, 15, 27
Schwartz, G. 2, 11, 51, 55
Scientific Organisation of Labour *see* Taylorism in Russia
self-reinforcement mechanisms 12; adaptive expectations 13; complementary effects 12, 23, 30, 43, 46, 68, 98, 170; coordination effects 12, 39, 57, 84, 90, 155, 175; interruption or weakening of 13, 15, 102, 173, 175, 176; learning effects 12, 39, 45, 68, 155–6, 174, 176–7
Shcherbina, V. 25, 26, 28
shop-floor management *see* blue-collar workers; leadership style
Siegelbaum, L.H. 27, 28, 29, 47n7, 47n9
Sochor, Z.A. 24, 25, 26
socialist competition *see* worker mobilisation
socialist industrial workplace *see* Soviet industrial workplace
Soviet automobile industry 25–6, 28, 32–8, 40–2, 44
Soviet ideology 24, 26–9, 32, 38–9, 45, 65, 128, 131, 136, 142; conscientious worker ethos 31–2, 39, 43, 45, 121,

126, 136–7, 141–2, 163, 167; labour competition 27–8, 34, 41, 47n7, 65, 133–7, 141, 145, 169–70; Stakhanovism 28, 47n7, 47n9; worker mobilisation 27–30, 43, 131
Soviet industrial workplace 44–7; brigade work (teamwork) 33–7, 39–43, 44–6; Coefficient of Labour Participation *(KTU)* 40–2, 44; quality control 23, 29–32, 34–7, 41–4, 138, 174; Taylorism 23–7, 29–32, 35, 45, 47n10; vocational training and qualification 25, 37–9; worker mobilisation 27–30, 43, 131; workers' self-organisation 43–4; *see also* Soviet pay and incentive systems; Soviet systems of organisation of production and work
Soviet pay and incentive systems: bonuses for amount of output 40, 41; bonuses for quality of work performance 41–2; Coefficient of Labour Participation (KTU) 40–2, 44; piece-rate pay 29, 30, 39–40; punish-but-retain logic 29; self-financing brigades 44; time-based pay 39, 40; Wage Rate and Qualification Handbook for Workers *(ETKS)* 37–40, 45
Soviet systems of organisation of production and work: brigade work 33–7, 39–46; Complex Systems of Management of Output Quality *(KSUKP)* 30–7, 43, 45–6, 53, 174; Saratov System of Defectless Work 31–2, 36–7, 40, 45; VAZ (AvtoVAZ) 32–5, 37, 40–1, 44; *see also* Soviet ideology
Stakhanovism 28, 47n7, 47n9
Stalin, Joseph 27, 29
Stark, D. 12, 14, 15
Streeck, W. 12, 13
Sydow, J. 12–13, 15, 27

Taylor, F. W. 23–5, 27, 35, 71
Taylorism 24–7, 29, 32, 45, 70–1, 77–8, 83, 128, 174; *see also* Taylorism in Russia
Taylorism in Russia 23–7, 29–32, 35, 45, 47n10; Central Institute of Labour *(TsIT)* 25; de-humanisation of work 27; humanistic vision of 24–5; timekeeping cards (time records) 25; *see also* Soviet systems of organisation of production and work
teamwork *see* brigade work; group work in the West

198 *Index*

temporary agency work 107
Thelen, K. 12, 13, 15, 114
Total Quality Management (TQM) 52, 72, 75–7, 82
Toyota 8, 50, 59, 63–4, 77, 115–17, 133; Toyota Production System 54, 70, 77, 115–17
trade unions: in the West 76, 79; at Westauto 134, 139, 141, 143, 147, 158, 165, 176; in the Post-Soviet era 50, 61, 64, 65–7, 136, 145, 161–3; in the Soviet era 27, 32, 34; *see also* works councils, resistance to change
training and skills development 147; 155–6; entry qualification requirements 147–8, 149–50; general (soft) competencies training 59, 76, 150, 152, 156, 176; in-house training 58–9, 148–55; mentorship 58, 146, 149, 150, 151, 155; Wage Rate and Qualification Handbook for Workers *(ETKS)* 57, 59, 148–51; *see also* blue-collar workers; pay and incentive systems

VAZ *see* AvtoVAZ
vocational education and training system 56–7, 109, 149–51, 152–3; Soviet legacy 25, 37–9; transfer of dual system from Germany 59
Volkswagen 8, 50, 59, 63, 64, 66

Wage Rate and Qualification Handbook for Workers *(ETKS)* 37–40, 45; at Rusauto 149–50, 158, 177; at Rusmet 150–1, 158, 161, 170; use after market reforms 56–7, 59, 147, 153, 155–6, 174; at Westauto 148, 168, 170
wages *see* pay and incentive systems
Wang, C.L. 28

Ward, C. 25, 27, 29
Westauto 17, 18, 20, 91, 105–7, 108–10, 113, 115–16, 117; deviation from Soviet legacy 169–72, 176, 177–8; group work (brigade work) 138–9, 142–4, 146–7; no-blame mentality 97, 138, 164, 172, 176; pay and incentives system 157–8, 163, 164–5, 167–8; personnel composition 107, 111; quality management 115, 118–20, 122, 124–5, 128–30, 132–3, 134, 137–8; requirements to Russian suppliers 91–3, 96–7, 99–101, 102; Westauto Production System (WPS) 92, 113, 115, 116, 137, 142, 151–3, 168, 169, 171; Westauto Quality Operation System (WQOS) 115, 152–3, 168; worker qualification and development 147–9, 151–3, 155–6
white-collar workers 39, 58–9, 60, 62, 107, 120, 143
Womack, J.P. 1, 77, 79
work discipline 2, 26, 28–9, 46, 49–50, 51, 62–3, 67, 135–6, 165–6; role of groups (brigades) in 44, 54, 141, 145; role of pay in 51, 60, 68, 157–68; *see also* blue-collar workers
work organisation *see* brigade (group) work; continuous improvement process
worker control in production 29–30; *see also* blue-collar workers
worker mobilisation 27–30, 43, 131
workplace competitions 133–7, 141, 145, 169–70
workplace culture 50, 59, 97, 144, 152; *see also* leadership style
works councils 66, 79, 134–5

Yin, R.K. 17, 18